BSU
BLACK STUDENT UNION

Celebrating Life

African American Women Speak Out About Breast Cancer

Sylvia Dunnavant

Edited by Sharon Egiebor

USFi

Published by USFI, Inc., 3001 LBJ Freeway, Suite 131, Dallas,
Texas 75234.

Cover photo by Sylvia Dunnavant

Cover design by Huge Image, Inc.

Edited by Sharon Egiebor

Manufactured in the United States of America

Library of Congress Catalog-in-Publication Data

95-60852

ISBN 0-9643211-4-9

First Edition

$\mathcal{D}$edications

This book is dedicated to my aunt, Annie Lou Lewis, who lost her life on March 19, 1994 to breast cancer. To my uncle Herbert, who stood by her side; my cousins, Barry and Sheila, who took care of her during her illness — I love you all.

I would also like to pay a special tribute to the woman who heightened my awareness of breast cancer, singer Minnie Riperton, and the many sisters who have lost their lives to this devastating disease.

— Sylvia Dunnavant

I thank God for the opportunity to have some input in a work that will ultimately save lives. My special thanks go to my son, Marcus, who was patient and considerate while I spent hours over the summer at the computer terminal.

I have read each and every page of this book several times. I have to remind myself as I go through the personal stories that these are survivors. They are not the ones who succumbed, who might not had enough information to adequately fight the disease or who received poor medical advice. It is my prayer that other women and men will take the time, get the mammogram, learn about the warning signs and begin to help themselves. Breast cancer is just one of the diseases that unfairly attacks the African American population — we're still battling Acquired Immune Deficiency Syndrome, high blood pressure, diabetes, and heart disease, to name a few. We should become soldiers, armed with information, in this fight to have a healthy, productive life.

These survivors have taken the first step. They have lifted the veil of darkness, brought in the light and told someone else how to make it through.

— Sharon Egiebor

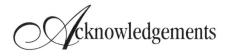

Acknowledgements

To My Creator: Heavenly Father, I thank you for giving me the vision for this project, the means and the resources to make it become a reality. I thank you for turning 36 subjects into 62. I thank you for allowing me to catch planes and make connecting flights that seemed virtually impossible. But mostly, I thank you for allowing your precious Holy Spirit to dwell in me.

Autria Robinson & Janet Walton: When I was younger I thought having two mothers was like having two heads. Now I know I was wrong. Having two African American women who are in a nurturing capacity in your life is like someone giving you the key to the universe and saying "go for it!"

Jaysen Scott: I could not have asked for a better son. Thanks so much for your patience and your unconditional love. But most of all, thanks for being you.

Mary Warren: Mary, you put the "F" in friend. I do not know what in the world I would have done without you. I will eternally be in your debt.

Faisal Ahmad: Every morning when I wake up I thank God for bringing you into my life. You are truly a remarkable man, and I will never forget the role you have played in my life. May Allah always be with you!

Frances Griffin-Brown: I have always believed in angels. Therefore, I know that God planted you in my life.

Curtis King: Now I know why they call you King Curtis. You helped me bring this one home, baby. Thanks!!!

Gerald Grimes: I have always known that photographers were great people, but I never met another one like you.

Pam Ferguson: If I had a thousand tongues I could not thank you enough. From the very beginning you gave me that extra kick to get me going, and now you see that was all it took.

Joyce Robinson & the women of First Baptist: Thanks so much for your prayers and support. It has been your prayers and your positivity that made this book happen as quickly as it did.

Sharon Egiebor: Thanks so much for stepping in and bringing this project home. You are a true gem.

Les Butler: Zora Brown is a lucky woman to have you as her right hand. If I could clone you I would, but I am sure someone has tried that already.

Giselle Fisher: Your coordination efforts are a blessing from God.

Nancy Wilson, Esther Rolle & Isabell Cottrell: Thank you so much for responding to my efforts, and giving me the encouraging words.

- Collen Allen
- American Cancer Society
- Elayne Anderson
- Ted Arrington
- Brandyn Barbara Artis
- Dorothy Ballard
- Royland Baptise
- Cheryl Basye
- Diane Beall
- Carolyn Beaman
- Gemeral Berry, *Our Texas*
- VonDonna Bircher
- Black American Community Connection
- Pat Brewer
- Charlotte Brewster
- Eric Brickler
- Nancy Brinker
- Felton Brown
- James Brown
- Thermalene Brown
- Zora Kramer Brown
- Susan Boucher
- Dennis Byas
- Dorothy Byas
- Wilma Carroll
- Paula Chalmers
- Cynthia Coleman
- Charisse Cossey
- Comer Cottrell
- Chrissy Daves
- Lillie Day
- Bobbi de Cordova
- Robert Donnell
- Yvette Eason
- Dawn Elliott
- Annie Pearl Foster
- Rev. J. Lee Foster
- Sheila Frazier
- Dr. Harold Freeman
- Fuji Film
- Augusta Gale
- Nancy Garner
- Yatta Gayljoy
- *Good Morning Texas*

- Darien Goode
- Kittie Gozlan
- Dr. Gwendolyn Goldsby Grant
- Wilhelmina Grant
- Joyce Green
- Dick Gregory
- Arthur Griffin
- Florence Griffin-Joyner
- Sheri Griffin
- Gwendolyn Hargrove
- Gloria Harmon
- Patsy Harris
- Dr. Cheryl Harth
- Carolyn Harvey
- Catherine Harvey
- Jesse Hornbuckle
- Huge Image
- Cassandra Iverson
- Karen Eubanks Jackson
- Karen Mayes Jackson
- Pam Jackson
- JBAAL
- Willis Johnson
- Dr. Al Jones
- Earline Jones
- Dr. Lovell Jones
- Dr. Marilyn Kern-Foxsworth
- Eric Key
- Shehzia Khan
- Eartha Kitt
- Karen Kloack
- Anita Knox
- The Susan G. Komen Foundation
- Dr. LaSalle Lafall
- Odell Lee
- Shirley Levingston
- Mary Lyons
- Branford Marsalis
- Virginia Martin
- Stephanie McKissic
- Audrey Montgomery
- Ernestine Montgomery
- Trudy S. Moore
- Janet Morrison

- Ruth Morrison
- Marian Mostiller
- Jim Olson
- Dr. Funmi Olopade
- Robyn Paige
- Jimmy Paige
- Theresa Patrick
- Nina K. Pettis
- Mae Phillips
- Kim Price
- Michael Price
- Minnie Pryor
- Adell Puckett
- Shawn Rabb
- Stephanie Reed
- Beverly Rhine
- Johnnye Ridley
- Don Robinson
- Dr. Bertha Roddey
- Emma Rodgers
- Dick Rudolph
- Jacqueline Russell
- Margaret Sanders
- Kitt Sapiero
- Myra Shelton
- J.J. Simmons
- Sisters Network
- Sheryl Siverand
- Cheryl Smith
- Lois Smith-Williams
- Carol Tapp
- Alpha Thomas
- USFI Staff
- Cynthia Vaughan
- P.J. Viviansayles
- Joseph Walton III
- The Warren Family
- Jim Washington, *The Dallas Weekly*
- Alice White
- Roxie White
- Karen Williams
- Women Of Color
- Stevie Wonder
- Deborah Green Woulard

Frances A. Griffin-Brown

President, Board of Directors
Celebrating Life Foundation

As I watched my friend and aunt, Barbara Doss, take her last breath, I vowed that I would, in her memory, dedicate my community service efforts to helping eradicate a disease that is swiftly killing African American women. Breast cancer is depriving African American communities across the nation of its mothers, grandmothers, sisters, aunts, cousins and friends. Our men are also being affected by this disease.

Working with Sylvia Dunnavant and establishing the Celebrating Life Foundation has been a very rewarding experience for me. Sylvia and I have spent many days and nights on the phone, in meetings, traveling, laughing and crying. She has earned my respect for her endeavors in writing this book and sharing her research about breast cancer with America.

I would like to thank the following people for their support: Giselle Fisher, my wonderful assistant; Kevin Schader, without whom I could not have done this project; his wife Mylene, who tolerated my interruptions to their home life; Ken and Kay Jarvis for all the knowledge they shared with me in putting the Celebrating Life Foundation together; Karen Love and Erica Christensen for volunteering their services whenever I needed them; Chrissy Daves, Mary Lyons, and Elayne Anderson of USFI, who assisted me whenever I needed help; The Plano Chapter of the Susan G. Komen Breast Cancer Foundation for their belief and support of this project; and my parents, Arthur and Earline Horton, for giving me the encouragement to do seemingly impossible tasks.

Special thanks to my husband, Felton Brown, my daughter Sheri Griffin and my son, Arthur Griffin, for volunteering their time and efforts to this project and for providing me with the strength and motivation to do it all. To Mr. Faisal Ahmad, who believed in Sylvia and me and gave his full support to this project, I give a very special thanks.

The Celebrating Life Foundation would like to express its appreciation to Delta Air Lines for their support of this project. As a major contributor, the spirit of Delta Air Lines is alive, well and growing.

able of Contents

reface

Celebrating Life is a most worthy undertaking. I come from a family of 18 children, and to date, I have lost three brothers and four sisters to cancer. I have two sisters in remis-

sion. We, as African American people, have not been trained to watch our health for this disease. Because we are generally not included in the studies on how cancer affects us, we come to doctors who know little about our body's reactions.

I have worked with Zora Kramer Brown in the Washington, D.C. area. She is doing wonders through her diligent work with African American women. She is a breast cancer survivor and so are several of the women who work with her organization, the Breast Cancer Resource Committee. These women exude an energy and intelligence that make us look out for the challenges of the disease. Their mental and spiritual attitude are inspirations to anyone who works with them. The job they are doing makes me feel safer as an African American woman. God bless the efforts that we are all making, and may we succeed in alerting our women to the dangers of this disease.

— Esther Rolle
Actress

reword

Seeing these gorgeous pictures of courageous women who transmit their strength, beauty, and the will to make their lives as fulfilled as they are meant to be, I could also see their faith shining through.

It also brought to mind the fact that so many of us, in the 90's, still don't take our lives into our own hands, by just asking questions ... gaining insight to our bodies and questioning decisions made by others. Take preventive measures, get that check up once a year, find out about good nutrition, find that physician that takes time to explain things fully and you feel comfortable with, exercise, take some time out for you, which is the thing we probably do least of. You are in charge of your own body and what happens to it.

You will have only one house — your body — while you're on this earth. Take good care of it, do all the necessary repairs, keep up its appearance: maintenance is the key to longevity.

— Nancy Wilson
Jazz Singer

Foreword

We, as African American women, have to be proactive instead of reactive when it comes to our health care.

Isabell Cottrell
President of Ethnic Gold

We have to realize that health is not something you can take for granted by avoiding it. We have to do our part by having regular mammograms and doing breast self-exams.

My mother-in-law, Helen Cottrell, was successful at combating breast cancer for over 40 years. She was diagnosed in her 30s. She lived a very happy, healthy and loving life until she was in her eighties. Most importantly, she was a true example of how breast cancer does not have to be a death sentence. By changing her eating habits, exercising and paying close attention to her body ... she was able to live a long healthy life.

It seems ironic that so many of us know much more about cars than we do our own bodies. We know the parts of cars and what it takes to operate them. Yet, we don't know what it takes for the body to run and operate at its very best. I think we need to learn all that we can about the body and the way it functions so that we can live a very happy and healthy life ... that is physically, emotionally, and psychologically.

There is currently not a cure for breast cancer so we have to look at the research and development that exists and support those efforts.

The key we have now is early detection. The sooner you can find the cancer, the better position you will be in to do something about it.

— Isabell Cottrell

ntroduction

When I first thought about writing this book my aunt, Annie Lou Lewis, had battled breast cancer for eight years. It appeared she was winning, at least until the doctors said the cancer had metastasized and was now in her liver. They gave her six months to live. She fought valiantly for another two years.

I began to do a lot of soul searching and research to find out why this disease was able to sneak back in and take over her life. When she passed the five year mark — the point doctors call remission — I sighed with relief. What had happened? I questioned myself, and I questioned others around me. I had studied a little about breast cancer when singer Minnie Riperton died in 1979. There was still so much I didn't know.

When I found out my aunt's cancer had metastasized to the liver, I later found out that was just *one* place breast cancer went after it left the breast. The other common locations for metathesis were the bone, the brain and the lungs.

My last visit with my aunt was here in Dallas for breakfast. I already had plans for the book by then, but I didn't tell her. I wanted to, but I couldn't. There was something precious about being in her presence. The laughter and conversation were going so well. I didn't want anything to ruin that moment ... definitely not cancer.

Her death on March 19, 1994 propelled me into action. I knew this book must become a reality. I began to question women that I loved and respected about breast cancer. Many of them didn't know that breast cancer was one of the leading causes of death for women in our community. Some said they thought the disease only affected white women. Another group said they would rather die than lose their breasts. It seemed so ironic. Throughout history the breasts of African American women have nourished an entire civilization, yet those same breasts have taken so many women to an early grave.

I pulled together my skills as a photographer and writer, and my desire to help other African American women learn about breast cancer, to do this book. Initially, I didn't think enough women would talk. But as you see, 62 breast cancer survivors shared their stories with me. They have all intimately touched my life and I hope they will touch yours. Many of them had multiple challenges to survive — the recurrence of breast cancer, other diseases, as well as deaths in the family.

Breast cancer is not limited to one race, family or ethnic group. One out of 8 women is at risk of developing the disease at some point in their life. My good friend Shirley Levingston, 39, was diagnosed with the disease as I was working on this book.

We African American women must become as aggressive with this disease as it is with us. We face more than twice the risk of dying of breast cancer compared to white women. Breast cancer is the leading cause of death for African American women between the ages of 40 and 50. Also, African American women under the age of 40 are 30 percent more likely to be diagnosed with breast cancer than white women. We have to know our bodies, have regular mammograms and do whatever we can to reduce our risk factors.

When most people think about cancer, they think about death. This book is not about death, it is about life, no matter how long or how short. It is about holding on to every precious moment that God allows you to have. It's about celebrating life!

— Sylvia Dunnavant

Listen to my prayer O God,
do not ignore my plea;
hear me and answer me.

My thoughts trouble me
and I am distraught
at the voice of the enemy,
at the stares of the wicked;
for they bring down suffering
upon me
and revile me in their anger.

My heart is in anguish with me;
the terrors of death assail me.
Fear and trembling have beset me;
horror has overwhelmed me.
I said, "Oh, that I had the
wings of a dove!

I would fly away and be at rest —
I would flee far away
and stay in the desert;
Selah,

I would hurry to my place of shelter,
far from the tempest and storm."

Psalm 55:1-8 (NIV)

Ten Things That Every African American Woman Needs to Know About Breast Cancer

1. *It can happen to you.* Many African American women don't believe they can get breast cancer; they assume breast cancer is relegated only to white women. That is the biggest fallacy going. Although not as many African American women are diagnosed with breast cancer, twice as many African American women as white women die from the disease. The latest statistics show that, since 1989, deaths from breast cancer are down 5 percent. However, in the African American female population, the death rate is up 2.6 percent.

2. *A breast self-exam can actually save your life.* In the 15 minutes it takes to perform, many women find their own lumps by doing a regular breast self-exam.

3. *The doctors may not remember to tell you everything.* If you have breast cancer, you need to empower yourself by learning as much as possible about the surgical procedure or treatment you are going to have. The more you know, the better off you will be in making choices that could affect the rest of your life.

4. *You don't have to be over 40 to get breast cancer.* Although some medical institutions say you should wait until you are 40 years old to have a mammogram, many African American women develop breast cancer much earlier. Some African American women have been diagnosed with breast cancer in their early 20s.

5. *There are exceptions to the rule.* Just because you don't fit into a "high risk" category for breast cancer, doesn't mean you can't get it. In fact, 75 percent of the women who get breast cancer don't necessarily fit the high risk profile.

6. *Men get breast cancer, too.* Your fathers, husbands and brothers are also subject to breast cancer. In fact, one percent of the people who are diagnosed with breast cancer are male.

7. *Getting breast cancer doesn't mean you are going to die.* Early detection is the key. Once you find a lump, you need to seek medical attention immediately. Some cancers are fast-growing, which means waiting could cost your life.

8. *Breasts do not make you a "woman."* Breasts are organs. They are part of the body, but they do not determine your womanhood. The loss of one or both breasts makes you no less feminine... don't let anyone tell you any differently. Always remember: The woman makes the breasts, the breasts do not make the woman.

9. *Sex does not have to change after having a mastectomy.* Some women have said that chemotherapy changed their desire for sex. However, not all women who have breast cancer need chemotherapy. Many women have normal sex lives after breast cancer. Some sexual partners even kiss or stroke the area where the breast has been removed.

10. *The most important thing you should know is:* Life goes on after breast cancer. Everything that was, still is. You may not have a breast, but the sun still rises in the morning and sets at night. For the most part, many women feel empowered and energized after overcoming breast cancer. It is almost like being immortalized, but left here to do a great deed. You have conquered the big "C" and nothing else can stop you. Now, you can go ahead and Celebrate Life!

$\mathscr{A}$ Tribute To Minnie Riperton

The wedding guests were slowly drifting into the conference center ballroom. As we waited this July 1, 1995 for the newly-wed couple to enter the room, the disc jockey went to his station.

The sweet sounds of little birds began to fill the room, and then Minnie Riperton's soft and soothing voice enveloped us. She was singing "Lovin' You," a song she composed with her musician husband, Dick Rudolph.

"That's MY jam," screamed a woman in her 30s.

Nearly 16 years after Minnie died from breast cancer and 21 years after the song began climbing the charts, audiences still are being brought to their feet with her music.

Minnie was at the height of her career in the 1970s when she was diagnosed with breast cancer. At the time, breast cancer was a whisper, the unspeakable disease.

She became a maverick. Undaunted and apparently no longer afraid, she shared her story on national television during the "Tonight Show" with Flip Wilson as guest host. Minnie Riperton, jazz singer, wife and mother had had a modified radical mastectomy.

Minni performed with such artists as Ramsey Lewis, Muddy Waters, Etta James, The Dells, Quincy Jones and Roberta Flack. However, it was her musical relationship with Stevie Wonder that lead to her first hit album, *Perfect Angel*.

Her influence continues through an annual American Cancer Society event, the Minnie Riperton Cancer Action 10K/5K Run. This event is sponsored by the Los Angeles Unit and has raised approximately $70,000 in the last four years for cancer research.

Minnie became a spokesperson for the American Cancer Society and traveled the country urging women to learn about early detection methods and prompt treatment.

In 1977, as a result of her courageous efforts, she received the America Cancer Society's Courage Award from former President Jimmy Carter, the Ebony Music Ebby Award and the NAACP Image Award.

The woman who was a Perfect Angel died July 12, 1979.

Her husband, her son Marc, 27, and her daughter Maya, 23, carry on her vision.

May her music continue to touch lives, and her memory linger on in our minds forever ... and ever ... more.

BREAST CANCER SURVIVORS

BY SURVIVORSHIP

As of

OCTOBER 1, 1995

ADELLPUCKETT *45 years*

ERNESTINEMONTGOMERY *22 years*

ANNIE*PEARL*FOSTER *22 years*

STEPHANIEMcKISSIC *11 years*

LOIS *SMITH* WILLIAMS *20 years*

ZORA *KRAMER* BROWN *14 years*

CYNTHIA *V.* VAUGHAN *14 years*

JANET MORRISON *13 years*

DOROTHYBALLARD *11 years*

CHERYL R. BASYE *10 years*

KIMBERLY ANN PRICE *9 years*

JOYCE GREEN *8 years*

DEBORAH *GREEN* WOULARD
6 years

AUGUSTA GALE
7 years

BRANDYN *BARBARA* ARTIS
7 years

VONDONNA BIRCHER
7 years

MARGARETSANDERS
7 years

ALICEWHITE
7 years

MARIANL.MOSTILLER
7 years

CATHERINEHARVEY
6 years

CHARISSECOSSEY
6 years

BEVERLYRHINE
5 years

PAULAJ.CHALMERS
5 years

VIRGINIAMARTIN
5 years

BERTHAM.RODDEY
5 years

ALPHATHOMAS
5 years

KARENWILLIAMS
5 years

ROBYNPAIGE
4 years

PATSYHARRIS
4 years

CAROLYNBEAMAN
4 years

P.J.VIVIANSAYLES
4 years

MICHAELPRICE
4 years

MYRA_HAYES_SHELTON
4 years

MINNIEPRYOR
3 years

CHARLOTTEBREWSTER
3 years

KAREN_MAYES_JACKSON
3 years

THERMALENEBROWN
3 years

ODELLLEE
3 years

YVETTEFRAZIEREASON
3 years

JACQUELINEJ.RUSSELL
3 years

ROXIEWHITE
2 years

CAROLYNHARVEY
2 years

JOHNNYERIDLEY
1 years

CAROLYNTAPP
2 years

KAREN*EUBACKS*JACKSON
2 years

EARLINEA.JONES
2 years

WILMACARROLL
2 years

NANCYGARNER
1 year

CYNTHIACOLEMAN
1 year

THERESAA.PATRICK
1 year

STEPHANIEA.REED
1 year

WILHELMINAGRANT
1 year

RUTHMORRISON
1 year

MAEPHILLIPS
1 year

GLORIAHARMON
1 year

DAWNELLIOTT
1 year

AUDREYMONTGOMERY
1 year

CASSANDRAIVERSON
1 year

PATBREWER
10 months

LILLIEDAY
9 months

SHERYLSIVERAND
9 months

SHIRLEYLEVINGSTON
5 months

Brandyn
Barbara
Artis

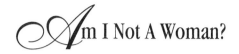m I Not A Woman?

Am I not a woman?

My shape has been changed.
My form has been revised.
My breast has been de-sized.
Am I not a woman?

My heart still loves.
My arms still hug.
My body still craves.
Am I not a woman?

My hips still swerve.
My lips still entice.
My eyes still allure.
Am I not a woman?

My fingers still caress.
My mouth still soothes.
My ears still listen,
tenderly.

Am I not a woman?

Sylvia Dunnavant

Too Young To Have Breast Cancer

Women that are diagnosed under the age of 40.

Stephanie McKissic

When the doctors told me that I was going to lose my second breast, it took me for a loop! One person told me, "You act as if you would rather die than to lose your other breast." I am not going to lie and say that thought didn't cross my mind. I am not suicidal or anything. All I could think was, "what was I going to have left." I had this thing where I associated my breasts with being a woman. Now it wasn't like I was going to have just one ... I wasn't going to have any!

I guess at the time I was more vain than I was concerned about my health.

Cancer had always been like this dark cloud hovering over my head. I had experienced three bouts with it in 24 years. I never knew when it was going to strike, and I was never surprised when it did.

I had my first bout with cancer when I was only 12 years old. I woke up one morning and I had this big knot on my head. It seemed that it had cropped up overnight. My mother asked me, "What happened?" She was wondering, had I been hit on the head or had I fallen?

All I could think of was that I had been hit in the head with a volley ball. She immediately took me to the hospital.

They found out I had a tumor on the left side of my brain ... it was cancerous. It had always been there, but the injury had brought it to the surface. In fact, they realized there

Stephanie McKissic

Age:	36
Stage:	1
Occupation:	Retail Merchandiser/ Free-lance make up artist
Residence:	Houston, Texas
Procedure:	Bi-lateral Mastectomy
Treatment:	Radiation
Survivorship:	17 years
Lymph Node Involvement:	None

was something wrong when I was a baby. Since I seemed to do OK, the doctors never pursued it. I had even been experiencing a problem with my vision in my left eye before the tumor was detected.

They told my mother I was definitely not going to live. And if I did live, it was going to be a miracle. Of course I didn't know any of this. I just knew I was getting all the ice cream I could possibly eat, and everybody in my family was coming to see me.

I never would have thought that seven years later cancer would strike again. This time, it would be in my breast.

I was 18 when my daughter Nichole was born. A year later I noticed that my left breast was considerably larger than my right one. At that point, my boyfriend and I both noticed that I had a lump in my breast. We both checked it out. Then I went to the doctor for a physical.

Even though I was 19, my doctor had a biopsy done immediately.

I freaked out when he told me it was cancer. I was originally from Peoria, and I happened to be living in Chicago at the time. Since I was only 19, I didn't want to believe this was happening to me. I went back to Peoria for a second opinion from a doctor that I knew.

He said the same thing. It was malignant, and I needed to have my breast removed. He even had several other doctors look at it because he couldn't believe it was happening to me.

I was so afraid. I was scared that I was going to die. I thought, "It's cancer, you are automatically going to get very sick, and you are going to die!"

At that point I wasn't really concerned about losing the breast. I wanted to get the operation over and get on with my life, with this one breast, and just hope that I lived.

They tested my lymph nodes and none were positive. It seemed the cancer had been localized.

Because I was so young, my doctor automatically assumed I was going to want reconstructive surgery. He had taken my

"Since I was only 19, I didn't want to believe this was happening to me. I went back to Peoria for a second opinion from a doctor that I knew."

nipple off and grafted it to my thigh. When I woke up and found my nipple on my thigh I lost it. It was the ugliest thing I had ever seen.

Needless to say, the nipple didn't make it.

I let them know that I didn't need reconstruction, all I wanted to do was to get back to normal with the breast I had left.

Stephanie and her 17-year-old daughter Nichole have both dealt with cancer. Yet, through everything their bond as mother and daughter has only grown stronger.

When I was 27, I found another lump in my breast. This time, they just treated it with eight weeks of radiation and it went away.

After I had my first breast removed, I began to have mammograms. I didn't have them on a regular basis, but I did have them. I went in for a mammogram when I was 28 and they detected some precancerous cells in my right breast. It was recommended that I have that breast removed as well.

When they told me that I was going to lose my right breast, I went through a lot of mental anguish. I knew I had dealt with the first one OK. I was happy to be alive. Nichole was a baby and I had a lot to live for. This time was different.

I even asked the doctor how many years would I have if I didn't do anything. He said, "Probably five to seven years."

At first I was willing to live out those years with my one remaining breast. Then I started counting. I was 29. In five years I would be 34. Was I going to be ready to die at 34? I don't think so!

Even though I was willing to take my chances, the reality of it made me change my mind.

The first time when I was in the hospital I had all my family and close friends with me. It seemed like I had so much support. This time, when I got ready to go to surgery, no one was there. I realized I probably needed them more the second time than I did the first. I guess, actually, I needed them both times, but this time was so traumatic for me.

It was amazing how things had changed in 10 years. For my first mastectomy I was in the hospital for at least a week. This time I was in and out overnight. It was almost like having day surgery.

Psychologically, I did not deal with having the second surgery very well. I spent the next three years in a rebellious state. I figured if I stayed in some type of a dream world, I would not have to deal with the whole turmoil.

One day, I said to myself, "This isn't working." I finally came to the conclusion that I wasn't going to die so I might as well be concerned about the life that I had left.

When I had my first breast removed, I thought I was going to die soon. So I would party and party and party some more. I did everything I could do to live it up. But Hell, after I reached 32, or 33, after all that partying, I was sort of tired. I figured, well, it doesn't look like I am going to die. Maybe I should try to live my life out the best I can since I have been blessed to live.

Now when I reflect on it, I truly feel that all the things I went through was God's way of preparing me for what my daughter Nichole was going to go through when she was diagnosed with leukemia at 13 years old. To me, compared to what she went through, my situation was nothing. After she was diagnosed, she had to go through chemotherapy. I had only experienced a little radiation.

I think that is what is unique about our relationship. She could talk to me about her cancer, and I really knew how she felt. I was very strong for her. I also became this very patient parent. I am not normally a very patient person. I think my illness helped me to deal with hers better. I always knew she wasn't going to die. I knew she would be OK.

Like myself, Nichole has had her bouts with cancer. At 2 years old, she had cancer of the adrenal gland. The tumor was pressing against her gland and secreting extra hormones. She started developing like a teenager. She had acne, pubic hair and hair under her arms. When the doctor examined her, he asked me if she had been having any blood in her Pampers. I was shocked, but he said based on her symptoms he wasn't sure if she had started her menstrual cycle yet.

We were very blessed in that situation. They removed the tumor and she was back to normal. She didn't have to have any type of after treatment, like chemotherapy or radiation. They found out the tumor was very contained in that one spot.

With my strong history of cancer, I feel I am not finished dealing with cancer yet. I am still ticked off by cancer, and I am not happy with how it has taken a part of my life and my daughter's life.

I see cancer as this entity. We have been hanging around together for a long time. It is sort of like a friend. A friend you love to hate. I hate it because it is cancer. But I have to respect it because it has never really taken over my body. We are not quite through dealing with each other. I know that there will be a day of reckoning. Even though I don't want it to win our battle, I know it very well may. But one thing for sure, cancer knows I will be kickin' ass all the way because I am a very good contender.

"We are not quite through dealing with each other. I know that there will be a day of reckoning. Even though I don't want it to win our battle, I know it very well may. But one thing for sure, cancer knows I will be kickin' ass all the way because I am a very good contender."

Audrey Montgomery

I have always been the strong one in my family. I have always been a fighter. When I found out I had cancer, I figured either I could fight back or I could crawl up in a hole and die. I chose to fight for my life.

I located my lump myself. I had a benign lump in my left breast when I was a junior in high school. So I have always been aware of checking my breasts. I know I never checked as often as I should have, but I was always sure to check some time or another.

Once I went to the doctor, everything seemed to go so fast. The doctor immediately scheduled me for a mammogram. A breast specialist gave me the results. He never came out and said I had cancer, but I could see it in his face. He told me that he had some concerns about what he saw, but he needed to be sure. The next thing I knew I was having a biopsy.

Audrey Montgomery

Age:	25
Stage:	2
Occupation:	Cosmetologist
Residence:	Grand Prairie, Texas
Procedure:	Modified Radical Mastectomy
Reconstruction	
Treatment:	Chemotherapy & Radiation
Survivorship:	7 months
Lymph Node Involvement:	1 / 13

I just knew something was wrong. It was like a bell went off. Before I even had the results, I told my family, "It's cancer, y'all."

I remember it like it was yesterday. I was waking up from a bad bout with the anesthesia. I couldn't stop vomiting. My husband was in the room with me. Then all of sudden a train of doctors walked in.

One of the doctors stepped forward and said, "Audrey, you have breast cancer."

I was sitting straight when they walked in the room. The moment he said it, I sort of lost my energy and just sunk down in the bed. My back went limp. But it was only for a second. Then I popped right back up, it was like the fighter in me kicked right back in just at that moment.

We have a history of cancer on my mother's side. It seems that everybody who had died on her side of the family had suffered from cancer. No car wrecks, no heart attacks. Just cancer.

I had the surgery with immediate reconstruction. I also had chemotherapy and radiation.

For me, losing my hair was hard, but I remember when I was a little girl my mother always told me I had the cutest little peanut head. She said she thought it would even be cute if I didn't have any hair.

I told her that we were going to be able to find out if my little head was cute with no hair because now it was going to be a reality.

Near the end of the chemo treatments, when I finally thought everything was over, I got sick while going for treatment. I ended up in the hospital. It seemed I had an infection in my blood stream. They ran several tests, later telling me the type of bacteria that I had in my blood could have killed me if it had not been caught in time.

For the first time I thanked God for chemo, because if I hadn't been going for treatment, I may have died from the bacterial infection.

I have to admit having children made this whole thing a little more complicated. With two boys, 3 and 7, I didn't quite know how to tell them Mommy was sick. So, I let them know gradually.

I thought it was important to let my 3 year old see the bandage when I came home from the hospital. Otherwise, he may have pounced on me while playing. I didn't just tell him "don't jump on me." I felt he needed to see that there was a big ouch there.

He is the friskiest child that you have ever seen, but after he saw the bandage he never jumped in my chest area.

My 7 year old and I talked before I started chemo. I knew he would notice my hair loss and I didn't want him to

"It seems that everybody who had died on [my mother's] side of the family had suffered from cancer. No car wrecks, no heart attacks. Just cancer."

freak out. I wanted him to know that it was because of the medicine.

I had two forms of chemo: Cytoxan and Adriamycin. From the moment I started the Cytoxan I experienced a weird burning sensation in my head. At first it bothered me, then I spoke with my doctor. He assured me that was one of the side effects, and some people even experience burning in their groin area.

I know that people are not always great with change. But my husband played an important role in helping me deal with all the changes I was going through. No matter what, he would not let me feel any differently about myself because he didn't feel any differently about me.

There is no doubt it is hard when you are married because you know that other person is going to notice the changes you are going through. However, you hope they don't lose sight of what is really important. You hope they love you for what is inside of you. Many people think that is the type of relationship they have, but never really know until something happens.

I just thank God for giving me a second chance. For the first time in my life I have become conscious of time. You go through life just piddling around, just like you are going to live forever. Everybody knows that there is such a thing as life and death, but you never really seriously think about your death until something puts it in your face. Then you realize what "here today, gone tomorrow" really means. It's a rude awakening!

Lillie Day

There is a member of my church who is always trying to make people more aware of health issues.

One Sunday afternoon she invited a representative from the American Cancer Society to our church to give a presentation about breast self-examinations. The afternoon turned into a complete seminar on breast health care. The presenter kept talking about factors that would put one at a higher risk for having breast cancer: having a family history of cancer, having a baby after 30, and being overweight were some of the factors she mentioned.

She also mentioned that the risk factor for breast cancer goes up as one gets older.

I began to tune her out because I didn't fit into any of those categories. I was only 29, so I knew this didn't have anything to do with me.

Lillie Day

Age:	29
Stage:	2
Occupation:	Court Reporter
Residence:	DeSoto, Texas
Procedure:	Mastectomy
Treatment:	Chemotherapy
Survivorship:	2 months
Lymph Node Involvement:	2/15

When I went home that night I kept thinking about everything that was said. I had never done a breast self-examination. Even though I knew that I was not going to find anything, I decided to examine my breasts.

To my surprise, I found a lump.

The first thing I did was tell my husband. He suggested I go to the doctor to get it checked out.

I thought it really wasn't any big deal, so I waited a couple of weeks before I went to my gynecologist. Although my doctor referred me for a mammogram, everyone kept insisting that I was too young. Finally, I was seen by a surgeon who told me that the lump did not feel cancerous. He suggested that we watch it for a couple of months and then do a biopsy.

My husband thought just the opposite. He didn't think it made any sense to watch it. He wanted me to have a biopsy right away.

Although there seemed to be a slight possibility that it might be cancer, I never focused on that fact. I kept thinking, "Whatever," because I just knew that I wasn't going to get cancer. Both my mother and my sister have had cysts, so I knew that was all it was, just a cyst.

After the biopsy, the surgeon let me know the pathology report confirmed my lump was malignant.

When he told me, I thought: "You've got to be kidding." After all, I didn't fit any of the characteristics that everyone is always talking about. I breast-fed both of my children, I wasn't over 35, and I didn't have any family history of cancer. They had to be talking about someone else.

Suddenly it hit me ... they were not talking about anyone else, it was actually me. I had cancer.

That is when I started to cry.

My youngest son was nine months old, so it was very hard for me to look at how this was going to affect my life. The doctors were not sure if something happened to my milk ducts during my pregnancy or if I had the cancer the entire time I was pregnant.

Probably one of the more trying things during this entire ordeal was when they went to insert the catheter into my chest for the chemotherapy and it kept popping out. They kept attempting; then they realized there was a mass in my chest that was preventing the insertion.

At that time they didn't know if the mass was cancerous or not. But they informed me that if it was cancerous, they would not be able to operate. You can't imagine how that made me feel. You go from having a normal healthy life to being sick. Then all of a sudden you find out you might be terminally ill.

Well, I am still thanking God that the mass was not

*"**I** breast-fed both of my children, I wasn't over 35, and I didn't have any family history of cancer. They had to be talking about someone else."*

cancerous, so they were able to remove it and start my chemotherapy treatment.

At first I thought about reconstructive surgery, but after they told me everything that was involved, I realized that I did not want to go through all of that. It was just another operation, and I was ready to be over with everything and get back to normal as soon as possible.

My husband finally told me that he really didn't want me to have reconstruction anyway. To him it was just a breast, and that didn't matter. Since he didn't have a problem with it, it was fine by me. The way I look at it, he and I are the only ones who have to know.

I was fitted with a good prosthesis, and I think it is wonderful. When I put my clothes on no one knows the difference. In fact, some people who are close to me have had to ask me which breast I have had removed, because they can't tell.

The two things that I know helped me make it through everything are the support of my husband and my belief in God. Without them I don't know what I would have done.

Yet, there is one thing I have to admit. Sometimes, at night, I get a little depressed.

As long as I have my clothes on I am fine. When I take my clothes off, it is then I am reminded that my body is one-sided, and that has been hard to deal with.

But that has been the only down side of this situation. Most importantly, having breast cancer has allowed me to appreciate life ... and truly value the time I spend with my children and my husband more. It seems like I always used to be so busy. Now, if I am cooking and one of my children comes up to me and wants to play, guess what? Everything goes on hold because I am going to play with my child.

Before my experience with cancer, I was somewhat superficial. I was a person who lived in a shell. Now, my first concern is doing what I think will please God, and that is my daily struggle and conviction. Despite how difficult it is, my concern is walking according to the ways of the Lord.

I believe cancer was not just something that happened to me, it was something that happened for me. Dealing with this disease has allowed me to become more in tune to myself, as well as those around me.

My transformation began the day I found my lump while doing a breast self-exam. The very first thing I did was show it to my husband to see what he thought about it. We both decided I needed to see a doctor. Within two weeks, I made an appointment to see my gynecologist so we could find out what was going on.

Because I was only 28 years old at the time, and I had no family history of breast cancer, or any other cancer, my doctor assured me there was nothing to worry about.

Charisse Cossey

Age:	33
Stage:	2
Occupation:	Human Resources Manager
Residence:	Houston, Texas
Procedure:	Lumpectomy
Treatment:	Chemotherapy & Radiation
Survivorship:	5 years
Lymph Node Involvement:	None

Despite his lack of concern, I still had a full physical examination and an ultrasound. Although the ultrasound came back revealing a mass, my doctor still assured me that there was nothing to worry about. I had no family history of cancer, I didn't smoke, I was at low risk of getting cancer — according to the checklist. There seemed to be no doubt that this had to be a cyst or some other type of benign tumor.

Even though my doctor scheduled me to see a surgeon, I still heard the same story, "You are too young, you have no family history of cancer. There is nothing to be worried about."

The story came to an abrupt end when the biopsy came back positive. Yes, I was young. Yes, I had no history of cancer. But, nevertheless, I had cancer!

It seemed that my whole life changed at that point. I became very strong. There was this powerful internal force that was guiding me and keeping me under control.

I now realize that force was God.

After reviewing my options, I decided to have a lumpectomy to remove the cancer. Although there was no lymph node involvement, my oncologist suggested chemotherapy and radiation as a precautionary measure.

Some people don't work while taking chemotherapy, but I decided to continue working on my job throughout my treatments. For the entire time I was going through chemo, even when my body felt weak, there was an internal strength that kept driving me through the day. At that point, nothing seemed unbearable to me.

As I was going through my treatments, my spirituality began to evolve.

"Now, I really don't spend a lot of time talking about my prognosis or my treatment. I am more concerned about how my soul has been altered and how my spirit has blossomed as a result of my experience."

I started to learn to love others beyond their flesh. For me, today is still a struggle, but I truly believe that my focus — how I deal with people — began to change after my diagnosis. Now, I really don't spend a lot of time talking about my prognosis or my treatment. I am more concerned about how my soul has been altered and how my spirit has blossomed as a result of my experience.

It seemed like I opened up and became very honest. I spoke very honestly about losing my sexual desire, due to the chemotherapy. I spoke honestly about losing a part of my breast.

It was at that time that I decided my husband was no longer able to love me the way I needed to be loved. He was used to buying things and fulfilling my material needs, but now I had a void that needed to be filled in my spiritual life. Although it was very difficult for me to deal with, I decided to file for divorce. In fact, I wanted to get my divorce while I was going through chemotherapy. However, my oncologist advised against it. I remember her saying, "Sister, not only are you losing your hair, you are losing your mind, too."

As a result of going through that experience, I still feel some loneliness. Sometimes I think when you learn to love people beyond a superficial level it becomes hard. It is easy to deal with people on the surface; it is more complicated to tap into their souls. I have still not remarried, and I still long for a true soul mate.

I do believe that I lost focus on myself as I looked toward God to pull me through this whole ordeal. Despite the divorce, I don't know that I ever really suffered because I always had this inner peace.

Through this experience I can truly say that I now know Jesus Christ and I openly speak about Him being the one who carried me when I thought I couldn't go on any more.

However, even today I have to admit, I struggle with the thought of death ... which is very difficult for a 33-year-old woman. I try to find some comfort in knowing that I am going to die. No one lives forever. Yet, I realize this is not just something that is hard for me to deal with but it is probably difficult for someone even twice my age. However, it is still something I am trying to come to grips with.

Sheryl Siverand

The day I found out I was going to have to have a mastectomy, I ran into one of my co-workers at the doctor's office. He walked up to me, yanked my jacket open and said, "Girl, I heard you were half dead and had both your breasts cut off."

I was so humiliated I didn't know what to do. Little did I know this was only the beginning of the discrimination I would experience after being diagnosed with breast cancer.

I was home recuperating from gallbladder surgery when I felt a lump in my breast. My mother just had surgery for breast cancer, so I did not hesitate to go to the doctor.

I had noticed a change in my breast a few months before I found the lump. I had never experienced a soreness in my breasts during my monthly cycle. For the first time in my life, my breasts began to get sore. At first, I just thought this was my body going through changes, and it was something I was going to have to start getting used to.

Sheryl Siverand

Age:	34
Stage:	3
Occupation:	Teacher
Residence:	Houston, Texas
Procedure:	Modified Radical Mastectomy
Treatment:	Chemotherapy & Radiation
Survivorship:	1 month
Lymph Node Involvement:	6 / 20

After my doctor did a biopsy and discovered I had cancer, he let me know that I didn't have any options. I needed to have a modified radical mastectomy. It seemed this cancer was very aggressive, and it wasn't going to allow me any time to doodle around. I had to move fast and be as aggressive with it as it was being with me.

I had a mammogram in 1992, but nothing had shown up. Two years later, the cancer was very distinctive and evident on my mammogram.

I guess most people would wonder why I would have a

mammogram at the age of 32. Well, I kept having a lot of ear infections and other infections. Every time I turned around my white blood cell count was very high. Finally, my physician ordered a mammogram. At that time they could find nothing.

When the doctors completed my surgery, they found out the cancer was in my lymphatic system and my vascular system as well. Fortunately, the involvement in my vascular system was confined to the area of my breast. They removed 20 lymph nodes and six were positive. As a result of the lymph node involvement, I ended up having to have both chemo and radiation.

They had a really difficult time installing the catheter in my chest for my chemotherapy treatments. I was told it was going to be a very simple procedure, but it ended up taking over three hours. My doctor said they ran into complications because I had very small veins and a very small chest cavity. Even when I went in for my treatments, they would have to find a radiologist to access the catheter first.

Having a catheter in my chest was very painful. In fact, I began experiencing muscle spasms in my chest area as a result of it. At first I didn't think the chemo was so bad, but every treatment seemed to get worse and worse. I had stomach cramps, headaches and vomiting. My tongue also turned purple and was swollen. I know that some people don't experience these things, but I think I had every possible side effect that you could have from chemo.

The most difficult part of the whole thing for me was being a single parent. My 5-year-old son was going from relative to relative as I went through my treatments. One day he told me, "Mom, you have to go to the doctor so much, why don't you just give me a key to the house? Then I can come in and make myself a snack and watch the Power Rangers while you have your treatments."

I just had to laugh. With him thinking like that, I didn't know when he would ever get a key to my house. I know that he was just trying to be helpful. As a result of my treatment, he knew more about breast cancer than most men.

Because I was so young, I thought about having reconstructive surgery. However, my insurance would not pay for

"One day he told me, 'Mom, you have to go to the doctor so much, why don't you just give me a key to the house? Then I can come in and make myself a snack and watch the Power Rangers while you have your treatments.'"

anything but saline implants. At this point, I felt funny about putting anything foreign in my body. I had heard so many women talking about having reconstruction with their own body fat. For me, I thought that would be the only option I would want. Since my insurance refused to pay for using your own body fat for reconstruction, I just totally forgot about it. Besides, when I really thought about it, I was tired of being cut on.

After going through what I have gone through, I can't tell large breasted women enough to be careful. I know it was always very difficult to examine my breasts. In fact, a few months before I had my surgery I had come very close to having breast reduction because they were so large and I had some much discomfort and irritation. My doctor had already consented to do the breast reduction.

As I planned to have the surgery they never said anything about doing another mammogram or blood work. The only thing that stopped me was the financial aspect. I had scheduled the surgery during a time I was only going to be working part-time. I finally decided the money could be spent better on my essential items. I guess it was the Lord's way of telling me, "Girl, keep your money in your pocket."

I keep thinking what would have happened if I had gone ahead with the breast reduction. In the back of my mind I think maybe my situation might have been fatal because no one seemed to be concerned about finding out if there was anything in my breast before doing the surgery.

Although my mom had been diagnosed with breast cancer two months before I was diagnosed, I still cringe when I hear women think they are safe because they don't have a family history of cancer. We have got to realize that with odds like one out of eight ... no one is safe.

Gloria Harmon

I went to a jazz concert one afternoon. I was trying to be cute, so I decided to wear something sleeveless. It got rather cool that day, but I didn't think much of it because I was having a very good time. Two days later my arm swelled up like a balloon. I had no idea what was causing it and thought I was going to go crazy. I went to the doctor and he told me I had lymphedema ... I had never heard of this. But little did I know this was just another word to add to my new vocabulary list since I had been diagnosed with breast cancer.

Gloria Harmon

Age:	37
Stage:	1
Occupation:	Postal Clerk
Residence:	Lynwood, California
Procedure:	Lumpectomy
Treatment:	Radiation
Survivorship:	1 year
Lymph Node Involvement:	None

I never thought I would get breast cancer. But when I went in for my annual pap smear, my doctor suggested I have a mammogram. I was only 36, but she thought I should get a base line. The mammogram showed something suspicious. They did a biopsy. And sure enough, it was cancer.

The surgeon who did the biopsy recommended I have a mastectomy. My mother totally freaked out. She thought we should get a couple more opinions before making a decision that drastic. I went to Long Beach, Calif. The doctors there thought I didn't need a mastectomy, and said that a lumpectomy with radiation would be sufficient.

One of my friends thought I should see another doctor. He even volunteered to pay for it. I saw the doctor he suggested. Once again I was told that a lumpectomy with radiation was all I needed.

After having two consistent opinions, I decided to go with the lumpectomy and radiation. I was very fortunate. I had no side effects.

Once I was diagnosed, no one could believe it. Even though my father had prostate cancer, no one in my family had ever suffered from breast cancer. I was the first. This totally blew my mother's mind. She kept thinking I was going to die before she did.

But I couldn't let it get me down. I kept thinking if I have to go, I have to go ... life goes on. You have to deal with it. Just because you have cancer nothing else stops, so you have to go on. You can't afford to stop.

Ironically, it seemed that I got more support from my male friends than I did from my female friends. One of my male friends wanted to take off work so that he could sit with me after my surgery. It seemed as if all of my male friends came to visit me in the hospital. Only two of my female friends visited.

In fact, one of my female friends crossed me out when she found out that I had breast cancer. After I called her and told her, she said, "I will talk to you later." Well, later just happened to be about six months later!

When I found out I had breast cancer I asked God to just give me another chance, and I would do whatever I could to let other women know about the disease. Now I feel that God gave me a second chance so that I can spread the news to other women and let them know they can make it. Breast cancer does not have to be a death sentence.

"This totally blew my mother's mind. She kept thinking I was going to die before she did."

# Stephanie Reed

When I first found out I had cancer I got down on my knees and said, "Lord, this is something I cannot handle. I am going to leave it in your hands, and I am not going to pick it back up again." Instead of saying, "Why me?" I was thanking God for letting me know something was there because I had no symptoms, no soreness, nothing.

I never found a lump, I had just gone in for my annual checkup. After the doctor did my pap smear, I told him I wanted a mammogram, just to have a base line exam. He said that because I was under 40, did not have a lump, and had no family history of cancer, he could not do a mammogram. But I was so adamant he finally gave in and did it. After I left his office I went on vacation, but when I returned home there was a message on my answering machine stating I needed to have another mammogram right away.

Stephanie Reed

Age:	37
Stage:	1
Occupation:	Technical Care Partner
Residence:	Los Angeles, California
Procedure:	Mastectomy / Reconstruction
Treatment:	None
Survivorship:	5 months
Lymph Node Involvement:	None

I went in and they took another X-ray of my breasts. This time they confirmed there was a distinctive spot. The area was like a capsule and had little leaves branching out from it. The doctor wanted to know what possessed me to have a mammogram in the first place. I really couldn't explain it. I just knew ... I thought it was time.

I went back two days later. After a biopsy, they told me it was cancerous. Because it was so small they did say that I could have a lumpectomy. But they could not guarantee that the rest of my breast wasn't affected.

I opted to have a complete mastectomy. For me, it seemed to be the best option. I did not want to go around wondering, "Did they get it all? Is there still some cancer in my breast?"

The night before the surgery I told my husband that one of my breasts was going to be gone tomorrow. I wanted to know how that was going to make him feel. He said to me, "Stephanie, if that means prolonging your life, I can deal with one breast."

After hearing his response I felt very comfortable with my decision. I went ahead and had the surgery the next day. Afterward, they let me know that there were no lymph nodes involved, which meant I did not have to have chemotherapy or radiation.

When I was recovering from the surgery, my husband was very conscious not to touch the area because it was tender.

After a while, I told him, "Baby, it ain't tender any more."

He eventually began kissing the top where the incision was, just as if my breast was still there.

"He said to me, 'Stephanie, if that means prolonging your life, I can deal with one breast.'"

Because he was so comfortable with me and I was comfortable with myself, I never thought about reconstruction. In fact, it wasn't until much later when we went on vacation to Las Vegas that I seriously started thinking about reconstruction. I wanted to wear a dress that did not require a bra. My prosthesis was nice, but I wanted that extra flexibility of being able to go without a bra if I really wanted to.

I have to admit, at first the idea made me nervous when they told me all that I would have to go through. It really seemed like a long, drawn out process. They originally told me it would take at least six months before I could even be considered for reconstruction. I was astonished when they called me after only a few months.

I was fortunate that my doctor had left enough skin around my incision, so it really wasn't difficult for them to do the reconstruction. The one thing that really shocked me was that it hurt more than the mastectomy did. I thought that the reconstruction would be a piece of cake, but to my surprise it was very painful.

Instead of taking the body fat from my stomach, my doctor did not want to bother my stomach muscles — he used a saline implant instead. I have to admit, I was very happy with the results.

I now have more flexibility when it comes to wearing what I want to. If I want to wear a bra I can. If I don't, I don't have to. I think most women like that option.

Because my cancer had no symptoms and I never had any history of cancer in my family, I am very obsessive when it comes to doing breast self-exams. Every time I think about it, I check my breast. I guess that is still my initial fear reaction. I don't want the cancer to come back. Maybe, after some time has passed, I will get back to normal and I won't think about it as much.

Nevertheless, I am very aware of my body. I also stress to other women that they need to pay attention to their bodies, to do their breast self-examinations and have regular mammograms.

I do know that dealing with breast cancer brought me closer to God. I have always had faith, but now I truly am a different person and my spiritual life is much stronger.

I am more aware of myself, and I take out more time for myself. Having cancer has let me know that if I don't sit down and take time for myself, I could be gone in a minute.

Alpha Thomas

I decided to join a support group after I was diagnosed. The first day I went I was very eager and excited. I walked in and looked around the room. All the women were white

Alpha Thomas

Age:	37
Stage:	1
Occupation:	Director of Health Coalition
Residence:	Dallas, Texas
Procedure:	Modified Radical Mastectomy
Treatment:	None
Survivorship:	5 years
Lymph Node Involvement:	0 / 8

and older. I thought to myself, "Where are the sisters? ...Where are the Hispanic women?" Not only were all the women white, but they were old enough to be my mother or my grandmother. I was wearing tennis shoes and jeans. There was no way that I fit in.

I headed for the door, but as I approached it, this mental light bulb went off in my head. Yes, these women were white. Yes, these women were much older than I was. But we had one thing in common. We were all breast cancer survivors.

I turned around and went back, and to this day I am glad I did.

When I first discovered my lump I was so caught up in denial that it took me a year to do something about it. I was so into my job and doing everything else that I felt I needed to do that I watched my lump grow from something I could feel to something I could see protruding from my chest.

At that point I thought, "Oh my God, what is going on?" I immediately went to the doctor and had a biopsy.

A few days later, I was all alone when the telephone rang. It was my doctor. He told me that he had gotten the results of the biopsy back and the tumor was malignant.

I could not believe this "fool" was calling me and giving me this type of information over the phone. He was a great surgeon but his bedside manner stunk. He had no idea what my emotional state was at the time. I could have tried to kill myself or anything.

At first, of course I thought he had made a mistake and gotten my lab results mixed up with someone else's. I went into denial, shock, and grief all at the same time.

After I got over the shock, I snapped back into reality and started thinking about what I had to do next.

I had always thought of breast cancer as an old woman's disease, so I wondered why I had it. I was only 32 years old. The one thing I knew for certain was that I couldn't tell my family because they would freak out.

I sat down with my doctor and went over all of my options. I knew early on that I could not deal with chemotherapy. I am sorry but the simple idea of losing my locks was not cool to me.

Because I live alone I had also ruled out radiation; I could not afford to be tired and unable to take care of myself. It seemed obvious that the only option I thought I could live with was a mastectomy.

I am used to being alone and I had pretty much decided that I was going to go through this alone ... all alone. I didn't have a good relationship with my family and had very few friends.

Then I got a call from an older lady in an organization that I am a member of; she informed me that she and another lady would be accompanying me to the hospital.

She was very stern and, in a matter-of-fact way, she let me know that she was not going to accept no for an answer. All I could say was, "Yes, Ma'am."

The day of my surgery, I had a new surge of energy like nothing I had ever experienced in my life. Without a doubt I knew that everything was going to be OK.

I was so energized that they had to increase my medication because my body was fighting the anesthesia. As I felt the medication going through my body I began to pray.

The first thing that I remember, when I awoke, is that I began to feel like I was going to live. I kept saying to myself,

"I knew early on that I could not deal with chemotherapy. I am sorry but the simple idea of losing my locks was not cool to me."

"I am going to lick this thing."

I quickly realized I had to recuperate, get back to work, and get on with the business of living.

I was never afraid of dying from breast cancer. My major concern was that I would not wake up as a result of the anesthesia.

After my surgery, I started talking non-stop. The nurse finally came in and insisted that I get some rest. She let me know that if I did not stop talking she was going to request that my guests leave.

I knew that I could not allow that to happen. Most of the women present were older African American women. They were very spiritual and I knew I needed them there ... I wanted to continue to connect with them.

After they left, I continued to focus on healing.

When my doctor removed the bandage, I looked at my scar and I realized this was the new me, all I had to do was to learn to cope with it.

I was given a prosthesis by the American Cancer Society, but I never really had a good experience with it. One day during the summer, it was really hot and I was sweating like crazy. I took it off, put it in the drawer, and I haven't worn it since. Now, to not wear a prosthesis is more like my political statement, to let people know that breast cancer survivors are real.

Breast cancer made me a very different person. I appreciate life more and I know that the Spirit of God is with me.

A few years later I adopted a baby who was born to crack cocaine-abusing parents. Despite her parents' destructiveness, she had a strong desire to live. Without a doubt, she is a survivor ... I guess we both are survivors.

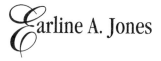

It was the end of September and I was on my way to church. My breast had been hurting really bad, so I reached up and touched the spot that was aching. I felt a lump. It was about 6:00 in the evening and I was on my way to evening mass. I totally lost it. I cried all the way to church, and I cried all the way through church. The next morning I finally pulled myself together and headed straight to the Emergency Room.

All I could think is, "Oh my God, it's cancer!" My mother, my father and my aunt had all died of cancer. Every time I had any type of ailment I always thought it had to be cancer. Little did I know this time I would be right. My greatest fear was about to become a reality.

The pains in my breast had really begun after I had returned from visiting my friend Ann in Richmond, Va. At first I thought it was all in my mind ... I had just helped her out while she was recovering after having some cysts removed from her breasts. When I first experienced the pain, I thought to myself, "Yeah right, that girl had me working like a dog, now my chest is hurting."

But I knew it wasn't anything more than my imagination running wild.

The next thing I knew I was sitting in the Emergency Room waiting to have a mammogram. After I had the mammogram, the doctor told me he would get back with me. I never heard anything, so I thought everything was fine. Then I had to go back to the Emergency Room to get some medicine for my asthma. At that time the doctor informed me that he needed to speak to me about my mammogram results.

Earline A. Jones

Age:	37
Stage:	1
Occupation:	Personnel Management Sergeant, US Army
Residence:	Houston, Texas
Procedure:	Lumpectomy
Treatment:	Chemotherapy & Radiation
Survivorship:	2 years
Lymph Node Involvement:	None

He told me there was definitely a lump in my breast. I let him know I knew that because I could feel it. I just didn't know what caused the lump or what the lump meant. He then referred me to a surgeon.

Because I was in the military, I had to go to Brook Army Medical Center in San Antonio, Texas to have the biopsy.

After they removed the lump, that same day they told me ... it was cancer.

Two months later I went in for additional surgery to remove the tissue around the lump and to check my lymph nodes. I was very blessed because they discovered the cancer had not spread to my lymph nodes. I was happy about that, but I had a real problem with everything else. The three people in my family who suffered from cancer, got sick, found out it was cancer, had their treatments and then they died. I just knew I was outta here. I knew I was not going to make it. I started willing stuff out. I was trying to figure out who could get this and who could get that. I just knew I was getting ready to die.

But Lord behold, I'm still here!

Because of my age and my family history, my doctor recommended that I have both chemotherapy and radiation. I was really nervous about having chemo, and I wanted to be with my family and friends in St. Louis so they could help take care of me. I was glad that the Army granted me permission to have chemo near St. Louis so that I could be with my family. Every time I would go in for chemo they would ask me where is my entourage — my family and friends who really helped me heal.

I was sort of looking forward to chemo because I thought it was going to help me lose weight. Being in the military I have to keep my weight down. Sister girl, I did not lose one single pound. I ended up having to see a nutritionist because I ended up *gaining* weight.

On the other hand, I really didn't have much of a problem with the radiation, it just burned me a little bit. I would tease the radiologist when I would go in for my treatments. I would tell him, "You got me cooking ... now I am well done."

Once they realized I was burning after my treatments, they gave me a cream to put on. It helped a lot. It even lightened up the scar.

The only thing that really bothered me was the thought of intimacy. My surgeon and I talked about this. She said, based on her lifestyle, if it were her, she would have had both of her breasts removed. She wouldn't want to have to deal with the possibility of a recurrence. I thought that might have been OK for her, but it wasn't for me. I was young, single, and a Black female and I still wanted to find a mate. I had heard all the stereotypes about Black men and how they wouldn't accept me now. All these kinds of things were things that worried me. I am proud of the sisters who don't have those problems, but these were things that were going on in my mind.

Luckily, the guy that I was dating kept encouraging me and he didn't have a problem with my surgery. Since my lump was under my breast you might not notice it unless you looked closely. The only thing is, it left my nipple a little cock-eyed. You know like when you are driving in a car and the front head light has been hit and you can read the addresses on every house as you drive down the street. Well, that's the way my nipple looks.

I still feel blessed. My nipple is a little cocked but it still works.

"I still feel blessed. My nipple is a little cocked but it still works."

Overall my male friend has been very supportive, he took me to my doctor's appointments and he has been extremely encouraging. I think he would have been the same way even if I had my entire breast removed. He is just that kind of guy.

Now I keep thanking God that I am still here. I know when they said it was cancer, I knew I was going down. I remember two years ago I had a miscarriage. Before I found out I was pregnant, I thought I had stomach cancer. I kept thinking I was having the same symptoms my mother had. When the doctor told me that I was pregnant, I jumped up and kissed him.

My biggest inspiration is one of my friend's mothers. She came to stay with me after my surgery. Miss Lucille has had both her breasts removed and she is still kicking butt ... she is steadily on the go. I guess there is nothing like somebody who has been there to let you know that you can make it.

Shirley Levingston

It didn't hit me until I had left the doctor's office that I really had breast cancer. All of a sudden, all of the emotions which I had been suppressing came to the surface. It was like a fountain of tears poured out. I cried all the way home.

When I got home, I finally pulled myself together. I have always been a very strong person and I knew that I couldn't let this get me down. At first I didn't know who to turn to or where to go. I had never known anyone who suffered from breast cancer. I had run in the Susan G. Komen Race for the Cure and I had the phone number for the Susan G. Komen Breast Cancer Foundation. Even though I knew it was after business hours, I called anyway and left a message. I said, "I have just been diagnosed today with breast cancer and I need someone to talk to."

Around 7 p.m. I got a call. Someone had gone into the office to pick up some paper work and they had retrieved my message. She had given my message to a breast cancer survivor who in turn called me that evening. All I could do was thank God because I knew I needed to talk to somebody.

Shirley Levingston

Age:	39
Stage:	2
Occupation:	Fleet Analyst/Secretary
Residence:	Dallas, Texas
Procedure:	Lumpectomy
Treatment:	Chemotherapy & Radiation
Survivorship:	2 months
Lymph Node Involvement:	None

It was comforting to speak with someone who had already experienced what I was just anticipating. I asked her all the questions that were flooding my mind. By the time she hung up we were both laughing and joking about bad hair days and scarves. It was like I had just met a new friend. I don't know what I would have done if she hadn't called.

Finding my lump at first was not a big shock because I never really thought it could be cancer. I was in the bathtub doing a breast self-exam, and out of nowhere, there it was ... a lump the size of a marble. I knew it couldn't be anything major because no one in my family ever had breast cancer. There was no doubt in my mind that I was going to be fine.

I told a friend about discovering the lump, and we both prayed over the situation. After that I really never focused much attention on it.

I watched it for two months. I then made an appointment with my doctor for my annual physical. At that point, I brought it to her attention. She ordered a mammogram without hesitation.

The mammogram showed nothing.

We both knew it was there. So, then she referred me to a surgeon to aspirate it. But he could not get any fluid. I finally had an ultrasound which revealed the mass. My next step was going to be a surgical biopsy to take a sample of the lump.

When I received a call on my job a few days after my biopsy requesting me to come back in, I knew something was wrong. I badgered the secretary because I wanted her to tell me what was going on. But she wouldn't say anything except that my doctor wanted me to come in.

Even when I went to the doctor's office I tried to keep a positive attitude, but there is nothing like when you hear the word cancer. It is like your entire mental process goes haywire. I could hear him talking but it was hard to interpret all that he was saying.

He let me know that he felt very confident with my option of having a lumpectomy. In fact, he assured me it would be just as effective as having a mastectomy. Although I was prepared to do whatever was necessary, I was happy with the possibility of preserving my breast.

Because I am used to dealing with things on my own, and I had to build up my internal strength, I did not tell my family until the day of my surgery. I could not deal with anybody killing me off before my time. Nor did I want to listen to all the negative things they may have heard about cancer. I had already decided that I wasn't claiming anything negative. I was depending on the Lord, and I knew with him I could make it.

At first, my sister was very disappointed that I didn't let her know right away. We are very close, and I knew that if I told her she would try to come to Dallas immediately. As it worked out, she got here when I finished my surgery and that was when I needed her most. I had drainage tubes in my breast and I could hardly move my arm. At that point I really felt like I was handicapped.

In fact, I thought I would never be able to stretch my arm out again. A friend of mine who had dealt with other women with breast cancer assured me that I would be able to stretch my arm out after time and doing my exercises. I thought I might be this rare case where my arm was stuck in this position forever.

Every night I would get in the shower and I would let the warm water hit my arm. Then I would try to do my "itsy bitsy spider" exercise as I worked my arm up the bathroom wall. I would even stand on my tiptoes and try to reach as high as I could.

After several days of repeated exercises, I finally did it. I could reach my arm over my head! Now, I had full use of my arm again.

Through this whole ordeal I put my trust in the Lord. I am not married, I don't have a mate, and most of my family is out of town. Therefore, the only one I could truly count on was the Lord.

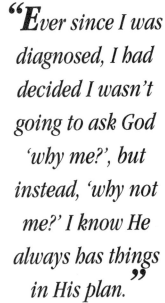

"Ever since I was diagnosed, I had decided I wasn't going to ask God 'why me?', but instead, 'why not me?' I know He always has things in His plan."

I remember being very nervous after my first chemo treatment. I was taking adriamycin, and I had heard all of the horror stories. I didn't quite know what to expect. I got up that morning and I went and sat on the porch. When I stood up to return to the house, I felt kind of weak. As I headed back to my bedroom, I just started talking to the Lord. "Lord, please don't let me be weak now." It was like He was sitting on my couch as I turned the corner. Before I reached my bedroom I felt my strength return.

Ever since I was diagnosed, I had decided I wasn't going to ask God "why me?", but instead, "why not me?" I know He always has things in His plan.

To show you how the Lord works, four years before my diagnosis I had taken out a cancer insurance policy. When I saw it on my check stub, the first thing I did was call payroll and ask them to cancel it. I don't know what happened, but they never canceled it, and I totally forgot about it. Now with all the expenses that I have incurred from having cancer, the extra insurance really comes in handy.

There is no doubt that God has been with me as I have dealt with this disease. But I am also grateful that I have met some other very wonderful women who have had to go through this painful disease we call breast cancer.

Love After Breast Cancer

Relationships that are enhanced
despite the trauma of cancer.

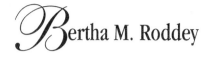

Bertha M. Roddey

My mother's grandfather was the son of a slave, and there was very little self-disclosure on her side of the family. Everything was always very hush, hush.

I was reared by my maternal grandmother. Now that I know more about self-disclosure and how people choose to share information, I understand how she handled it when I began to develop breasts at the ripe age of 9. Instead of having me wear a bra, she put a wrapping around my chest that not only protected my breasts, but it also concealed them. This was her way of keeping my development a secret. It probably was also her way of protecting me — with my fully developed breasts — from any kind of sexual abuse.

I started having cysts when I was in my 30's. I ended up having two operations to have them removed. It really didn't concern me at the time. Later, I ended up having breast reduction because I wanted to be able to wear a strapless bra.

Bertha M. Roddey

Age:	65
Stage:	1
Occupation:	Professor Emeritus, University of North Carolina at Charlotte
Residence:	Catawba, South Carolina
Procedure:	Lumpectomy
Treatment:	None
Survivorship:	5 years
Lymph Node Involvement:	None

During the reduction they removed as many suspicious masses as they could find. I was quite comfortable at that point. I thought maybe I wouldn't have any more cysts ... maybe they had gotten them all.

At this point I had a very false sense of security.

I went along merrily thinking nothing about cancer or anything like that, even though I had a family history of cancer. My father had prostate cancer, my grandmother had colon cancer, and my mother had stomach cancer. But I never entertained the thought of getting cancer myself.

Nevertheless, with the amount of cancer I had in my family it made me very conscientious about going to the doctor, having my breasts examined and having regular mammograms.

Ironically, as I did workshops around the country, I would tell people, "You better be prepared to deal with cancer in your life." Little did I know this would be a self fulfilling prophecy.

The oncologist who took care of my mother when she was sick was so nurturing that I took him on as my general physician. Finally, he suggested I have a mammogram. It wasn't anything he could feel in my breasts. He just thought it was time.

I didn't hear anything about the results of the mammogram so I was sure that nothing was wrong. Then I got a call from him saying that something had showed up on the mammogram. Even though he thought it might not be malignant, he felt it needed to be checked out further.

Being the very busy woman that I am, I told him I didn't have time. I now realize that was a very dumb thing to say. When it comes to your health, you have to make time to take care of things.

As I rambled off my itinerary for my doctor, he quickly reminded me that we were talking about my health. Finally, he agreed to let me go to a workshop I was giving in Cleveland, if I agreed to have the lump removed under a local anesthetic.

My surgeon and I had such a great rapport. When he removed the lump, I got up off the table, looked him straight in the face, and said, "Your singing was terrible!" Then I headed out the door to have lunch with my secretary.

A week had passed since my return home and still I hadn't heard anything about the biopsy. I was sure the lump was benign. I waited another week before I called about the results. I told the receptionist that I hadn't heard anything about my test results and I just wanted to know what had happened.

The nurse called me back very excited. "Oh, my God," she said. "We need you to come in right away." I knew then there was something wrong.

When I went in my doctor gave me my options. I could have a mastectomy with chemotherapy or I could have a lumpectomy with radiation. Right away I let him know that I was opting to have a lumpectomy.

I can honestly say the first thing you think when you hear the

> *"Ironically, as I did workshops around the country, I would tell people, 'You better be prepared to deal with cancer in your life.' Little did I know this would be a self fulfilling prophecy."*

word cancer, is "I am going to die." I was totally immobilized once I found out the lump was malignant. Before that I had been very cavalier, very *laissez faire* and very flip.

My first concern was my husband, Ted. I had only been married to him for nine months. That's why I chose a lumpectomy. I wanted my husband to wake up and see as much breast as he could sitting up there.

His first wife had died. I kept thinking, "Here I am. I am going to die and make him a widow again." I kept thinking, "I bring this into this man's life and he is going to have to go through a grieving process again."

Despite my anxiety, my husband was very calm and supportive through everything. His family also was right there by my side.

After the surgery, things took a turn for the better. I had caught the cancer in a very early stage, and there was no lymph node involvement. My doctor gave me a recovery rate of 95 percent.

For a while after my surgery I went through a stage of denial. It was as if the portion of my breast that had been operated on didn't exist any more. I didn't want to look at it, and I definitely didn't want to touch it.

Nine months after Ted and Bertha were married she developed breast cancer.

It was the support she received from her husband and in-laws that helped her recover.

I ended up having to call my friend Marva one day to help me change the dressing on it because I was determined not to touch it. Most of us perceive ourselves as being super women. We feel we are so strong and so independent that we don't need anybody to do anything for us ... that was me. When I got to the point where I didn't want to touch my wound, I had to call for help.

The cancer made me stop for a moment and re-evaluate everything I was doing. I realized I could stop and say, "I have got this" and just sit here and die, or I could continue to go on about my life.

I have a great deal of faith. I know there is a Master's plan to everything, and I feel that I am part of it. I realize it is not my will, but God's will ... whatever happens in my life.

I think once you have dealt with cancer, you are more in tune with your body. Everything that happens sort of triggers a nerve and you wonder if maybe the cancer has returned.

I bumped my leg. When I went in to the doctor the first thing I told him was, "I just know it's cancer."

He just looked at me and laughed. "I have been in this business for a long time. I have never known anybody to have cancer of the breast and have it to come back where you are saying it is," he jokingly responded.

I think it is great to have a good relationship with your doctor because then you are not inhibited. You are very comfortable in letting him know exactly what is going on with your body.

I remember one visit I was joking with my doctor. I told him, "My mother always called you her little boy doctor. But you are not a little boy doctor anymore. You are fat, and pudgy, and you really don't know all the things you think you know about what's going on with me."

He just sat there silently and took all that I was dishing out at him. Then he said, "Your test results all seem fine." He paused and added with a smirky grin, "But I must inform you, you only have two weeks to live."

That was all I needed to get cranked up again. I said, "OK. But let me tell you something. I am going to live to be 100 years old. I know that you are a little bit younger than I am, but you are going to be running around in a wheelchair trying to find me."

After dealing with cancer, I have developed a greater appreciation for the little things in life, like waking up in the morning and looking out my window and seeing the robins and squirrels chasing each other. It has brought me back to the point I was at when I was a child and wanted to find the key to how the universe worked. Now I have a deeper appreciation for small things and little creatures. At one point in my life I was too busy to even notice them.

There is no doubt that I have learned to turn negatives into positives. There was no way that I could treat cancer as a death sentence. I think if the doctor tells you that you only have 10 months to live, you need to live those 10 months to the fullest.

My doctor once told me, "You might get hit by a car before you die from cancer."

"I think if the doctor tells you that you only have 10 months to live, you need to live those 10 months to the fullest."

68

$\mathscr{O}$dell Lee

In my early 20s I found myself a single parent with two children. I was divorced, and I had taken on four younger siblings after the death of both of my parents.

Odell Lee

Age:	41
Stage:	1
Occupation:	Medical Records Technician
Residence:	Dallas, Texas
Procedure:	Mastectomy & Reconstruction
Treatment:	None
Survivorship:	3 years
Lymph Node Involvement:	0/13

Because of all this, I always worked two jobs and went to school at the same time. From the very beginning, it was evident that I had to develop a lifestyle of being on the go ... if I was going to survive. Therefore, I never saw my house during the light of day, except on weekends. In order to keep up with my tight schedule, many times I would go straight from work to school. I held down many different part-time jobs because I knew I had to do what I could in order to pay tuition and take care of my family.

A month after I had a complete physical, I found a lump while doing a breast self-exam. I moved around in a different angle, but the lump was still there.

Based on my knowledge of breast cancer as a disability liaison, I knew then that I needed to act swiftly. When I went to the doctor he recommended an ultrasound and a mammogram. As a result of both tests he referred me to a surgeon for a biopsy.

The surgeon told me, "It's cancer, Miss Lee."

I was so calm. He asked me if I understood what he had just said.

I told him, based on my job, I had probably read 100,000 cases where women had been diagnosed with breast cancer. It was pretty clear what diagnosis he had just given me. I didn't go into shock, but it was like I was dropped into this deep well. Then I realized I was going to have to accept this as I had so many other painful experiences in my life.

My doctor gave me two options: One was to have a modified radical mastectomy, the other was to have a lumpectomy removing tissue around the lump and radiation for six weeks. I realized after a few days that the best option for me was a modified radical mastectomy with reconstructive surgery. I knew this would take several phases and would also mean having a saline implant before it was complete.

This was an extremely hard time for me and I had to draw on everyone's strength around me. I had to pray for guidance on how to deal with this. I went back to work and handled things as if nothing was wrong. I told my boss I was going to need to take a leave of absence because I was having "female surgery."

I did not tell anyone about my disease except for my immediate family. I didn't even tell my co-workers. It was taking every bit of my strength to keep from breaking down emotionally about it, I didn't need to deal with other people's fears.

I had the surgery and I went home the next day.

There was no doubt that I had to get my life back to normal as soon as possible.

Breast cancer by far is one of the hardest things I have had to go through alone. Sometimes I did not share information because I felt that others would not understand my plight. I waited until two days before my surgery before I even told my family. I had enough to deal with. I did not want to also have to overcome their fears. You know, everyone has this hang up about the big "C." Therefore, I knew that I had a battle to fight. I knew where my faith in God was; I couldn't risk worrying about where their faith lay.

I needed strong women surrounding me who could join me in prayer and proclaim the victory with me. I found some prayer warriors that were truly ladies of wisdom. One lady was from Africa. Although she could not even speak English, she prayed for me with the help of an interpreter.

Truly, after my experience with breast cancer I have never been the same. Now I am always going to community meetings and I am involved with several organizations. I feel that God gave me a new life and he has a purpose for me here and I really want that purpose to be fulfilled.

I know that I have a story to tell, but I am not my story. I think my life stands for itself. I have successfully picked my life up. I have had to live through quite a few crises in my life. I have had to feed myself with the fruit of positive books. I know that tragedies are a part of my life. But they are not my total life.

Despite the things I have had to encounter, I believe I have been successful. My daughter Shelby is now on the Dean's list at Howard University, and my son Robert is very involved in music and is about to release his first album.

Through the years I have heard many people say, "If you take one step, God will take two." But my family literally bears witness to that fact. I have had to overcome so many different things, whether it was being robbed of my dignity by a marriage gone bad, or someone not giving me a job that I felt I rightfully deserved and desperately needed to take of my family.

"My having breast cancer made no difference to him, because I was still a Black woman."

Being single, I have to admit I had second thoughts about intimacy. It was challenging when I did date. I was overly sensitive when it came to dealing with my breasts. I had learned to live with my body for 38 years and all of sudden it had changed. Then finally I resolved within myself just to say, "This is me, take it or leave it!"

I also began to realize that being a Black woman approaching 40 the chance of my not marrying was very high. I wondered if a Black man would be willing to commit to me knowing the type of surgery I had. I guess that is why I fell in love with my husband, because it really didn't matter to him.

He is a very religious man. My having breast cancer made no difference to him, because I was still a Black woman. He realized that I had caught the disease early, and had an excellent prognosis for recovery.

He also is very conscious of his eating habits, and has a very healthy diet. His lifestyle complements mine tremendously. We take natural vitamins and eat a lot of fresh foods. I can truly say that I feel that odds of my having to deal with breast cancer again are slim to none.

Cynthia Coleman

The first thing my mother and I did after I finished chemo, was to head for Florida.

Cynthia Coleman

Age:	42
Stage:	2
Occupation:	Assistant Store Manager
Residence:	Dallas, Texas
Procedure:	Modified Radical Mastectomy
Treatment:	Chemotherapy
Survivorship:	1 year
Lymph Node Involvement:	2 / 30

I was bald, I had no eyelashes, but I had this big black wig. Up until that point, I had just worn the wig for other people because being bald did not bother me.

One day we were walking along the beach and a friend of mine asked to take my picture. All of a sudden, I yanked the wig off and I flung it in the air. I didn't care if anybody saw my bald head, and I definitely didn't care what they thought. I was just happy to be alive. After that the three of us just walked along the beach totally carefree. I was proud of myself: bald head, missing eye-lashes and all!

Reflecting back, I have to admit I first realized something was wrong after I had started working out. I had finally decided to go on this diet and to get in great shape.

I thought the best thing to do was to go back to the gym full force. I used to be really involved in working out, so I didn't give myself a chance to gradually build up ... I went back full steam ahead.

After a few weeks of working out, I noticed a tenderness under my right arm. At first I just attributed it to my strenuous regimen. It also was a couple of weeks before my period. I know that sometimes before your period your breasts can get tender, so I didn't think much of it.

But it continued to bother me. I asked my boyfriend, J.R., to feel the side of my breast because I thought I felt a lump. At the time I wasn't sure if it was just my imagination or if something was really there.

J. R. told me that it felt odd to him.

That was the only confirmation I needed. I went to the doctor immediately. Within no time I was referred to both an oncologist and a surgeon. The surgeon did a biopsy and diagnosed that the lump was malignant.

I could not believe it! Just a year before I had a complete physical and my gynecologist assured me there was nothing to worry about, that my breasts were very easy to examine. She had suggested that I wait until I was 40 to get my mammogram.

Well, I turned 40 in April and I found my lump in October.

Once I was diagnosed, I got busy trying to find out everything I could about breast cancer. I decided the best thing to do was to get all the information you can.

I called the toll free number for the American Cancer Society, and a woman on the telephone told me about all kinds of books. She even asked me what my symptoms were. In actuality I learned more from this woman on the telephone than I did from my doctors.

"I had not had a child before the age of 30, I carried a disproportionate amount of fat on my body, I had an early menstrual cycle. I was like an accident waiting to happen."

Once I got the literature and started reading, it seemed the writing was on the wall. I had not had a child before the age of 30, I carried a disproportionate amount of fat on my body, I had an early menstrual cycle. I was like an accident waiting to happen. Based on all these factors, I was at high risk for cancer. I also had been under a tremendous amount of stress at the time. But I realize there are people who don't fit into any of these categories and they still get breast cancer. I just think maybe these things contributed to my case.

I think the most difficult thing for me to do was to tell my mother and J.R. I knew that both of them would take it harder than I did. And it was true.

My mother came down the day of the biopsy, and she stayed with me the entire time. My mother and I have a special relationship — there is no doubt that she played a major role in my healing process.

Then things took a sharp turn for the worse between J.R. and me. He left the day of my surgery.

I later realized that it had nothing to do with me losing my breast. Instead, it had to do with the fact that he wasn't ready to lose me. His reaction was like that of many people; he had never dealt with any one who had cancer, and it scared him to death. We continued to talk about things over the phone, and gradually I was able to relieve his fears, and he began to realize he wasn't going to lose me after all.

During my operation the doctors discovered that instead of having one lump, I had two ... so that ruled out my option for a lumpectomy. The lumps were very close to my chest wall; therefore, they had to do a radical mastectomy and remove my entire breast along with the lymph nodes under my arm.

My oncologist introduced me to a cancer study. The study allowed me to receive a double dose for three months instead of a single dose for six months. Needless to say, I was glad to get the chemo over. I was also happy, because as a result of this study, I will be watched closely for the next five years.

As for J.R., once he realized I wasn't going to die, he came back. I had just finished my chemotherapy treatments. I still remember when he first walked through the door. Although I was no longer feeling very sick, I still looked sort of sick. My head was bald, and of course I had no eyelashes. But the best thing for me was when he walked up to me, lifted my blouse and kissed my scar. Then I knew he was ready to accept me for who I was now. I knew everything was going to be all right.

We got married the month after I finished my chemotherapy.

Robyn Paige

I never thought I would want to have any children after I was diagnosed with breast cancer. I had one physician who told me not to even think about it because of all the hormonal changes you go through during pregnancy. Then another physician said, "There are children after breast cancer." But she recommended waiting two years after my treatments were completed.

It hadn't even been a year since I completed chemotherapy when I found out I was pregnant. I wasn't afraid at first. Then I had a doctor's appointment. The first thing the nurse said was, "I think I would always be afraid with chemotherapy that something would happen to my baby." I thought to myself, "Gee, if I wasn't afraid, I am now."

I couldn't wait to deliver my baby. All my anxieties really hit me when I went into labor. I started panicking. I didn't know what I was going to see when the baby was delivered. I kept worrying — was I going to be elated or was I going to be devastated? I thank God that I was elated. I gave birth to a healthy baby boy.

Robyn Paige

Age:	35
Stage:	4
Occupation:	Homemaker
Residence:	Charleston, West Virginia
Procedure:	Mastectomy
Treatment:	Chemotherapy & Radiation
Survivorship:	4 years
Lymph Node Involvement:	None

I had already prepared myself for breast cancer by dealing with my sister Kim. I had been by her side in Houston when she had gone through a bi-lateral mastectomy. Her experience made me very conscious of breast cancer and doing self-exams.

In fact, I examined my breasts right after her surgery and I found a lump. Based on our family history, her physician cautioned her to have me check it out.

I returned home and immediately had a mammogram. My doctor informed me that one area looked highly suspicious, with calcification around it. I had the lump removed and found out it was cancerous.

I think that I had unknowingly been preparing myself to deal with this when I spent time with Kim. I sort of went through a rude awakening with her surgery. As I saw her going into the operating room, I started to examine myself. I wanted to see if I could deal with something so traumatic.

I was devastated when they wheeled her away for the surgery. I thought, "How is she going through this? What is she thinking? If I had to do this would I be able to?"

Once I was given my diagnosis, it didn't bother me because I had already gone through it with Kim. My doctor knew I had been educated about breast cancer from dealing with my sister, and that I was also a nursing student. Therefore, he was very direct in giving me my options of having a lumpectomy or a mastectomy.

The only thing I had a problem with was whether or not to have chemo. My oncologist thought I should have chemo but I opted to have radiation instead.

After my lumpectomy, I had to go back to the doctor because he had removed my lymph nodes under my arm and my arm began to swell. My doctor did not initially put a drainage tube in. I guess he thought that he had done such a good job there wasn't going to be a problem. It would drain itself. As a result of the poor drainage I developed a large knot under my arm. I am one of those people who never wants to be a problem patient, therefore I didn't say anything about it until it literally grew to the size of a baseball. At first I remembered that he had said there would be some swelling so I didn't think much of it. Finally, I thought this was getting out of hand. I went in to have him check it out. He ended up having to make several incisions to get it to drain properly.

To this day I still have a little swelling in my arm. I now realize that it is lymphedema and it is something I will have to live with.

A year later, I noticed a lump in my sternum area. I watched it for a while. Then I noticed it was getting bigger. I told myself, "No, it is not getting bigger, I'm just getting smaller."

I went to see my oncologist. He assured me it was nothing. I went to my family doctor and he also agreed it was nothing. However, he did a mammogram anyway and the mammogram was OK.

A year and a half later, I went back for a checkup. This time my physician was very concerned. I couldn't understand —

"A year later, I noticed a lump in my sternum area. I watched it for a while. Then I noticed it was getting bigger. I told myself, 'No, it is not getting bigger, I'm just getting smaller.'"

this was the same man who told me I didn't have anything to worry about. He did a needle aspiration, but it was inconclusive and it looked suspicious. I had a biopsy to remove it.

It was cancer. This would be my second bout with cancer.

My doctor suggested I have a bone marrow transplant. I thought that was too extreme. I was not willing to expose myself to that. I opted for a second opinion. I knew that I would have to have a mastectomy, and I was willing to do that. I was also willing to take chemotherapy, which I had not looked forward to before.

After my second opinion, they recommended chemotherapy. That was OK ... I had anticipated that and felt I could deal with it.

After the mastectomy they removed lymph nodes underneath my sternum area that I didn't even know existed. Thank God all of them were negative.

At this time they were diagnosing me in stage 4 because of the location of my lump. I didn't ask the doctor about my prognosis. I already knew what stage 4 meant. To me, that didn't carry any weight. I don't think anyone can determine your life expectancy but God. I put it all in God's hand.

Chemo was definitely the hardest part of this whole thing. It was a very different feeling. When I was going through it I was strong, I knew that God was going to carry me through. I was a real trooper. After a lot of prayer I went ahead and did what I had to do.

After my first treatment, I felt like a million dollars. I called my mom and said, "Let's go get some Chinese food." I sat down and ate it. I felt fine. I went home and I was deathly sick. I threw up all night long.

The next time I went in for treatment I thought, this time I will be fine. I blamed the first illness on the Chinese food. Every time I convinced myself it would get better. Then I would go home and throw up anyway. But I kept psyching myself up for the next time.

Because Kim and my brother Michael had both dealt with breast cancer, I got a lot of support from them. They were very open when it came to discussing their bouts with breast cancer with other people as well. At first their openness bothered me a lot because I was always hoping they wouldn't bring my name up.

I thought my breasts were a part of my body and that was a very private thing. I was single and I didn't want them to hamper me getting in a relationship in any way.

Before I finished my chemo treatments I got a job at the James Paige III Learning Center as the executive director.

At first I was very nervous. I was scheduled to have my fifth chemo treatment and I was just starting my new job. I was having my treatment on Friday and I started my job on that following Monday.

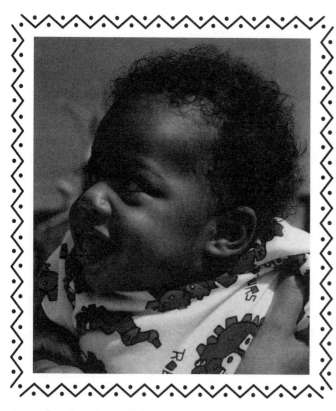

A year after chemotherapy Robyn Paige found out she was pregnant. She later gave birth to a healthy baby boy, James Harvey Paige IV.

Since I was still taking chemo and I didn't know how I was going to feel, I knew I had to tell my new boss, James Paige that I had breast cancer.

I remember his eyes got really big when I first told him. I knew that he was thinking, "This poor girl, this must be a hard thing for her to deal with."

We later became very good friends. I learned to respect his opinion, so when I first had to start wearing a wig, I stopped by to see him and get his reaction. But I was really shocked because it didn't bother him at all.

I thought at first when he saw the wig he would ignore it. But he didn't. He told me that he thought it looked nice. He never treated me like I was a person with cancer. In fact later, he told me that he was attracted to my strength and marveled at the positive attitude I had while I was going through everything.

Even though I was a widow and had two children, he didn't have a problem with that either. After being friends for so long our friendship turned into a relationship. We later realized we wanted to be a family. We got married in August and now besides our two children, we have a beautiful baby boy.

My Mother Had Breast Cancer
Having the trait in the family.

heryl Reneé Basye

After my surgery I decided I wasn't just going to sit around looking any kind of way. I got up from the hospital bed and went into the bathroom to put on a little lipstick. I just wanted to jazz myself up. If I had to be in the hospital, at least I didn't want to have to look sick. While I was in the bathroom, I fainted and the lipstick went up one side of my face. A nurse came in and found me laying on the floor. Needless to say, she was very upset. For my punishment, she said she was going to leave the lipstick on my face because I had no business trying to go to the bathroom by myself anyway.

I guess I never really considered myself vain. Buy I think you begin to challenge everything about yourself when you have something taken away. I have heard someone refer to women's breasts as their "badge of femininity." I never really thought of it in that way. But when you lose one, whether you thought of it in that light or not, it starts to take on a different meaning.

I found my lump by doing a breast self-exam. I stupidly did not do anything for a year hoping that it would go away. Breast cancer was not anything new to me. My mother Zora Talbert Basey died from the disease while I was in college. The year after she died, I felt a lump in my breast. I panicked and went to the doctor right away. My doctor said it was just a swollen milk gland and it would go away. Sure

Cheryl Reneé Basye

Age:	48
Stage:	2
Occupation:	CEO
Residence:	Garland, Texas
Procedure:	Modified Radical Mastectomy
Treatment:	Chemotherapy
Survivorship:	10 years
Lymph Node Involvement:	None

enough, it did go away. Fifteen years later I discovered another lump. I thought maybe it was the same thing, but this time it did not go away.

It seemed like the more I touched it the more it appeared to grow by leaps and bounds. At first I thought it was all in my mind. I kept envisioning it becoming the size of a basketball. Finally, I decided to go to the doctor.

Although the physician's assistant didn't think it felt like anything to worry about he scheduled me for a mammogram anyway. I had never had one.

The mammographer saw something that concerned him, so he ordered an ultrasound. Then they asked me what was I doing for the rest of the afternoon. Those words were enough to make me panic. They sent me to a surgeon for a needle biopsy, but they couldn't get any fluid. The next day I had a surgical biopsy.

As I was coming to from the anesthesia, I heard the doctor telling my brother he regretted to say that it was cancerous.

The next day I walked around in a daze. I went to Neiman Marcus because I decided that if I was going to the hospital I was going to be cute. Like most women, spending money to me was therapeutic.

After the surgery they found out that I was only feeling the tip of my lump. It was actually the size of a baseball and it was resting on my chest wall muscles. But fortunately, there were no lymph nodes involved.

Due to the size and location of my lump, my doctor did not want me to take radiation. He did recommend chemotherapy.

After my surgery, I had a sigh of relief that the cancer was not in my lymph nodes. But to physically look at myself and see this huge scar was a sad sight.

At that time the AIDS scare had just started and my doctor did not want to give me any type of transfusion because he was not convinced that they had a way of making sure the blood was tested to be free of the HIV virus.

As I began to recuperate the first thing I started thinking

"As I began to recuperate the first thing I started thinking about was dating. I wondered, 'How would I date now? How do I explain to men that I am going to be a little bit different than your average woman?'"

about was dating. I wondered, "How would I date now? How do I explain to men that I am going to be a little bit different than your average woman?" I had all of that racing through my mind. But all in all I was just happy to be alive.

The one thing I had in my favor was a role model to watch — I had seen how my mother dealt with breast cancer. She had dealt with it very well. Even though she had a radical mastectomy she never let that slow her down. She had a lot of strapless gowns, so she just modified them. She would have chiffon added to one side and drape it over her shoulder. Because she dealt with breast cancer so well, I developed a foundation in her honor.

I remember the doctors had told her not to worry about her lump, so she waited a year. When they finally went in to do the surgery it was too late, the cancer had already spread. She only lasted two years after that.

My only really big scare since my diagnosis came when I was in a car accident a few years ago. The only thing that bothered me was that my arm had swollen. It frightened me, because I remembered when my mother's arm swelled it meant that her cancer had returned. I later found out that I had just developed lymphedema. Now, I realize that it is just something that I have to live with. Some days it is more swollen than others. There are probably things that I could do to make it better, but I have never been one to set limitations on myself. Unless it is going to kill me, I am going to do it.

I think as a result of having breast cancer I have learned to appreciate life more. When you go through a life threatening disease you always think of the things that you wish you had done.

Now I tend to devote more time to myself. I get manicures and pedicures every two weeks. I get a regular massage and I go to the health spa whenever I can.

I have also developed an incredible amount of patience. I tend to take a lot of time with other people. Tomorrow is not promised. I don't think you need to live your life fanatically, because of dealing with cancer. But I think if you take something on you should finish it.

I have always been the type of person who liked running around the house in my underwear ... boobs hanging out and all. I would always wait until the very last minute before I got dressed. After my mastectomy, I went back to that same process, except I was always careful to make sure I had a towel wrapped around my chest. I later realized that my towel was my way of avoiding looking at my scar, which was my reminder that I had breast cancer.

I have fibroid cysts in my breasts, so having lumpy breasts was never a real issue for me. But one day I started have a shooting pain through my breast. At first I was determined to ignore it; if anything was wrong I did not want to know.

After dealing with the pain for a week and a half, it got so bad that I was grabbing my breast in meetings. I immediately went to the Emergency Room.

I now know that was not the thing to do because doctors never associate pain with cancer. Even though I had a history of cancer, they just gave me some Ibuprofen and sent me home.

Patsy Harris

Age:	47
Stage:	3
Occupation:	President of Sister's Breast Cancer Survivor Network
Residence:	Los Angeles, California
Procedure:	Modified Radical Mastectomy
Treatment:	Chemotherapy
Survivorship:	3 years
Lymph Node Involvement:	4 / 20

Finally, I ran into a friend while I was out getting something to eat. I told her about the pain I was experiencing in my breast. She suggested I get a mammogram. I took her advice.

By this time I had a lump that was three inches long and I was diagnosed as being in the third stage of cancer.

I ended up having to wait three weeks before I could actually have my surgery. I think that is the best thing that could happen to me. I accepted the fact that my breast was going to be gone. And it was really OK. Each day when I would get in the shower, I would have a conversation with my breast. I know it sounds crazy but, yeah, I talked to my breast. I would tell it, "We are good friends, but you are going to have to go."

By the time I had surgery I was definitely OK with giving up my breast. I wasn't OK with what I was going to be like as a human being and as a woman. I didn't quite know what I was going to do, or how I was going to adjust. Undoubtedly, the hardest part for me was looking at the scar and having it be a constant reminder that I had breast cancer.

It was very fortunate that I ended up connecting with a group of upper middle-class white women. They were all searching for truth. They accepted me, and I learned a lot from them. I started hearing about lymph nodes, different types of chemotherapy ... before, chemo was just chemo.

At that point I realized that color didn't have any relevancy at all. The doctors were treating white women the same way they were treating us. We all had the same questions.

We couldn't understand why they were telling us not to worry about lymphedema and they were cutting up our nerves.

The one thing I did find out was that there were 50 different opinions out there. Yet there weren't any real, conclusive answers. You had to go for what you knew. You had to be empowered to ask the doctor the right questions in reference to your situation.

All these things started me to dream at night that there was something that I could do to make a difference for other African American women, and for all women ... because I had to remember who helped me at first.

At one point, I had come to the realization, "I have lost my breast so what do I do now?" Undoubtedly, I needed a prosthesis. My insurance paid for protheses, so that should not have been a problem. But it was. I found out that I had to pay for my prosthesis up front, then they would reimburse me. I was on disability and I couldn't afford to pay for one. So my friend put it on her charge card. She said, "Girl, if we can get you back to looking normal, I think you will start feeling better."

Although my mother had breast cancer, I still didn't have a role model to reflect on because she never talked about it. She never shared any of her emotional trauma. I don't know why women stay in the closet. It seems to be a stigma or an embarrassment, even in my church. I could have stomach cancer or a brain tumor but not breast cancer. The one thing you don't do is stand up in church and say, "I have breast cancer." It's like we are getting a little bit too personal here.

I felt like I was caught in a maze. I didn't know who to run to. I would go to my minister and try to tell him how I felt. All he would say was how good I looked. I guess he would look at me and since I didn't look sick he felt everything had to be OK, but it wasn't.

As I continued to look for someone to understand what I was going through, the one person I definitely learned to depend on was my 16-year-old son.

I didn't know it at the time, but my doctor was giving me the highest dosage of chemo he could possibly give me without being hospitalized. As a result of this I developed peripheral neuropathy, which is severe nerve damage. I would come home from my treatments and I was temporarily paralyzed. My son would have to help me get undressed and put me to bed.

It finally got to the point I felt like taking chemo was driving myself to the electric chair, and what fool is going to drive themselves to the electric chair? I said to myself, "To Hell with this, I am not going anymore." When a friend of mine called, I let her know that I decided I wasn't taking chemo anymore. She made me realize it wasn't the chemo that was the problem. I just didn't want to go alone. I would sit there for two hours as this stuff went through my veins, and this was too much for me to deal with. She decided to go with me ... and that helped me make it through the rest of chemo.

Cancer brought me back to my spirituality. It was hard at first, because God and I had a real serious battle. I felt He had put a lot on my plate at that point.

I went through this point of wondering, was I so bad? Why was he allowing all these things to happen to me? Besides having breast cancer, I was diagnosed with a herniated disk, arthritis and several other conditions. Because of my conditions, 24 hours a day, seven days a week I am in pain. At any given point in time some part of my body is hurting. I have learned how to disguise it because people don't want to be around someone who is always in pain.

I don't know if it is in spite of or because of the pain, but I have become a much stronger person. Some days when the phone rings and it is someone who has just been diagnosed I am able to ignore the pain because I know I can be of help to someone else.

I cannot allow myself to be hung up on the negative aspects of dealing with breast cancer. I have to channel my energies into how I can make a difference in someone else's life.

Janet Morrison

When I took a trip to Egypt, I was really concerned about losing my passport. I thought the best thing to do was to stick it in the pocket of my bra behind my prosthesis. Lo and behold, when we got to the airport the tour guide wanted to collect all of the passports. I tried to slip my passport out without bringing any attention to myself, but it got caught behind my prosthesis. As I continued to try to unhook my passport, the tour guide seemed to be getting very uncomfortable. I don't know what he thought I was going to pull out, but he finally said, "Lady, I am only asking you to show me your passport. I don't want you to show me anything else."

I assured him that was the only thing I had to pull out.

That is just one of the humorous things that I have encountered since I was diagnosed with breast cancer.

I went to my gynecologist because my breast started to show a flakiness. He suggested I have someone else look at it. I went to another physician who said that everything was OK and I didn't have anything to worry about. I really wanted everything to be OK. I watched the flaking for another year, but then my nipple started oozing. That was enough to send me back to the doctor for a biopsy.

I was all by myself when I went back for the results. I wasn't expecting to hear I had any form of cancer. Then the doctor told me I had Paget Disease and, as a result, I needed to have my breast removed. I just got in my car and started to cry.

After I pulled myself together, I went to a cancer center for

Janet Morrison

Age:	48
Stage:	Paget Disease
Occupation:	Field Representative for Teacher's Union
Residence:	Mount Laurel, New Jersey
Procedure:	Mastectomy
Treatment:	None
Survivorship:	13 years
Lymph Node Involvement:	None

a second opinion. I was very excited to know that I was being seen by the noted surgeon Dr. Susan Love. But I knew even she couldn't work miracles.

She asked, "What can I do for you?"

"Tell me there is nothing wrong," I responded.

Once I realized that I needed a mastectomy, I started reading everything that I could about Paget Disease. I couldn't find anything that remotely related to Black women. The one thing that stuck out about all the books I was reading indicated that the women were very dependent. I couldn't relate to that because I was very independent. In fact, I think my independence caused a problem to people who loved me.

I started sharing with my family what was going on. I was surprised to find out that my mother had had breast cancer. I knew that my mother suffered from a number of ailments caused by a lung condition she had since early childhood. I guess I had always focused on the lung condition. After my father told me that she did have breast cancer, I still wondered if it in any way played a role in her death, which I had attributed solely to her lung condition.

I also had an aunt who suffered from breast cancer. I now realize that breast cancer was not something strange to our family. I remember when I was younger members of the family would come in to change the bandage on her chest. I guess I had put that in the back of my mind.

Overall, I think I felt the worst for my father through all of this. He had already dealt with breast cancer with my mother, and now he was having to deal with breast cancer with me. When it comes to breast cancer, I don't think anyone attends to the concerns of men. It seems like they are the third party. Yet, many times they are very much involved.

My doctor offered to put me in touch with support groups after surgery. He also recommended a psychologist. I was determined that wasn't going to be necessary. I had a very strong support network, and I always knew that my father was there if I needed him.

Before I dealt with breast cancer I never thought about

how your mental condition could affect your healing. I was determined to keep a positive mind set, and to keep my sense of humor, no matter what happened.

I have a friend who had a mastectomy and she was always leaving her prosthesis somewhere. She would forget about it and leave it on her bar downstairs. When I first heard about the prosthesis that sticks to your skin, I cut the advertisement out and sent it to her in the mail. I wrote a little note inside letting her know that now she could make sure her prosthesis went everywhere she did.

The day after my surgery I was out in the rain attending a meeting for Affirmative Action. I was determined I wasn't going to let this hold me back. And that is the way I have been living my life ever since.

I thought about reconstruction but that is all it was ... a thought. The one time in my life when I felt completely out of control was when I had my mastectomy. I don't ever want to experience that feeling again. Besides, I don't want to go under the knife any more.

Before I went to Egypt I did a lot of reading. One of the things I remembered reading about was Amazon women. I shared what I learned with one of my friends who also had a mastectomy. I wasn't sure if it was just a myth or reality. It was reported that the Amazon women cut off a breast to be better warriors. They would cut off their left breast as a sign that they were related to nobility. They would cut off their right breast for the purpose of being a better archer.

All of a sudden my friend had a burst of energy and said, "I guess we are all warriors in this thing."

"It was reported that the Amazon women cut off a breast to be better warriors. They would cut off their left breast as a sign that they were related to nobility. They would cut off their right breast for the purpose of being a better archer."

$\mathcal{M}$ae Phillips

Basically, I think personalities have a lot to do with how you deal with things ... and that includes cancer. I have always been a spontaneous person. I don't have to have everything calculated and figured out before I do it. I just do it! Some of my friends that are more conservative and withdrawn haven't done as well as I have.

I also believe that spirituality plays a key component with how you cope with the outcome of things. Regardless of what you believe, you need to believe in something. I think that is what makes a difference in those of us who survive and those of us who don't.

I felt a knot and a soreness in my right breast one day. I was concerned about it so I made an appointment to see a doctor. He recommended a breast specialist. The specialist did an ultrasound and a needle aspiration.

Mae Phillips

Age:	56
Stage:	2
Occupation:	Teacher
Residence:	Houston, Texas
Procedure:	Bi-Lateral Mastectomy & Reconstruction
Treatment:	Tamoxifen & Radiation
Survivorship:	1 year
Lymph Node Involvement:	2 / 9

I was told that everything was OK. I was told I had nothing to worry about, just to see my primary physician for a mammogram the following year. I just put it in the back of my mind because at the time I was on my way to Virginia to visit with my family.

I later changed health insurance. When I developed a rash under my breast, I went in to see my new doctor. He did a surgical biopsy. He asked me to come in the following week for my results. To my surprise ... I had cancer. By that time I was completely out to lunch! I thank the Lord that my husband went in with me to get all of the information because once I heard the word cancer I didn't hear anything else.

They performed the surgery the next week. I was so angry, and so frustrated. I could not believe that I had gone to the doctor, done all the things I was supposed to do and now, all of a sudden, I have cancer. And it is in the second stage.

I was so overwhelmed I told him to just go ahead and take both breasts. Normally, he said he wouldn't do that but because of the history of breast cancer in my family he thought it was a good idea.

Fortunately for me it was a good idea because they found precancerous cells in the other breast as well.

After my surgery, I was too busy being angry, and upset about not being able to get up that I never dealt with the fact my breasts were gone.

I later found out that the first ultrasound I had revealed some suspicious cells. Also, my cancer was present on my first mammogram. The more I found out the angrier I got because I realized I almost slipped through the cracks of the system.

I still have a lot of anger about the way my situation was handled.

Because of my age, my doctor suggested that I take tamoxifen. I take it as directed but I just pray that it does the right thing and does not stop off at the uterus or the liver where it could be dangerous. When I started taking it, I had a complete physical with base line data on everything so I would be able to trace any changes.

My only after treatments were the tamoxifen and radiation. For me the radiation was a piece of cake. I did develop a little cough and I lost my appetite. But I didn't have any bad skin burns. Overall, the medication and I have done very well. I can't say that I have had any real problems.

Despite the fact I was angered at the way my situation was handled, I can't let breast cancer get the best of me. I realize that as a result of dealing with this disease I do have some limitations. I can't use my arm the way I used to so now I have to pay someone to come in and help around the house. I also realize that my immune system isn't what it used to be. I know that now I am more susceptible to disease than I ever was.

"I was so overwhelmed I told him to just go ahead and take both breasts. Normally, he said he wouldn't do that but because of the history of breast cancer in my family he thought it was a good idea."

Yet, I have decided to take the focus off of me and put it on other people. I have always been a people person. I want my focus to be on working with people and educating people about breast cancer and cancer, period. I know it is important to get people to discuss and share their situations.

I do volunteer work with the American Cancer Society. I also teach women how to do breast exercises after their surgery. But basically I want to get in the trenches and work with the people. I don't just want to limit myself to working with middle-class women, I want to work with the women that don't have access and don't have the information.

As an educator, I think we also need to put breast health care in our health programs at the high school level so that our young girls can start becoming more aware of their bodies.

I had only been married nine months before I had to have my surgery. So that posed a new dilemma in my life. I would not have put my husband through this if I had known there was a possibility of me having breast cancer. His mother died from breast cancer. But I have to admit, he was there for me when I needed him most. He was a great source of support.

My being breastless didn't affect my husband one way or the other. Even though he didn't say anything, I think my shape may have bothered him a little. I later had reconstruction because it was something I wanted to do for myself. I was surprised at my husband's response when he first saw me. He said I looked sexy. He hadn't used that phrase since I had my surgery.

Since I have had cancer I now realize that there is an inner light that travels throughout me. I know that it is the Christ within me. When I am at home I like to listen to spiritually healing tapes. I know that I don't go to church any more or any less than I did before. But I do know that there is something very different about me.

Zora Kramer Brown

After several years of great anticipation, I finally found the lump I had been waiting for. My great-grandmother, my grandmother, my mother and three of my sisters all had breast cancer. I knew I was bound to get it. I just didn't know when.

Because of my strong family history of breast cancer, I started having mammograms when I was 21. At that time, my doctor informed me that I had dysplasia in a section of my right breast. Five years later I had another mammogram and it was still there.

My doctor recommended I continue doing monthly breast self-exams. I finally found a lump by the time I was 31.

I felt I had pretty well prepared myself psychologically for what was about to happen. I had already spent a lot of time arming myself with as much knowledge and information as possible.

Zora Kramer Brown

Age:	47
Stage:	1
Occupation:	Vice President, Development & Public Relations
Residence:	Washington, D.C.
Procedure:	Modified Radical Mastectomy
Treatment:	None
Survivorship:	14 years
Lymph Node Involvement:	None

I felt that I was very fortunate to already be very familiar with breast cancer. I think when you know a lot about cancer, when it actually happens to you it is not as traumatic. I know that nobody wants to get breast cancer. I certainly didn't. Yet, I made sure I was as prepared as I could be, so when it happened I wouldn't be caught off guard ... and I wasn't.

I had already assembled a team of doctors to treat me. I had also obtained the best insurance coverage I could possibly afford at the time.

My doctor told me I had caught my cancer at an early stage and that I could have a lumpectomy. Sixteen years ago information on lumpectomies wasn't readily available. I also was told I could just be treated with radiation and chemotherapy. At that time I did not know enough about the outcome of women who had treatment without surgery.

What I did know was that my grandmother had survived breast cancer for 40 years and she had a mastectomy. My mother was still alive and she had a mastectomy. I chose what I thought was best for me and what I thought was going to offer me long term survival — a modified radical mastectomy.

When I had my surgery I was married to a very wonderful man. He was extremely supportive. Even though we are no longer married, he continues to be supportive of me.

I think after I got breast cancer, I began to get restless. I kept thinking there is more to do and there is more to life. As a result, my husband and I ultimately divorced. I became methodical and began chasing this great career.

I later remarried someone else. He had never seen me with both breasts. I think psychologically that was very good for me, to be in a relationship with someone who was accepting the new me, who never knew the old me.

The one message that I strongly try to convey to women is that there is life after breast cancer, and there is sex after breast cancer. In fact, sex can be very good after breast cancer.

Even though my second marriage ended in divorce, I know it had nothing to do with breast cancer. In fact, we are still very good friends.

Cancer has taught me not to hold on to grudges. I don't hold on to anything anymore, especially things that are tangible. I now know that those things you can hold on to are things that don't last.

Ten years after I was diagnosed with breast cancer one of my sisters had a recurrence. She already had two bouts with breast cancer. This time, her prognosis was not so good.

Before she died, she encouraged me to do more about

"The one message that I strongly try to convey to women is that there is life after breast cancer, and there is sex after breast cancer. In fact, sex can be very good after breast cancer."

making other African American women aware of breast cancer. She kept saying, "We have got to get the word out, particularly to other Black women, about early detection and early treatment for breast cancer."

The two of us and five other women formed the Breast Cancer Resource Committee in 1988. We were formally incorporated in 1989. We have tried to put together a comprehensive breast cancer awareness message targeted to African American women. We act as a conduit for those who need information and for those who have information to give. I know we are not experts by any means, but we do know how to get information and how to connect people with resources.

The Breast Cancer Resource Committee is a miracle to me. We had no funding, we never got any assistance from the government, and I never got any grant money for the program that we operate. I just believe if it is the right thing to do, God will provide. I tell everyone that I don't worry about it. If I run into a obstacle, I just cast it away. I tell everyone that, "no weapon formed against me shall prosper." As long as I have God on my side, I know I can make it, and God is always on my side.

I have a very active life. I do all the things that most women do: I go to church, I go to work, I play, I travel, I read, I make love.... I do all the things that I have ever wanted to do in my life. I think now I probably do those things more abundantly because I have had to deal with breast cancer.

I guess my mother put it best when my sister was dying. She said, "A long life might not be good enough, but a good life is certainly long enough."

Augusta Gale

The protocol for the hospital I was going to was to call and let one know there was a bed ready before being admitted. The day of my admittance I sat there by the telephone, just waiting.

When the phone finally rang, I grabbed it in great anticipation. I was totally shocked when I received the message: "Augusta Gale, we cannot admit you today, because you do not have insurance."

I panicked.

I sat on my bed just wondering who in the world could help me. I didn't know anybody. Then it came to me, Nancy Reagan had a mastectomy. I picked up the telephone and called the White House.

When I asked for Nancy Reagan the gentleman on the phone thought I was crazy. He said, "You don't mean the President's wife, do you?"

I responded, "Her name is Nancy Reagan, is it not?"

Augusta Gale

Age:	54
Stage:	1
Occupation:	Registered Nurse
Residence:	North Andover, Massachusetts
Procedure:	Bi-lateral Mastectomy
Treatment:	None
Survivorship:	7 years
Lymph Node Involvement:	None

I finally cut through all of the red tape and got to her personal assistant. She insisted I calm down and told me to inform my doctor there had been a slight delay. She assured me I would be in that hospital before the day was over ... one way or another.

Ten minutes later I received a call.

"Augusta Gale, we have a bed ready for you."

I believe in going to the top. This time it had definitely paid off.

I was not alarmed when I first discovered my lump. As a

nurse, and also having a mother who had died of metastatic breast cancer, I was always very aware of breast self-exams.

I watched my lump carefully for a month. When it did not change the next month, I went in for a biopsy.

I was totally new to the New England area at the time. I was going to a new doctor and a new health facility. I didn't even know any one to get a recommendation from.

The doctor called me on the phone to give me the results of the biopsy. It was "carcinoma." In other words, it was cancer.

Due to the casual way my doctor chose to give me the news, it did not take me long to realize that not only was I going to need a second opinion, but I needed another doctor. After doing some research I chose a cancer facility in New York. It was like night and day. The doctor I selected was very warm and concerned and we carefully went over all of my options.

Based on a 30 percent possibility of a recurrence in the other breast, and the fact my chest was a double F, which is like Dolly Parton's, and it would be difficult for them to reconstruct it ... I opted for a bi-lateral mastectomy, which meant having both of my breasts removed.

The one good thing about the facility I had chosen is that every one around me was also having a mastectomy, so I didn't feel threatened or intimidated.

Once I had made my decision I felt very comfortable with it, and I stuck to it.

I do recall one uncomfortable situation. One of the doctors came around to check on me and he didn't close the privacy curtain. After I insisted that he do so, he couldn't seem to understand why I was concerned. I simply responded, "I have a right to privacy. Now, if you had surgery on your penis, I don't think you would like to be lying here on the bed totally exposed."

I never again had a problem getting the privacy curtain closed.

When the big day came and it was time to take off my

*"**I** simply responded, 'I have a right to privacy. Now, if you had surgery on your penis, I don't think you would like to be lying here on the bed totally exposed.'"*

bandage for good, I was so excited that I helped the doctor remove it. Because of my enthusiasm he said, "I know you are going to be O.K. with everything."

It was an emotional day for me when I left the hospital. A Reach to Recovery volunteer came around to see me. She had reconstructive surgery and she showed me how it looked. It was at that moment I made up in my mind I was going to be a Reach to Recovery volunteer. I knew other African American women would want to see someone like themselves who had made it through the same thing they were going through.

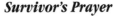

Survivor's Prayer

*God, We thank you
for this day,
Our family, friends and
support groups,
Help us to forget the pains
of yesterday,
Help us to relax and to realize
we are Beautiful and
very precious.*

— Augusta Gale

It was only a few months after my surgery when I opted to have reconstruction. Instead of saline or silicone, I decided to use my own tissue. The doctor told me it would be easiest for him to take the tissue from my stomach area. At first when my friends heard about it, I got offers for stomach all around, black stomachs and white stomachs. Unfortunately, I had plenty for the doctor to work with ... so that never became an issue.

One day, I remember getting a call from the young lady who was my roommate in the hospital. She was concerned about going on a date and she only had one breast. I just told her to put on a pretty top and go on about her business.

She was so excited when she called me back she exclaimed, "Augusta, it worked!"

I am so glad that women are coming out of the closet and admitting they have had breast cancer. What you should really be ashamed of is if you don't do breast self-exams.

The Second Time Around
When cancer returns.

Charlotte Brewster

I can still remember the oncologist telling me that I was going to lose my hair on December 19th. I asked him how in the world he knew I was going to lose my hair on a certain date. He assured me that he had administered enough chemotherapy that he could pretty much tell when a person would go bald. In spite of his experience, I was banking on him being wrong. I let him know that there was no way I could lose my hair. I had a party to attend on December 20 and I needed my hair!

He jokingly said, "On December 20, you can wear any color hair you want to the party."

I fixed him. The night of my party my hair was intact. But eight days later it all came out. I was caught completely off guard. I had my hair for so long that I thought maybe I might not lose it. But sure enough I did. I lost every strand. This was the first, but not the last time that breast cancer would catch me off guard.

Charlotte Brewster

Age:	50
Stage:	1
Occupation:	Administrative Assistant
Residence:	Dallas, Texas
Procedure:	Lumpectomy
Treatment:	Chemotherapy & Radiation
Survivorship:	3 years
Lymph Node Involvement:	0/30

One afternoon I picked up a pamphlet from a local drug store advertising a mobile unit that would be in the community doing mammograms. Since the mobile unit was going to be in the neighborhood, and it was about time for me to have a mammogram anyway, I went ahead and signed up. Several times I tried to cancel because I really didn't have the time. Once the mobile unit was set up I saw that the girls who were working there were so young. I figured they didn't know what they were doing.

Finally, I went in on a Thursday. The very next day they called and told me that my results were sent to my gynecologist, who immediately referred me to a surgeon. I thought, "Wait a minute. Let's see what it is first."

My doctor told me this was the best surgeon in the area, and that was who he wanted me to see. Of course he did a biopsy. But the entire time I never thought it would be malignant.

I remember waking up from the anesthesia and hearing the doctor say, "We have got all the cancer."

I couldn't believe it. It really was cancer. I starting crying. You hear of other people getting cancer, but now I had it.

The next day my doctor wanted me to talk about my treatment. I had my very close friend Jeff go with me when they talked about my options.

Because we caught the cancer early, my doctor felt I could get away with a lumpectomy followed by six months of chemotherapy and six weeks of radiation.

The radiation made me feel really tired. I also experienced a skin burn that was pretty uncomfortable. But once I stopped my treatments, the burn started to heal right away.

One of the most unexpected parts of my chemotherapy treatment was losing my eyebrows. I was prepared to lose my hair but I never really thought about my eyebrows. I never wore much eyemakeup anyway, so it was kind of hard to draw in eyebrows that weren't there.

Just like everybody else, I had some good days and some bad days. I never let it get me down. I was afraid if I let myself get too down it would be hard to pull myself back up again.

For me the shocker was having a mammogram a few months ago and finding a spot in my other breast. This time I was sure it wasn't cancer. The spot was so small they had to insert a small wire in my breast before they did a biopsy to insure they got the right area. Ironically, this was around the same time of year I had originally been diagnosed. I was still sure it was not cancer. But once again I was wrong. It had not spread from the original site. This was a completely different cancer.

> "*One of the most unexpected parts of my chemotherapy treatment was losing my eyebrows. I was prepared to lose my hair but I never really thought about my eyebrows.*"

I have to admit, it was devastating when once again I heard the word "cancer." But my doctor told me he could handle it, that he had everything under control ... I figured OK, what do I need to do. I knew then this was going to be something that I was going to have to deal with.

This time I was more emotional than before. The first time I didn't know what to expect, and I was going along with the program because I was anticipating that everything was going to turn out OK. This time I am impatient. I know where I am going to end up, and I am ready to get it over and get back to normal so that I can stop thinking about it.

I wasn't sure what my options were going to be because I had already had a lumpectomy in the other breast. But my doctor said that a mastectomy didn't offer any more protection than a lumpectomy. I really didn't want to have a mastectomy unless I absolutely had to. But I told my doctor if there ever came a time that he felt that was going to be necessary, just tell me and it was done.

Even though I don't become obsessed with having breast cancer, I have to admit it is hard not to think about it. When I wake up in the morning and I look in the mirror and I don't have any hair, I think about it.

I didn't have any family history of breast cancer, but my mother had died when I was three years old from improper medical attention. Since my mother died so young, my doctor thought she might have been a potential candidate for breast cancer.

After I was diagnosed the second time my daughter was very scared, and angry. I guess she kept wondering why it happened to me. But I thought just the opposite, "why not me?" Breast cancer does not discriminate. It can happen to anybody.

Body Parts

I never thought to thank you
For the hair upon my head,
It wasn't such a big deal,
Just a cover-up instead.
But now I'm more than grateful
For my woolly little tress;
Before I take for granted
Let me thank you for the rest!

So thank you for my feet
Upon which I so impose
To carry all this body,
And to keep me on my toes.

Thank you for my elbow
Which justifies a mean,
I don't use it very often
But it's right there when I lean!

Thank you for my neck,
Though swan-like it is not,
It helps me turn the other cheek
When someone makes me hot!

There are so many body parts
I never think about;
I use them and abuse them,
With never a doubt
That they are a given,
"They're supposed to be there!"
But thank you, Lord,
for all of them,
Especially the hair!

— Charlotte Brewster
12/16/92
7:05 am

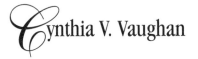

Cynthia V. Vaughan

One night before I went to bed I read the book of Joshua. That night I dreamed I was going up a steep mountain. I was sitting in the back seat of a car. There was a man and woman sitting in the front seat. As the car approached the end of the cliff, the woman disappeared. The car fell over the cliff. Down at the bottom of the cliff I could see this dirty muddy water. I just knew I was going to die because I was going to hit the bottom. By the time the car hit the water and the water began to come into the car, I reached for the door. Suddenly when I opened the car door, I realized the car had turned into a boat.

I was saved! I didn't die, I didn't drown, the car had turned into a house boat. I later realized the man in the car was Jesus Christ. Yes, I was going to hit rock bottom, but I was going to be all right because God was going to be with me. A few months later I found out that my cancer had returned in the same breast.

Cynthia V. Vaughan

Age:	43
Stage:	1
Occupation:	Minister
Residence:	Atlanta, Georgia
Procedure:	Mastectomy & Reconstruction
Treatment:	Radiation & Chemotherapy
Survivorship:	14 years
Lymph Node Involvement:	0 / 30

I had a history of fibroid cysts. When my doctor suggested I get a lump in my breast removed, I really didn't pay it much attention, because the cysts had been there for seven years. I decided to wait a while longer. Then my grandmother was diagnosed with breast cancer. At that point, I decided it was time to get it checked out. I went to another doctor. He assured me it was nothing to worry about, but he found another lump and he felt that I did need to get that one checked out.

I went back to my original doctor and he insisted it was nothing but a clogged milk duct. He wanted me to watch it and come back in six months.

I started to watch it, and it started to grow, and grow, and grow. After three months I went back. My doctor still assured me there was nothing to worry about because of the statistics — there was nothing that showed I should be susceptible to breast cancer. After all, I was only 29 years old.

Nevertheless, he referred me to a surgeon who performed a needle aspiration. The surgeon told me he would call me back at the end of the week. Two days later he called and said that there was abnormal cell growth and he wanted to know when I would be available for a surgical biopsy.

A few days later I had a modified radical mastectomy. He had also given me the option of a lumpectomy with radiation. For my own peace of mind, I felt better off going with a mastectomy. Before the surgery I gave them permission to do the surgery if it was malignant. I didn't want to wake up and then go through it.

Because of my age I was a candidate for reconstruction. I had the reconstruction with silicone implants. It wasn't the best reconstruction, but you know nobody is perfect but God. Therefore, I guess it was the best possible reproduction.

Last January, I had rubbed my hand across my breast and it wasn't smooth like it had been. It felt sort of strange. It was in the same area of my surgery. At first I thought it might just be a pimple. Nevertheless, I made an appointment with my gynecologist, my oncologist and my plastic surgeon.

I wanted my gynecologist to check the lump. It was time for me to see my oncologist anyway and I wanted to see my plastic surgeon because the implant was getting uncomfortable.

My gynecologist told me that it was a sub-contained cyst, don't worry about it. My oncologist said he didn't think it was anything to worry about, but because of my history I should have a biopsy anyway. That worked out fine because I was scheduled to see my plastic surgeon anyway, who in turn did the biopsy.

It seemed my worst nightmare had come true. My cancer had returned.

The first thing I did was call my pastor. I wanted to know if this was going to interfere with my ministry. He assured me it would not.

For a brief second I was concerned. Then I was fine with it. I went ahead and had the surgery with reconstruction again. This time I got a tummy tuck, and used my own tissue to rebuild my breast. I was pleased with that.

The only thing I had a problem with was having chemotherapy. The first time I was diagnosed I didn't want chemo because I had this fear of being so sick that I could not take care of myself. This time, because it was contained in the same breast, they did not want to do radiation. I had already had radiation in that same area.

I said to myself "I want to live," so I went ahead with the chemo. It wasn't as bad as it could have been, but I wouldn't wish it on my worst enemy.

It seemed the time between my treatments went so fast. Just as I would get over one treatment, they would knock me back down with another one.

When it was over I felt like I had lost six months of my life.

When I finished radiation after my first bout with cancer I went to the Bahamas. This time I went on a cruise with my family.

Dealing with cancer has made me appreciate life more. After my first incidence, I just wanted to do things and be around people. Up until that point, I was the type of person who could get a good book and be by myself and be happy.

From my second bout with cancer, I not only realized how much people mean to me, I know how much I mean to them. There were so many people in my hospital room that they could not all sit down. Friends, family and people from the church were surrounding me. I know this was God's way of showing me His love. My love for people has increased considerably.

Cancer has also made me have a better appreciation of time. I no longer want to be bound by time. I haven't worn a watch since my second surgery. I don't even use an alarm clock unless I have a plane to catch. I just relax and allow my body to wake up naturally.

"Cancer has also made me have a better appreciation of time. I no longer want to be bound by time. I haven't worn a watch since my second surgery."

Paula J. Chalmers

I got married in 1989, moved to Florida, was hit by a truck and then discovered I had breast cancer.

I had been married only two months when I found a lump in my breast. I had never really done breast self-exams. And this lump seemed to just pop up overnight.

Although I had just relocated to Jacksonvile, Florida, I decided I had to make time to get to a doctor and have this checked out.

After a week, I finally got in to get some tests run. They said they wouldn't have the results for another week. Well, I got really busy and forgot all about the test results until I found myself in the hospital recuperating from a broken leg.

While I was walking on the side of the road I was hit by a truck which sent me to the hospital. As I lay in my hospital bed with my broken leg propped in a cast, the doctor came in and told me that I had breast cancer.

Paula J. Chalmers

Age:	33
Stage:	3 / 4
Occupation:	Credit Analyst
Residence:	Dallas, Texas
Procedure:	Bi-lateral Mastectomy
Treatment:	Chemotherapy
Survivorship:	5 years
Lymph Node Involvement:	13 / 30

He said they were going to have to take my right breast. And because the tumor was so large — 13 centimeters — they were going to administer chemotherapy before they could even begin the surgery.

I was quite devastated with this news. I ended up going through chemo while I was still on crutches for my broken leg.

If you have any good veins at all, chemo destroys them. I always had small veins anyway. By the time I went in for my fourth treatment, they could no longer find my veins. So they started me on tamoxifen.

Four years later I went in for my regular check up and they discovered I had cancer in my left breast. They suggested I remove it as well. Of course, this time I wanted a second opinion. The second opinion confirmed my first diagnosis.

As much as I hated it, I knew this would mean that I would no longer have any breasts. I was only 31 years old!

Now this was going to be my third bout with cancer. At 12 I had suffered from Hodgkin's Disease, which is a lymphatic cancer. I remember waking up with a swollen face. After that happened a few times, my grandmother became concerned. She was a nurse. She didn't hesitate to take me to the doctor to find out what was going on. They ran several tests and found that the disease was affecting my spleen. Doctors removed my spleen and a part of my liver.

I had radiation for six months which caused me to lose half a head of hair. At the time I was going into eighth grade, and this was a little traumatic for me to deal with. Kids can be a little vicious when you are different.

I came through that just fine. I never had any more problems. It didn't keep me from engaging in activities that most children did. I went on to high school, and college ... I was just fine ... until I started having my bouts with breast cancer.

Since I didn't have any veins left after my second mastectomy, they inserted a catheter in my chest. My chest cavity is so small it couldn't hold the catheter. I ended up with a bad infection that took three surgeries to get it all out. They grafted the skin back, but I now have a large scar in that area. I can't ever wear a scoop necked blouse because the scar will show.

I transferred back to Dallas almost two years ago. Shortly afterward, I had a blood clot in my right lung. I was treated by a pulmonologist for the blood clot. He ran several tests. After the last set of tests, he said my chest X-ray looked abnormal. Then he started with an entire new series of tests.

This time they informed me that the cancer had metastasized and was now in my bronchial area, near my lungs.

They wanted to administer chemo again, but needless to say my access was very bad. This time they wanted to insert a catheter in my groin area and have it rest in my side. It was in the shape of a small disk. I could feel it, so I thought that would be OK.

After they inserted the cather, I came home. I was very sore that night. I finally called my doctor to ask him if I was supposed to be sore. He said that was abnormal.

It got so bad the next day that I could hardly walk. I had to take pain pills because the pain had become unbearable. After being sick so much, when your body starts to change, you can detect it right away. I started feeling really weird. I took my temperature and it was 104 degrees. At that point I headed to the Emergency Room.

I didn't know what was going on. All of a sudden the next day fluid started coming out of my side. It seems that an infection had built up where they had inserted the cather. Once again they had to do surgery to remove it.

I took this as my sign from the Lord that I didn't need anything foreign in my body.

While I was lying in my hospital bed recuperating from the surgery, the surgeon walked in. He said, "Miss Chalmers, we are going to have to find another rare spot to put the cather for your chemo."

I looked at him like he was crazy. I told him I didn't want to talk about that now.

The next thing they suggested was a bone marrow transplant. But I wasn't going for that either. I think the Lord had made it clear this was the route for me to take. I decided to continue to look up to Him, as I had been doing all along.

When I went back my oncologist was so excited. He laid all my chest X-rays out for the last two years. He showed me my first one and the two taken while I was taking chemo, which were the worst. Then he showed me my current X-ray. It was just fine.

I am still considered a cancer patient, but they can't find any cancer. I feel well and I am not taking any drugs. But the main thing is I'm still here!

I think I am the best example that regardless of what kind of hand you are dealt ... you can still make it.

"I am still considered a cancer patient, but they can't find any cancer. I feel well and I am not taking any drugs. But the main thing is I'm still here!"

VonDonna Bircher

One night I had a dream that I had gone to a coaching convention and there was a doctor there speaking about health issues. One of the issues he addressed was breast cancer. He talked about doing breast self-examinations. As I was walking out of the meeting, I felt my breast and it felt like there was a lump. I had another coach touch the spot, and sure enough she said it felt like a lump.

VonDonna Bircher

Age:	38
Stage:	1
Occupation:	Physical Education Instructor/Basketball Coach
Residence:	Houston, Texas
Procedure:	Modified Radical Mastectomy
Treatment:	Chemotherapy
Survivorship:	7 years
Lymph Node Involvement:	0/18

I decided I was going to find the doctor who was speaking at the convention the next day. I wanted to ask him what he thought about the lump. After the convention the next day, I did find the doctor. I let him know that I had discovered a lump in my breast. He felt my breast and agreed there was definitely something there. He asked me to come to his office immediately. After he examined me, the next thing I heard him say was, "Mrs. Bircher, you have breast cancer."

At that moment I woke up and I put my hand on my breast. Sure enough, there was a lump there.

That morning I didn't go to work. I called my doctor and scheduled an appointment right away. He, in turn, sent me to a surgeon. Three times they unsuccessful tried to do a needle aspiration, but they could get no fluid. As they kept attempting to aspirate the lump, I told the nurse not to bother because I had breast cancer. She asked me, "how did I know?"

I told her I had a dream. She looked at me like I was crazy.

I kept saying, "I am trying to tell y'all this is breast cancer because God had already showed me." It took them three weeks to determine what I already believed to be true ... I had breast cancer.

My doctor suggested I have a mastectomy. "Will this save my life?" I asked. My son, Rickey, was only 6 years old, and I very much wanted to live.

This was going to be my second time around with cancer. Ten years before I had been diagnosed with Hodgkin's Disease, which is a cancer of the lymphatic system. So my husband had already gone through chemotherapy and radiation with me. He knew what we were in for this time.

When I first had cancer he didn't deal with it very well. We hadn't been married that long, and we were very young. This time our relationship was 10 years older, we were more mature and he was extremely supportive.

I think he really went out of his way to make me feel better because I was losing a part of me ... with the other cancer I didn't lose anything.

The more I thought about losing my breast, the more I felt sorry for him. He would tell me, "Donna, it is only a breast." But I kept thinking to myself, "This man has to look at this woman with one breast."

It seemed through this entire ordeal I thought about everybody but me. I really didn't think about myself. I thought about all those people who had to deal with me.

I never expected to get a completely different type of cancer 10 years later. It was a complete shock to me. At 31, all I could think was, "Why me?" I wondered what I had done in all my life to deserve all of this. I thought it just wasn't fair. I looked at cancer as coming in 10 year increments — 21, 31. I started to dread turning 41.

I had taken several weeks off work after my surgery to recuperate. When I finally returned to school, it was only a few weeks before school was going to be out for the summer. At that time I only had limited use of my arm, so I was very glad all I had to do was a little paperwork.

There was no doubt that my biggest challenge was ahead of me. As a basketball coach, I needed to be able to lift my hand over my head. I was determined to do whatever I

"I looked at cancer as coming in 10 year increments — 21, 31. I started to dread turning 41."

needed to do to make sure I was in shape for the next school year. I realized I only had the summer to make that happen.

I was in a great deal of pain each time I tried to regain the use of my arm. It felt so heavy. It seemed as if someone had added extra weight to it. I thought I would never reach my goal of getting my arm over my head.

I kept thinking to myself, "If I can just get my arm over my head before basketball season, I will know I am back. I will be totally recuperated."

That summer, I continued working on my arm and doing my exercises as I went through chemo.

I returned to school and began preparing for basketball season to start the second week in October. I still wasn't sure if I had complete use of my arm. The last week in September I went in the gym all by myself. I got a basketball. I decided if I made the basket, then I knew I was back ... because I would have to get my arm over my head in order to do that.

I got to the free throw line. I stared at the basketball hoop as I began to make my shot. As the basketball went flying through the air, I watched with great anticipation. When it went through the net, I threw my hands up in the air because I knew I was back!

That year I had my best season ever. I took my team to the state championship game.

Dealing with breast cancer definitely changed my perspective on life. The things that I took seriously and that meant so much to me, aren't serious any more. The things I took for granted became serious. I don't spend a lot of time worrying about things that I know I can't change; that's not a problem any more. But things like visiting my mother, or spending time with my son ... those are the things that matter to me now.

I now realize that nothing is guaranteed. I am not guaranteed to see my son grow up.

I had always been very open with my son, but I was very careful not to let him see me undress after my surgery. Then one day he hid under my bed. When I walked in the room

> **"A** *little while later, I looked around and there were six little boys in my living room. With great enthusiasm, he said, 'Mamma, show them! Show them that you only have one breast.' I was so embarrassed I thought I was going to go through the floor."*

after taking a shower, he jumped out and yelled, "Surprise." There I was standing totally naked. I was so upset. I started yelling for him to get out of my room. I had never wanted him to see me with one breast. Finally, my husband let me know that I was going to have to sit down and talk to him about it.

I explained to him what had happened, and now, "Mommy only had one breast." He seemed to understand and accept it with no problems.

A little while later, I looked around and there were six little boys in my living room. With great enthusiasm, he said, "Mamma, show them! Show them that you only have one breast." I was so embarrassed I thought I was going to go through the floor.

My husband pulled him aside and let him know that you don't go around and tell everybody in the neighborhood that your mother only has one breast.

My son is 13 years old now, and I know that he has grown accustomed to the fact I only have one breast. In fact, one of the little girls in the neighborhood teased him by saying, "Your mother only has one breast."

He simply responded, "My mother may have one breast, but I still have her. She's still alive."

I guess that's the way I feel. I am just happy to be alive, one breast and all.

P. J. Viviansayles

It was a beautiful morning. I was listening to Franky Beverly and Maze and just chilling out as I started my day.

I was also pretty excited. After a big struggle, I had finally landed a great job. It seemed I had so much to be happy about. I was just groovin' along in my own little world. Then I stepped into the shower.

Having fibrocystic breasts since puberty, the lump I noticed wasn't anything new to me. In fact, I had discovered my first lump at the age of 12. It was finally removed four years later when it became completely unbearable during my monthly cycle.

But there was something different about this lump.

As I began to reflect, I realized that some strange things had been going on with my body. For the first time in my life I had developed an unpleasant body odor. In fact, my co-workers had given me a beautiful basket of feminine hygiene products, powders and soaps because they had also noticed this odor. They wanted to show me they cared. But by that time, I already knew there was something definitely wrong.

Even though I was relatively new on my job, I went into the office and told my boss I was outta there because I had to get to the doctor.

My doctor immediately referred me to a surgeon, and ordered an ultrasound and a mammogram. I was having surgery before long.

P. J. Viviansayles

Age:	46
Stage:	2
Occupation:	President, Women of Color
Residence:	California
Procedure:	Lumpectomy
Treatment:	Chemotherapy & Radiation
Survivorship:	4 years
Lymph Node Involvement:	2/25

I didn't know anything about mastectomies or lumpectomies. All I knew about was breast health care. Yet, when I was given my options I told my doctor if there was any way for him to preserve my breast I wanted him to.

I admit to not being familiar with anything that was going on. This was a very fearful experience. However, I was fortunate because I had excellent doctors.

They recommended I get the sandwich treatment — chemotherapy and radiation. I had very small veins in my left arm. Between treatments I had to get one of those Silly Putty balls from the exercise store to help build up my veins to make it easier to insert the IV.

My biggest problem was dealing with the side effects of chemotherapy. For me, chemo caused an excessive amount of depression. I had some unresolved issues with my father, and chemo brought them to the surface.

"I kept thinking I could not be the only Black woman going through this."

I believe that I became so preoccupied with my feelings about my father during my initial treatments that it may have very well contributed to my recurrence.

When going through cancer treatments, you need to be focused on healthy stuff. You should be thinking about exercising, healing and giving yourself personal attention, but I was preoccupied with my father. He had disconnected himself from me earlier in my life and I could not understand why.

The chemo had me going through these severe mood swings. For a few days I would be totally, psychologically out of it. But when I was up, I was getting on with the business of living.

Normally I don't believe in support groups but this entire experience set me on a venture to find other African American women who were going through the same thing. As I reflected on an experience I had in 1974, I was more driven to find other Black women that were going through the same thing. It seemed that I was propelled by this experience. I kept thinking I could not be the only Black woman going through this.

In 1974 I had gone to see my friend Vickie in San Diego.

Her mother Mary was in this dark room with a tattered curtain in front of it. I spoke to Mary but she didn't respond. I asked Vickie, "What's up with your mom?" Vickie let me know that her mother was dying from breast cancer.

At that point I knew I had to do something. I had to do something for Mary, for all the sisters that had gone on, and for the sisters who were in the closet and didn't want any one to know they have or had breast cancer ... because breast cancer was supposed to be this hush hush thang.

"The Tamoxifen had made me feel so hot that I thought I had died and gone to Hell, because now I was going through menopause due to the treatment."

That's when I decided to start the Women of Color Breast Cancer Survivors Support Project. I have been blessed with the ability to speak so I started speaking to community based organizations about the breast cancer epidemic.

I have two daughters and a son. My son was very supportive, but he was still into this "male" thang. Once he walked up to me and asked, "Why are the dishes still in the sink?" Even though he cared, I knew he really didn't understand that I was going through treatment and I didn't care if the dishes ever got washed.

On the other hand, my daughters never saw the real me. I was into the Super Woman syndrome. You know, how Black women carry the weight of the world on their shoulders but don't think it is OK for someone to take care of them. We always put ourselves last on the totem pole. I had to let everybody think I was strong and could take care of myself.

While I was hung up on being Super Woman I found a second occurrence under my right arm. At this point, I decided to throw off my cape with the big "S" on it. I began to share some of things I was going through with my daughters. I no longer felt I could go through this alone. This was really devastating for me. I had just started a new job, and I was finally making decent money. My health insurance had just kicked in. Now, once again, I was going to have to go through treatments.

The doctor decided to use a catheter this time because my veins weren't very good. Honey, that thing popped out and the medicine spilled into my breast and swelled my breast to the size of a damn cantaloupe. They tried to give me medication to stop the swelling but the swelling would not go down. Finally, with Aloe Vera and cocoa butter, I was able to reduce the swelling.

During my treatment I was unable to pay my rent and health insurance in full because now I was on disability. When I finished my treatments, I was evicted from my apartment. My landlady knew I had cancer. But it didn't matter to her. I knew I needed to keep my insurance paid so that I could continue my treatments ... so that I could stay alive!

After my treatments I was put on Tamoxifen. The Tamoxifen had made me feel so hot that I thought I had died and gone to Hell, because now I was going through menopause due to the treatment. Then I found out my vision was blurring and I didn't know what was going on. I went to the doctor and she said, "P.J., didn't you know one of the rare side effects of Tamoxifen is that it can cause permanent retinal damage?"

I know now that I can no longer be concerned with the quantity of life, I am more concerned with the quality of my life.

I drink an herbal juice which contains Aloe Vera, and I also take vitamins. Now I feel better than I did before I was diagnosed. I live my life to the fullest and if there is a party, you can bet I will be there.

Finding It At Forty
Women who were diagnosed in their forties.

Sometimes I get a sensation in my chest, and I do not feel like I have lost a breast.

One morning, I got dressed and went to work. Once I got to work I went to the ladies' room, and I was shocked when I looked in the mirror. I could not believe that I had forgotten my prosthesis!

I called my boyfriend and he brought it to me in a paper sack.

There is no doubt that the one thing I have realized throughout this whole ordeal is that you have got to keep your sense of humor. I may have lost my breast, but I can still laugh at myself!

My experience with breast cancer started one morning when I was in the shower and found this big lump under my arm. I had never heard about breast cancer, so to me it was just a lump. After a while it started feeling like it was pulling. So, I went to the doctor to find out what was wrong.

Joyce Green

Age:	48
Stage:	3
Occupation:	PBX Operator
Residence:	El Segundo, California
Procedure:	Mastectomy
Treatment:	None
Survivorship:	8 years
Lymph Node Involvement:	Unknown

The first thing he did was order a mammogram. I had never heard of a mammogram, so I still didn't have a clue to what was going on. He did some other tests, and examined me further but he couldn't find anything. He told me to wait a couple of weeks and then he would do a biopsy.

I waited three months.

I really did not know what was going on, I didn't feel that I was in any danger. I finally decided to go in for the biopsy. The real shock for me was when I awoke seven and a half hours later after my "biopsy," and I did not have a breast! I didn't know what had happened. Supposedly I was only going to have a biopsy.

No one ever explained to me that I might lose my breast.

All I can remember is being so frightened. The first thing that came across my mind was that I was going to die. I was only 41 years old, but I believed I was getting ready to die. It was like walking into a nightmare.

I had just gone through a divorce. I had three children, two were in high school at the time. Then, like a stranger in the night, breast cancer decided to slither into my life.

When the doctors suggested chemotherapy I told them there was just no way. I had three children to take care of, and there was no one else to help me. I know my family pulled back because they were scared. They had never had to deal with cancer before. I knew this time I was going to have to be my own source of support.

At first I thought about reconstructive surgery, but after they told me about the process I thought it would make me sicker than actually losing a breast.

Having a significant other helped me get through the whole ordeal. We finally moved in together about two years ago.

I also joined a support group called Women of Color. As a result of my involvement with the group, I started going around and talking to other African American women about health care. Now that I know what is going on, I want to share as much information as I can with my sisters.

I decided I wasn't going to let cancer run my life, I am going to run it. I still wear my "V" cut blouses, I just don't let them dip as low as they used to. Sometimes I even wear a regular bra.

Now I just live my life one day at a time because I never really know what is going to happen. After my surgery was complete, the doctors said they thought they got it all. I know that I could wake up one morning and they could just as well say, "Joyce, it's back" ... but I know I have lived my life to the fullest. It's been eight years since my surgery, so all I can figure is either they did get it all, I'm in remission or God has a greater plan for me. Whatever the case, all I know is ... I'm still here. I am just happy to be alive. I wear a good bra and I wear a good prosthesis. Therefore, having one breast is not an issue.

Cancer has made me realize you don't take anything for granted. So, I make sure that every now and then I step back and take time for Joyce.

"The real shock for me was, when I awoke seven and a half hours later after my 'biopsy,' and I did not have a breast!"

Karen Mayes Jackson

Age:	42
Stage:	1
Occupation:	Accountant
Residence:	Houston, Texas
Procedure:	Modified Radical Mastectomy
Treatment:	None
Survivorship:	3 years
Lymph Node Involvement:	0 / 12

It was really interesting. I didn't think my 3-year-old son Girard was old enough to be aware of what was going on. But he kept asking me why I was in the hospital. Since my arm had swollen after my surgery, I just told him I had a problem with my arm. I know it sounded stupid, but that was all I could think of at the time. I don't know if it was the tone of my voice, but it seems he really knew I wasn't telling him the truth. He kept right on asking me over and over again. Finally, six months later, I told him I had breast cancer. He seemed fine with that and he never asked me again.

Doing breast self-exams was something that was second nature for me. I had already had three fibroid cysts. In fact, I had my first one when I was in the 7th grade. The other two I had five years apart. I had a biopsy after I discovered each one of them. They were all benign.

Based on my history, when I discovered this lump, I was pretty complacent. To me this was no big deal. My doctor wasn't even concerned about it. He suggested I watch it for a while. I watched it for a year, then I decided I wanted a biopsy.

I just went in for day surgery. When I woke up, I overheard the nurse saying she was getting ready to move me to my room. I knew she had made a mistake. Then she said my doctor had instructed her to admit me. I still could not figure out what was going on.

When I saw my husband, I asked him what was going on. He sort of whispered to me, "It's cancer." He could barely get the words out of his mouth.

"It is a shame that we are so secretive about breast cancer. My grandmother had breast cancer almost ten years before I was diagnosed and I didn't even know it until I was in the hospital."

Of course I freaked out. At that point, I found out that my doctor had scheduled me for surgery the next day. I was so frustrated I didn't know what to do. Finally I screamed out, "Just hold it! I didn't have any idea it was malignant when I came here. Things are moving too fast for me."

I got real assertive. I started calling every 800 number dealing with cancer that I could get my hands on.

I told my husband I couldn't go through with the surgery. But my doctor insisted. He said I was already cut and it wouldn't be a good idea to wait. My husband was so afraid he didn't know what to tell me to do. He had just lost a cousin to brain cancer two weeks before I was admitted and he definitely didn't want to lose me. So I went ahead with the surgery.

I had a complete mastectomy. It was caught in the early stages, so I didn't have to have chemotherapy or radiation.

My husband has been really supportive. I thought it would bother him at first, but he didn't have a problem with it. I was the one who didn't even want to look at my scar.

It is a shame that we are so secretive about breast cancer. My grandmother had breast cancer almost 10 years before I was diagnosed and I didn't even know it until I was in the hospital. One of my aunts called me and said, "Oh, you'll be OK, Grandma had it in both breasts and she did just fine."

As a result of dealing with breast cancer, I have a greater appreciation for life. The little things that are petty, I don't let them bother me anymore.

It was strange — when the doctor said I had cancer, I just knew he had to be talking about someone else. I had my daughters with me as well as another friend, all of whom got emotional. However, I remained calm and I started consoling them because I felt he wasn't talking about me. I just wanted to shout, "You don't understand, I can't have cancer. I don't fit into any of the categories. I am at low risk for cancer."

I was overwhelmed with denial. It seemed as long as I could stay in my own little world, then maybe it wasn't happening, maybe it didn't exist, maybe I didn't have cancer. But the reality was that I did!

It all began when I went in for my annual physical. While examining my breasts, the doctor asked if I had noticed any changes. Although I had not, from that point on I became very conscious of doing my own breast self-exams.

Minnie Pryor

Age:	49
Stage:	2
Occupation:	Registered Nurse
Residence:	Dallas, Texas
Procedure:	Mastectomy & Reconstruction
Treatment:	Chemotherapy & Tamoxifen
Survivorship:	3 years
Lymph Node Involvement:	4 / 18

One morning I awoke and did an exam, and I noticed something. I felt a distinctive lump. I couldn't wait until the clinic opened that morning.

My doctor thought I was not old enough to have a mammogram. However, after examining my breasts he changed his mind. Even though I had the mammogram, he said there was no problem and that the results were negative.

I kept thinking to myself, "I'm OK, there is no problem ... but what is this thing in my chest?"

My doctor didn't seem to know the answer. We talked about it further, and finally he recommended a surgeon. So,

I took the "negative" X-rays to a surgeon. He did a biopsy, but it took a week before I got the final results.

Once the doctors told me the lump was malignant, I decided I would not let the terror of cancer touch me. I quickly jumped into a real self-help mode.

I started reading everything I could get my hands on. I bought a juicer and started making my own juices — I decided I was going to really punch my immune system up. Of course none of this made a difference. The thing I did not want to accept was a reality.

I had a trip planned to the National Black Women's Health Project Conference in Atlanta, and I decided I was going to take this trip. For all I knew, this might be my last trip, actually my last chance to celebrate life.

The one thing that stood out about this trip was that there were at least 100 women there. I had shared with one woman that I had been diagnosed with breast cancer ... gradually others began to find out. There was one session where we were all standing on top of this mountain in Georgia. It had to be one of the most incredibly powerful experiences that I have ever encountered in my life!

One by one, each woman came to me and said something. As they individually approached me, I felt that they did not see me — Minnie Pryor, who had been diagnosed with breast cancer. Instead, I felt they tapped directly into my soul, which itself was totally untarnished by cancer.

The last woman to come up to me was Marge. She was in her 70's. Marge had also had an experience with breast cancer. It seemed the moment Marge touched me I connected with all of the feelings I was avoiding: sadness, terror, uncertainty. Who was I going to be now?

I remember Marge sharing with me that she was worried about cataract surgery she was going to have when she returned home. I told her that it was nothing. I had that surgery a few years ago.

I still remember this 70-year-old woman looking at me like I was crazy. She asked me if I was ever going to have children again. I simply replied, "No."

"She said, 'Do you mean to tell me that you are more attached to your breasts that you are not going to use any more, than you are to your eyes that you need every day?'"

Then, with the wisdom that only a woman of her age and experience could have, she said, "Do you mean to tell me that you are more attached to your breasts that you are not going to use any more, than you are to your eyes that you need every day?"

Wow. That gave me a sharp jolt of reality. Finally, I began to put things in perspective. I was ready to have my surgery.

I still remember them wheeling me into the operating room. I was yelling out as I went down the hall, "It's the right one. The right one. It's the right one!" I had heard horror stories before. The last thing I wanted was for them to remove the wrong breast and then have to remove the other one.

After my surgery, the doctors told me that four out of 18 lymph nodes were positive. Although that was a small amount, it was significant enough that they wanted to do chemotherapy.

I elected to have reconstructive surgery immediately. Then I started the chemo. I still remember having the worst headaches in my life while I was taking chemo. Once when they put the IV in my arm, the pain was so intense I felt like they had blown the top of my head off!

Despite the headaches, I did make it through chemo ... but my surprises were not over. I told my doctor I had been bleeding for two months. He was surprised because I was not supposed to be bleeding at all. When I went in for an exam they found a fibroid tumor on my cervix and they thought it might be cancerous.

I thought to myself, "Been there and done that."

Fortunately, it wasn't cancer but I did have a hysterectomy. Now it seemed the *two* things, that I *had* associated with "being a woman" my breast and my uterus were gone. That was hard to deal with.

However, the main thing for me, after I got out of a state of denial, I was incredibly grateful to be alive. I had survived! No matter what kind of things are going down, nothing can go down like that again. I totally believe that now I can deal with anything!

*M*arian L. Mostiller

The phone was ringing off the hook. My in-laws were calling, my mother was calling and my brother was calling. It seems that everybody in my family was trying to get to me. They were even calling my doctor at work. It got so bad, the secretaries became concerned about me. Everyone who was remotely interested in me thought I had lost touch with reality. I was in a complete state of denial, and I was trying to avoid a very real fact in my life ... I had breast cancer.

My husband had been working out of town for a while. When he came home, we had a very passionate lovemaking session. He touched my breast in a certain spot and a pain shot through my breast. From that moment I thought to myself, "Oh no." I had no history of cancer, but I just knew something was wrong. It was like what I never wanted to think about was right there with me.

Marian L. Mostiller

Age:	48
Stage:	2
Occupation:	Lawyer / Teacher / Mediator
Residence:	Houston, Texas
Procedure:	Mastectomy
Treatment:	Chemotherapy & Radiation
Survivorship:	7 years
Lymph Node Involvement:	Unknown

My husband wanted me to check it out. Three weeks later, I ended up spending all night with my daughter who was having her first child. After the baby was born I decided it was time to see about myself. So, the next day I went in for a biopsy.

When they told me that it was cancer, I slipped right into denial. I said to myself, "If you don't think about it, then maybe it will go away."

That is when my family kicked in and tried to make me come to my senses. My mother told me she had prayed about it and the Lord had let her know that it was OK to have the surgery. My brother is a minister and he was telling me to have the surgery.

I said to my mother, "I went back and they said it had not grown in size. Isn't that a sign it is going away?"

My mother just said, "No, God is just with you. He understands your mind set and He is giving you time."

The day before I went into the hospital I saw Sister Gabriel from my church. When I told her what was going on she said right away the Lord had revealed to her everything was going to be OK.

Once my mother told me she was coming, I knew it was time to go to the hospital. She got on a plane in New York, came to my house, grabbed me by the hand and took me to the hospital. I was in denial the entire time. I didn't care about anything. It was not in my mind whether I was going to live or die. All I can remember is that on the way to the hospital everything seemed to be so beautifully green.

When I got there I started crying. They asked me if they were hurting me. I said, "No, you all do what you have to do, just accept the fact that I am going to cry all the way through this. Now I understand what is happening – I am getting ready to lose a part of my body."

Then mysteriously this wonderful woman appeared. To this day I do not know where she came from or what her capacity was. She held my hand and asked me what I was going to have done. Then she just began telling me about her mother who had the operation 30 years ago, and she was doing fine. I remember nothing else.

When I woke up I was in this nice little world all to myself. I had this big bandage on, and I thought to myself, "Just suppose it didn't happen and they did not have to remove my breast."

Two days later the doctor shattered my little fantasy world when he announced that she was going to remove my bandage. Once again the tears started to fall.

My mother came in while the doctor was removing the bandage and I told her, "If you are going to sit there and tell me I can't cry then you are going to have to leave." Bless her heart, because she didn't say anything. She just sat there in the corner holding her hands. And I just lay there crying.

When I went home, I got a letter stating I had been accepted into Law School. The same day I also got a letter from the School District stating that unless I completed the requirements for special education certification I no longer had a job.

It was at that point that I realized that the world did not stop because I had breast cancer. If I had died on the operating table everything was still going to go on. The sun was still coming up, and people were going on about their business. So, I decided it was time for me to get on with the business of living. I was going to law school.

I had not realized how removed I had been from everything until my 6-year-old daughter Phoenix saw me in the bath tub and said, "Mom, what happened to your boob?"

Finally, it hit me that I hadn't explained to her why I had been in the hospital. I talked to her and let her know what happened. When we finished talking it dawned on me that she never said how gross my scar looked.

In the fall I went in for some tests and the doctor said my tumor markers were high. I asked what that meant. She said, "Possible bone cancer."

I said, "Are you saying that could shorten my life?"

She said, "No, I am saying it could end your life."

I went home and I looked at my children and I talked to my husband about death that night. Then all of a sudden it was like a light bulb went off in my head. I said, "I am not going to accept this." I looked at my children. I wanted to live. My children needed me.

I knelt in the closet and I prayed for myself. "Lord, please don't take me from my children. Don't let that happen." I told my husband, "I know I've been delivered."

On the way to the hospital hymns came to me and I started humming them. I was just thanking God. I had the CAT scan, and everything was clear.

Breast cancer truly forced me into a new mind set. I could no longer just go on with the mundane tasks of life. I had to live my life.

> **"I** had not realized how removed I had been from everything until my 6-year-old daughter Phoenix saw me in the bath tub and said, 'Mom, what happened to your boob?'**"**

Cassandra Iverson

I have always been a very inquisitive person. I like asking questions and trying to find out the "whys" of a particular situation. I never really like to accept things at face value.

Cassandra Iverson

Age:	48
Stage:	1
Occupation:	Teacher
Residence:	Los Angeles, California
Procedure:	Mastectomy
Treatment:	None
Survivorship:	1 year
Lymph Node Involvement:	None

For me breast cancer presented a new challenge of unresolved questions that I was to seek the answers to.

The complex world of breast cancer became a wake up call for me. It seemed like I was always so very busy, but I realized it was time to stop wasting time and take care of business. I now have to live with the thought of a recurrence in my other breast lingering over my head. That is enough to make you know how precious time really is. I am not saying that I have to be doing something every minute of the day, but there is not a day that goes by in which I don't find something to enjoy.

I went in for my annual physical with my gynecologist. I wasn't having any problems, it just happened to be time to have my pap smear. My insurance also required that I have a mammogram.

After they did the mammogram, the technician noticed that there was an unidentifiable spot in my breast.

I keep thinking that it was the Lord that made me have the mammogram in the first place. Because I had such a bad experience with one four years ago, I had vowed not to have another one. If it hadn't been for the stipulation by the insurance company, I would never have broken that vow.

My doctor let me look at the X-ray. The spot was so small I could barely see it, but it looked like little grains of salt. In fact, the surgeon requested another mammogram before the biopsy so that he could make sure he got the right area.

I was expecting to wait a few days for the results of the biopsy, but my doctor called me the same night at home. He informed me that the area was malignant and I needed to schedule surgery as soon as possible.

I guess nobody is prepared to get that kind of news. I was so glad my husband was able to go with me to go over my options. I didn't know what to do. I thought about all the pros and cons. And what I didn't think of, he did. I felt like he went through the entire ordeal with me.

There is no doubt this was a very trying experience. Fortunately I felt my doctor was very up front with me and he did not hesitate on recommending what I should do. I still requested a second opinion.

I wanted to make sure I was making the right decision. I had heard there was a possibility of a lumpectomy or a mastectomy. But in my case I knew a lumpectomy wasn't going to be a good option because there wasn't a lump ... the cancer was in the tissue.

When I finally got in to see another doctor for a second opinion, he bombarded me with information. In fact, he gave me so much information it became confusing. He started talking about reconstruction before he explained my surgical options or possible treatments. I was so overwhelmed that I knew that he was not the one.

I started to pray and ask the Lord to help me make a decision and calm me down. But most of all, I wanted Him to help me deal with whatever that decision was. All at once I felt this calmness go through my body. I realized God had answered my prayers and it was time to go ahead and have the surgery.

Once I made my decision, I was at total peace. I remember sitting on the table reading the newspaper and a doctor came up to me. He questioned my visible tranquillity. "You are just calmly reading the paper knowing what you are facing?" he asked.

It was then I knew beyond a shadow of a doubt that I was at peace with the decision I had made.

It became evident, after the surgery, that I had made the right choice because there was cancer in another area of my breast. But fortunately there was no lymph node involvement.

> *"I started to pray and ask the Lord to help me make a decision and calm me down. But most of all, I wanted Him to help me deal with whatever that decision was."*

The entire time I kept thanking God. I knew that if it was left up to me I wouldn't have had another mammogram and the cancer would have been growing in me all the time.

Now that I look back at it, I realize that there was a family history of cancer that I really hadn't paid much attention to. My cousin had breast cancer and my grandfather had lung cancer. My mother had also had a benign cyst. I know those aren't really uncommon because you hear of a lot of women having cysts all the time. But still, these are issues I really never thought about until after I was diagnosed.

The one thing I will never forget is how supportive my husband Aaron was through this entire thing. The mastectomy didn't bother him. For instance, after the surgery the doctor told me I was going to need to change my bandage. I could not even look at it, let alone change it. My husband ended up being the one to change it for me. It really didn't bother him.

He kept telling me that I was so strong to make the decision to have the mastectomy. But I thought to myself, "That was the easy part." I thought he was strong for looking at my scar everyday.

Even though he is pastor of our church, he also helped out a lot with the children. I have two daughters, Lauren 16 and Camille 17, and I was usually the one running around with the car pools getting them where they needed to go. But after my surgery he fell right in place and started taking care of everything. Because of the genetic link for breast cancer I wanted to make sure I educated my daughters about the disease, but I didn't want to frighten them.

I did not want to have another surgery at the time, so I never even thought about reconstruction. But now, after talking to other women in my support group who have had reconstruction, I am becoming more curious about it. It has made me interested enough to check with my doctor to find out what it will entail.

It seems that after you have breast cancer you start noticing other people around you who have been through the same thing. My husband has an aunt, Nancy Friend, who has had a double mastectomy, and she is really active. She has been a role model for me. I know that nothing has to stop after breast cancer — it can be business as usual.

Catherine Harvey

After I found out I had breast cancer, I was determined that I was not going to spend my birthday in the hospital again. Once before I had spent my birthday in the hospital. I thought to myself, "Not this time!" I have a form of Sickle Cell Anemia and have experienced several blood crises in my lifetime.

I had always had to adjust my lifestyle because of my illness. I remember when I was in college everyone would go home to celebrate Christmas vacation with their families. I would go home, spend Christmas Day with my family and then check into the hospital for additional tests. At this point they had not diagnosed my blood condition and I was constantly being tested. This was the only way that I could deal with my blood crises and not have to lose so much time during the school year.

Now that I had breast cancer, once again I was going to have to change my lifestyle in order to accommodate my health.

Catherine Harvey

Age:	44
Stage:	1
Occupation:	IRS Problem Resolution Officer
Residence:	Dallas, Texas
Procedure:	Bi-lateral Mastectomy, Reconstruction
Treatment:	None
Survivorship:	6 years
Lymph Node Involvement:	None

I have always had fibroid cysts in my breast. Therefore, I was extremely conscious of doing breast self-examinations. Because my job as a revenue officer with the IRS required me to move around a lot, I found it very difficult to keep track of my base-line data. In fact, for a while, it seemed that I was moving every 18 months.

In 1988, I moved to Lubbock, Texas. A year later I discovered lumps in both of my breasts. I went in to have a mammogram at a diagnostic center. Since I had not established a base-line in Texas, the technician suggested that, even though the lumps looked suspicious, I wait six months and come back to have them checked out.

I was very uncomfortable with that.

I had already established a relationship with an internist because of my blood condition. I went to him for advice. He agreed that the situation required immediate attention. I took him my X-rays and he coordinated a second opinion along with a needle biopsy.

My doctor was very concerned when they couldn't get any fluid from the needle aspiration. He suggested we take further action. He told me then that generally, when they were unable to aspirate fluid from a lump, that was a good sign of a possible malignancy.

Since this was very close to my birthday, and I was determined not to be in the hospital, I decided to wait before taking any action. I called my sister in Hawaii and spent the Thanksgiving holiday with her.

I was single and I had no children, so I knew that I was going to have to get to my family and let them know what was going on. My parents had always been very protective of me because of my illness. I knew that they would want to know that I was OK.

We all gathered together at my brother's house for Christmas dinner. After dinner was over, I made my big announcement that I had breast cancer. I kind of shocked everybody at first. No one knew what to say.

They all knew me, and they all knew how I looked at illness. I looked at breast cancer the same way I looked at my blood condition — as just another challenge. It was just another opportunity for me to be the best that I could be.

The most difficult decision for me to make was whether I was going to move back home to Virginia or stay in Texas and go through this by myself. At this point, all I knew was to trust in the Lord, and believe that everything was going to be OK.

I did have some friends in Texas and I also had a great relationship with my employees, so I decided to stay.

I worked up until the day before my surgery. My staff handed out duties while I was gone. They even conducted a blood drive just in case I needed blood. Even though I was away from my family, there was no doubt that I had a lot of support.

At the time of my surgery, it became evident that I was going to have to have a bilateral mastectomy. My left breast was showing cancerous cells. Thankfully, it was the very early stages of cancer. Due to the fact I had already had cysts removed from my right breast, there was no longer any fatty tissue there. In the absence of fatty tissue my doctor felt it was very likely that the cancer would return there.

I opted to have immediate reconstructive surgery. I was very disappointed because when they showed me all of the tapes of what it would be like, they had no African American women as models. I have keloid skin, and I felt I did not have a very accurate picture of what it was going to look like.

After my surgery, my family seemed very cautious not to talk about it. Nobody asked me what it felt like. They didn't ask what it looked like. Finally, two years later, I was joking around and trying on clothes with my sisters and one of them broke down and asked me what it looked like.

Now that I think about it, I realize that cancer had run through my family. My mother had cervical cancer. My two sisters had vaginal cancer, but I never really thought about it. With all of the other health problems I had, cancer was never a real issue for me.

When I was a kid, besides having Sickle Cell, I was asthmatic and I was allergic to everything, including dirt. I could never do the normal things that children do. I remember praying and asking God to just give me 25 years. I told Him that if He would just bless me with 25 years that would allow me enough time to grow up, go to school, get my degree, and prove that I could make it in the American way.

I felt that 25 years was enough. Anything after that was a gift. I would spend the rest of my days sharing and caring for people. That's the way I look at it now. I feel that I am truly blessed and every day is a gift from God.

"I felt that 25 years was enough. Anything after that was a gift. I would spend the rest of my days sharing and caring for people. That's the way I look at it now. I feel that I am truly blessed and every day is a gift from God."

Jacqueline J. Russell

Ever since I was diagnosed with breast cancer, I never really dealt with it. I was going along doing my everyday tasks, but I was holding a lot of anger within me. Little did I know I was like a walking time bomb.

Jacqueline J. Russell

Age:	43
Stage:	1
Occupation:	Legal Secretary
Residence:	Channelview, Texas
Procedure:	Lumpectomy
Treatment:	Chemotherapy & Radiation
Survivorship:	3 years
Lymph Node Involvement:	0 / 11

During the Christmas holidays my friend Karolyn and I decided to go shopping. I hadn't taken any treatments yet. So, I knew that chemo and radiation were still things that I would to have to deal with. It was like there was a big ball inside of me. I didn't know what was going to happen with my life at this point. All of this was going on in my head as we were shopping. We were standing in the check-out line when this lady bumped me with a box in my spot where I had surgery. Before I could think about it, all this pent up frustration came out. I swirled around and hit her with my good arm.

I think I released all of my frustration at the time. Later we laughed about it, but it really wasn't funny. I could have gone to jail for that. I am not the kind of person who would have ever reacted that way under normal circumstances.

Right before I turned 38 I decided to have a baseline mammogram. My doctor never recommended it. I just thought it was something I should do. Two years later my firm offered mammograms to employees for a very minimal cost.

I really didn't think there was a reason to have one. I just thought I would take advantage of it. I waited until the last minute. Finally, I paid my money. When I went in to have the mammogram, I drew the technician's attention to one part of my breast under my arm. She asked if she could get a film of it. Two weeks later my doctor called me at my office and said my mammogram looked suspicious. He said he had already scheduled me to see a surgeon the next day.

I went in for a biopsy and found out it was malignant. I thought it was very ironic — this was October 1, and the beginning of Breast Cancer Awareness month.

Because it was in the first stage, I was told I could get away with a lumpectomy, and that is what I opted to have along with chemotherapy and radiation.

Like every one else, I had this big fear about going through chemo. I really thought all of my hair was going to fall out. The Friday before my treatment, I decided to have it all cut off. I went to my sister who is a beautician and asked her to cut my hair. She started cutting my hair until it was really short. Then she said, "OK."

I looked at her and said, "You don't understand, I want you to cut it all the way off."

"Jackie, is this something you really want to do?"

"Yes. This is something I have to do for me. I cannot go through waking up every morning and looking at my pillow to see if my hair is on my head or if it is lying in the bed with me."

The whole time she was cutting my hair she was crying. She said, "I don't want to do this." But I let her know that she had to do it ... for me.

Every year on March 1, I cut my hair very, very short. It is my reminder of what I have been through, and that I am glad to still be here.

My mother went with me for my first chemo treatment. I really didn't want her to stay in the room, but she insisted. When they hooked me up to the IV, I started to cry. She said she knew that was going to happen; that is why she didn't want to leave. The only bad thing about chemo was that I didn't want to do it. Really, the worst thing that happened to me was that I gained weight.

"This is something I have to do for me. I cannot go through waking up every morning and looking at my pillow to see if my hair is on my head or if it is lying in the bed with me."

Throughout my treatment I had to keep a positive attitude. For a long time I didn't really deal with the cancer. All I could think of was that my daughter was in college and I was a single parent. She was totally dependent on me. She didn't have any other sources of support. So it was important for me to be able to go to work. I knew I had to live ... because I had to live for her.

I think everyone realizes that cancer is a very serious and dangerous disease. It can wipe you out. Even though my family and I have always been close, through this it brought us to a totally different level.

Because of my experience with breast cancer, I have become more aware of life's goodness. I have become more of an advocate because of the changes I have gone through. I try to talk to everybody who is willing to listen about my cancer. I have never been a very talkative person about anything like that at all.

One evening I came in from work and turned on the television. On the news they had something about Sisters Breast Cancer Support Group. I knew this was a group for African American women and I thought this was the perfect thing to get involved with. At my first meeting I had a hard time dealing with it. I saw people I knew, but I never had a clue that they had been sick ... that did something to me. But it was great to be around people who had the same experience.

Now I realize that at any given point in time it can be the end or it can be the beginning. I choose to make mine the beginning. I live every day as it comes and I live one day at a time. I just continuously thank God for allowing me to be here.

Virginia Martin

The guy I used to date had an ex-girlfriend who had breast cancer. I remember him making a lot of crazy comments about her. He even said he would boil the glasses to sterilize them after she drank from them. Well, needless to say, I realized he was someone I could do without.

One day I called him up and told him that I had been sick. I had started re-evaluating things and thinking of the people who were important in my life ... and his name didn't come up.

I hung up the phone, and that was it. I never told him that I had breast cancer.

I discovered my lump in the shower one day. I had been feeling it for a long time, but I kept pretending that if I ignored it ... it would go away. Finally, I realized it wasn't going away, so I decided to get it checked out.

Virginia Martin

Age: 47

Stage: 2

Occupation: Retired

Residence: Los Angeles, California

Procedure: Lumpectomy

Treatment: Chemotherapy, Radiation

Survivorship: 5 years

Lymph Node
Involvement: 4/14

But, I never let myself conceive the thought of cancer. I just thought this was a little inconvenience I was going to have to deal with, having this lump removed.

I should have known that something was wrong when they asked me to come back for my biopsy results, on Friday the 13th. I remember just sitting there waiting for someone to confirm that there was nothing wrong with me. Then the doctor walked in and said, "Oh, it was cancer."

From that point on I started arming myself with as much information as I could get from the American Cancer Society. All my doctor had told me was that it was cancer, and it was treated by a mastectomy.

Well, I had already spoken with a nurse who had suggested that if my lump was malignant I needed a second opinion. She had also recommended a cancer specialist who would do everything in his power to preserve my breast. When I went in to see him, he told me that I could get by with a lumpectomy. He let me know that the recovery rate would be the same, the chance of a recurrence was the same, so there was no need to take my whole breast. I went with that option.

Because I had four positive lymph nodes, it was recommended that I take both radiation and chemotherapy. I had no idea what chemo was going to be like, but I totally freaked out when they brought the IV in the room. I was in the chair, the nurse had put the IV in my arm, then I decided I could not go through with it. Everybody looked at me like I was crazy.

After my first treatment, I thought it wasn't so bad after all. By the time I got home I started throwing up. I must have thrown up everything that I had ever eaten in my life.

Unfortunately for me, it did not get any better. I felt like I was throwing up poison and chemicals all the time. That went on for a week after my treatments. Finally, I decided to make a pallet on the bathroom floor after I had a treatment.

Of course, I lost every strand of my hair. It was like watching a movie, I started brushing my hair and it just kept falling until there wasn't any more left. I remember my granddaughter rubbing my bald head and saying, "That's OK grandma, it will come back."

But if it never came back, I realized losing my hair was a small price to pay for saving my life.

One day I went in for a treatment and a nurse said, "Thank God there is chemo here to help you." And I said to myself, "Yeah, right."

Radiation, on the other hand, was tolerable for me.

My boss had called to let me know that I had picked a bad time to get sick. I wanted to tell her if I had known the promotion was going on, I would have told the cancer to wait.

"But if it never came back, I realized losing my hair was a small price to pay for saving my life."

But I went back to work, while taking radiation every day. I was still really tired and I only wanted to work part-time. At first she was insistent on my working a full 8 hour day, until she realized my doctor was going to put me on complete disability. Then she thought part-time was just fine.

When I went back to the doctor I thought my treatments were over, then he suggested that I take a few more chemo treatments. I was so upset. I couldn't believe he would let me think it was over, only to pull the rug from under me. I took two more treatments, then I told him that was it. He finally agreed. He said, "I guess that would be just gilding the lily; we probably got everything."

Now when I think about it, I guess I get a little upset at myself, I never did breast self-exams because I was afraid I would find something. But it is like being a little bit pregnant. If it is there, it is there. Whether you acknowledge it or not, it will just keep growing.

The one thing I do know is that breast cancer made me put things in a different perspective. I used to be so practical, and I was definitely a penny pincher. I never bought patent leather shoes for my daughters when they were little girls because they were not practical. But now when we go out to lunch I leave this big tip, and my daughters look at me with their mouths hanging open. I know they want to say, "Mom, is that really you?"

I now realize that money is only money. I know that I may not get all the things that I want to get, but life is precious ... and I have to enjoy my life.

Thermalene Brown

When I found out I had cancer I was totally devastated. I went into a complete state of shock. I was really caught off guard because the doctors had insisted that it was "nothing" for so long. It was only through my persistence, based on a gut level feeling, that my lump was removed. I kept thinking of what would have happened if I wasn't so persistent.

Now, I am insistent that my 21 year old daughter be conscious of proper breast care. I want to make sure that she takes care of herself.

Although I had no family history of cancer, I had my first cyst at 17. And by the time I was 22, I had another lump. Four years ago I developed yet another cyst. The doctors assured me that the growths were nothing to worry about, but because of my history I kept having mammograms every six months.

I don't know why, but I just had this gut feeling that there was something different about this latest "cyst." This one bothered me. Finally, I told my doctor that I wanted him to remove it.

When the lump was removed, they did a biopsy. That is when they told me that it was malignant.

It took me an entire month to get over the news and finally come to grips with it.

When it finally settled in that I had cancer, I reviewed my options and elected to have a modified radical mastectomy. Because there was no lymph node involvement I did not have radiation or chemotherapy treatments.

I adapted to the surgery very well. For me it was a total

Thermalene Brown

Age:	42
Stage:	1
Occupation:	Post Office Supervisor
Residence:	Humble, Texas
Procedure:	Modified Radical Mastectomy
Treatment:	None
Survivorship:	3 years
Lymph Node Involvement:	None

re-birthing experience. I had a new beginning ... a chance to start all over again.

One of the best things for me was that I had a very understanding man in my life. He still saw me as a total woman. He looked at me as being a strong woman who could adjust to a part of her body that was no longer there.

It seems the men in my life were there when I needed them most. My ex-husband even came to my side after I was diagnosed. Before I had my surgery, he took care of things for me. He even went as far as to leave his apartment and stay at my house until I was back to normal. Because some things around the house were difficult for me to do for a while, he made sure that those things got done. For me, his commitment was something unexpected, but it was very appreciated.

"... It is still hard for me to believe that I was doing all the right things, and my cancer almost went undetected."

Even today I keep thinking that if I weren't so persistent I might not be here. I remember every time I would make a wrong move I would feel this tenderness. It is still hard for me to believe that I was doing all the right things, and my cancer almost went undetected.

I have become involved with Sisters, a support group for African American women that are breast cancer survivors. I think it is so important for African American women to be properly educated about breast cancer. It is extremely important that our women know the seriousness of this disease.

My mother is 63 and she still will not get a mammogram. Her mother is 89 and she has never had a mammogram. Without a doubt, this bothers me because these are very important women in my life and I want to make sure they are taking care of themselves.

I think they may be afraid of what they may find out. Maybe fear is an issue with a lot of women that won't have mammograms done, or don't do breast self-exams. But as women, we have got to get past the fear issue because it is what we do not know that can do us the most harm.

Years ago, African American women would not come out and say they were breast cancer survivors. It was like there was some type of stigma attached to it. Once I had my surgery I wanted to speak out about it. I was not ashamed of having breast cancer because I was glad to be a survivor.

Carolyn Harvey

I had a partial mastectomy two years ago, and I thought everything would be fine. Then last year the doctors said I needed another biopsy. This time I became frightened and concerned that I would become more disfigured. I was so concerned that to compare the differences, I took a picture before the surgery.

Before I had the biopsy I had a talk with the Lord. First, I told Him that He had promised me that the disease would not come back. I let Him know that I truly did not want to lose my breast, but if I had to I was willing to accept that fact.

After the second biopsy, I realized the deformity wasn't that bad. I have a little more dimpling than I had before.

My physician found my first mass during a routine physical. He sent me to have a mammogram. However, the mammogram didn't show anything. He also referred me to a surgeon to have a needle aspiration — that proved to be negative as well.

Carolyn Harvey

Age:	47
Stage:	1
Occupation:	Advertising Billing Coordinator
Residence:	Largo, Maryland
Procedure:	Partial Mastectomy
Treatment:	Radiation
Survivorship:	2 years
Lymph Node Involvement:	None

Then we took the "wait and see" approach.

Hindsight has taught me that wasn't the best approach. I went back every two months for him to check it. Six months later, he decided to do a biopsy. At that time they found out it was cancer.

At first I had these big crocodile tears. When I had the initial biopsy everything looked clean. Once they told me it was cancer, I was caught off guard. I had never even entertained that thought.

I thank God that even though I had waited, it was still caught in stage 1. I did not have to have any chemotherapy. Yet, I still had to have 27 treatments of radiation.

Two years after my initial surgery I went back for my regular mammogram. This time the mammogram was questionable. There seemed to be a remarkable change from my last X-ray. My doctor wasn't sure if it was scar tissue or something else.

I was really afraid. I kept thinking to myself, "I wish I had a significant other to help me go through this." I didn't want to have to deal with it by myself. Other times I was glad. I had heard so many stories about women who were rejected by their mates. I don't know how I would have dealt with that. It seems that so many men can't handle this kind of thing.

I don't have a problem talking to anybody about what has happened to me, and I also believe breast cancer is something we should address with men. I truly believe the more we talk to men about it, the better they will be able to cope with us.

God had been my source of strength through all of this. I embrace every day. I try to live each day to its fullest. I don't take life for granted because with cancer you never know. There is always the threat that it could happen to you again. At that point, you don't know what stage it could happen to you in.

Nowadays, I try to give more. I try to make myself more available. I am now certified by the American Cancer Society for the Special Towel Program to teach breast self-exams. I think education and early detection is the key to the successful fight for the breast cancer survivor. I know you can't save the world by yourself, but I try to share with other people as much as I can.

I try to make sure every day counts.

"I also believe breast cancer is something we should address with men. I truly believe the more we talk to men about it, the better they will be able to cope with us."

$\mathcal{W}$ilma Carroll

When I found out I had breast cancer, I was in the process of terminating a relationship. My friend didn't abandon me; instead, he was very supportive. He took me to the doctor and to chemo. He stood by my side the entire time. Later on I met someone else, and my breast cancer didn't make a difference.

I have come to realize that your breasts do not make you a woman. They are only a part of you ... they are not all of you. You have more to offer a man, to life, to society and your community than just your breasts or your physical appearance.

For me, as a single woman, having breast cancer has only enhanced my relationship with men because I do not look at myself as less of a woman.

I had gone in for my routine mammogram. At that time I didn't do breast self-exams, so I had never noticed a lump. Thankfully, the mammogram picked it up. Yet, by the time it was detected, the lump was already 3 centimeters.

Wilma Carroll

Age:	45
Stage:	2
Occupation:	Teacher
Residence:	Uniondale, New York
Procedure:	Lumpectomy
Treatment:	Chemotherapy & Radiation
Survivorship:	2 years
Lymph Node Involvement:	None

I had a baseline four years before and it showed no problems. I was expecting this X-ray to go fine as well. The next day, I got a call from my gynecologist who said he thought I should see a surgeon because something showed up on the film that we might need to take a look at.

The first thing that came into my mind was the fear of cancer. Cancer is one of those things you never want to catch. It is one of those diseases that you sort of hope passes you by. It is the fear of death that causes the major trauma. At that particular time, all I could think of is that I was going to die. It is like a monster movie when this big hand comes from nowhere and rips a piece of your heart and soul out.

This was my first experience with any kind of disease. I had never been sick, and I had never been in the hospital.

I had no family history of cancer. I always figured since I didn't smoke cigarettes, I was never going to get cancer.

I was very satisfied when the doctor gave me the option of having a lumpectomy. Even though my lump was relatively large, there were no lymph nodes involved so I knew that was a good sign.

Because of the size of my lump, I ended up having both chemotherapy and radiation. I went through the majority of my treatment with a certain amount of denial. I couldn't understand why I was doing these things when I knew good and well I wasn't going to live.

My hair loss was a real shock for me. Like my breasts, it was a part of me and I had set certain standards on how I wanted to look. I was upset because now I no longer looked that way.

"My hair loss was a real shock for me. Like my breasts, it was a part of me and I had set certain standards on how I wanted to look. I was upset because now I no longer looked that way."

From that point on my life began to take on a different form. It was like being a prisoner on Death Row. We all know that eventually we are going to die. However, once you are diagnosed with cancer you feel that your death is going to come a little sooner. It seems that constant fear of death is lurking over your head.

I didn't have any children or a husband to lean on. I had to go through everything by myself. I think that is where support groups come into play. They help give you a sigh of relief that life will return to normal ... that someone else has gone through this too.

Even though some people make it OK on their own support, I think support groups are very important for those who don't have a lot of family or close friends. Also, support groups provide a source of information and better awareness.

The one thing that I feel compelled to do is to reach out to other Black women who have had this disease. I have a strong desire to give back. If my having a lumpectomy can save one sister out there, then it was all worth it.

When I had my surgery, I was the only Black woman around. So, I knew there was a need that was not being fulfilled. I knew there had to be other women who felt like me and who didn't want to feel like they were the only ones out there. As a result, I eventually started a branch of the Sisters Network in the Long Island area.

I am very conscious about what I believe in now. I think that having cancer may have made me a little bit selfish because I realize that life is really short. You could be driving down the highway and it could be the end. Life becomes more of a personal experience. You began to evaluate it and think about what you really want to do with it.

There are things that I used to put on the back burner. I have now begun to accomplish those things. I think when you are given a limited time to accomplish something, it gives you more energy to do it.

It is said that cancer takes a part of your soul. For some it may, but it does not devastate you to the point you cannot function. You are still a viable functioning woman. From my experience, I feel it makes you more exciting and more interesting. You take on a different zest for life. Once you come around and get your strength back, you are more energetic about life in general.

Pat Brewer

I have always had very large breasts, but I never looked at them as playing a major role in my sexuality. When I realized that I was going to lose one, I became very concerned at how that was going to affect my relationship with my husband. This was a man who had married a woman with a 38-4D chest, and now that was about to change drastically. I wanted to make sure that didn't affect our relationship in any way. But if it did, I was very open to having counseling.

Yet, I was surprised at the support I received from my husband. He loved my breasts only because they were a part of me, but the main thing was that he loved me. He let me know that he had taken the vows "for better or worse" and that had come to pass. And "in sickness and health" and we had dealt with that, too. Breast cancer just seemed to make our marriage stronger.

Pat Brewer

Age:	47
Stage:	1
Occupation:	Employment Interviewer
Residence:	Tuscumbia, Alabama
Procedure:	Mastectomy
Treatment:	None
Survivorship:	4 months
Lymph Node Involvement:	Unknown

Because of my age, I had regular mammograms. When I went in two years ago, they found some calcium deposits that my doctor thought needed to be checked out. I didn't have any lumps or any other way to identify them outside of the mammogram. So they suggested I have a biopsy. The area was so small they had to mark the mammogram to insure that they got the sample from the right area.

After the biopsy, I was told that everything was fine.

The next year I went back as usual, but my mammogram was the same. Again they recommended a biopsy. This time, my gynecologist said, based on my report, they had missed the correct spot last year. They had collected the wrong sample. Right away this let me know I needed another surgeon. There is no way I wanted to risk that happening again.

After I selected another surgeon, I asked him what was the possibility of them missing the spot again. He assured me that there was only a 2 percent possibility of it happening again. I felt very confident with that number. So I decided to have another biopsy. This time they got the spot right off the bat.

Based on the fact I had no family history of breast cancer, I was told there was a good possibility that it was not malignant. So none of us expected cancer.

When they called me in and told me the tissue was malignant, I didn't freak out, I didn't get emotional; I just wanted to have the surgery the next day.

At first the doctor asked if I wanted him to step out of the room so my husband and I could discuss it. I let him know there was no need for him to step out. I just looked at my husband and told him I was having the surgery the next day if there was any way it could be arranged. My husband had no problem with that. All I wanted to do was remove the cancer and get on with my life.

My doctor explained to me that I could have a lumpectomy with chemotherapy or I could have a complete mastectomy. I was very unfamiliar with chemo except for the bad things I had heard about it, so I opted to have my breast removed.

After the surgery, they told me the tumor was the size of a grain of popcorn. They had also removed some lymph nodes, but none of them were positive.

My doctor recommended I take Tamoxifen. He said one of the side effects was hot flashes, and also it could cause uterine cancer. I couldn't see giving up one form of cancer for another. I knew whether I took chemo or hormones there was no guarantee that the cancer would not return. I realize that there are some things that we don't have any control over. No matter what we do or how many preventive measures we take, there are still things that are going to happen to us. So, I don't worry about the cancer coming back in my breast or anywhere else.

*"**I** am just glad that I was having regular mammograms. My breasts are so large I probably would not have found a lump anyway. And by the time I did feel a lump it might have been too late."*

Every time I think about my situation, I am just glad that I was having regular mammograms. My breasts are so large I probably would not have found a lump anyway. And by the time I did feel a lump it might have been too late.

I don't know if it is normal or not, but I never really had any problem dealing with breast cancer. At first I was wondering what was wrong with me because I wasn't acting like the women you hear about or you see in the movies. They wake up and find out they don't have a breast and they lose their minds. I guess because of my awareness of the disease that didn't happen to me. And I never looked at it as if I couldn't get breast cancer. I thought it could happen to anybody.

I tried very hard not to look at this as being sick. Before my surgery I didn't feel sick, and I certainly did not want to feel sick after it. The day after my surgery I got up and made up my bed because I was determined I wasn't going to stay in it.

After my surgery, I didn't miss a beat. I had my surgery on a Tuesday morning and I was at church on Sunday morning. I know a lot of the women must have looked at me like I was crazy because they didn't understand how in the world I could be at church after just having a mastectomy.

I have not allowed myself to be preoccupied with having one breast. Overall, I feel really good about it. Of course I am reminded of it when my blouse raises up, or something doesn't fit right. And it is hard not to think about it when I remove my clothes. But it is definitely not something I allow myself to dwell on.

My mother was upset when I was first diagnosed. I tried to let her know that this is life. It could happen to me just like it could happen to the lady up the street. No one is exempt.

Carolyn Beaman

Carolyn Beaman

Age:	47
Stage:	1
Occupation:	Teacher
Residence:	Lake Jackson, Texas
Procedure:	Bi-lateral Mastectomy
Treatment:	None
Survivorship:	4 years
Lymph Node involvement:	None

I had seven surgeries in my breasts by the time I was 43 years old, three in one breast and four in the other. That had just been part of my history as a result of suffering from fibroid cystic disease. Biopsies had just become a part of my life from an early age. So when I found another lump, my doctor thought it wasn't anything to be concerned about. According to my history, it too was supposed to be benign. To everyone's surprise, this one was different.

At first when I found this little pea sized lump, I immediately went to the doctor. He suggested that I watch it for three months before having a biopsy ... after all, that's when I was scheduled to have a mammogram anyway.

I couldn't believe his carefree attitude. I sat up on the table and told him that I really didn't want to wait. I wanted to have a mammogram now. With my insurance, you can't just request a mammogram. It has to be done by a doctor's referral.

In a very irritated voice he told me, "No, we will wait. It doesn't feel like anything that we need to be concerned about."

By this time I was just as irritated as he was. I told him, "I don't know, but from all of my readings you can't tell a benign tumor by your fingertips."

I know this angered him. He threw his pad on the desk and said, "If you want to give those people $50 to $100 for a mammogram then you go right ahead and do it."

When I left his office, I found out he had not ordered a mammogram and his nurse wasn't sure if he was going to.

Anyway, three days later he did order one. The results revealed that the area was cloudy, and the doctor suggested a biopsy. At first they tried to do a needle biopsy. But every time they tried to aspirate fluid from it, it would move. Finally the doctor let me know that even if they were able to get fluid from the lump it was only going to be 85 percent accurate.

Since this was my health I was dealing with, I asked him what was it going to take to be 100 percent accurate. The only thing they could suggest — the one thing I didn't want — a surgical biopsy.

"I figured if my husband could grow that patch of hair back on top of his head, then I would work on perfecting myself."

The next day I flew to California for the biopsy. My sister was an oncology nurse and she had recommended a surgeon for me to see. When I woke up, I remember him saying, "You are a little groggy now, so I will talk to you later."

Well, I knew that wasn't what the doctors say when everything was OK. I had been down this road several times. I know they were always happy to wake me up and give me the good news. I remembered in the past them saying, "Mrs. Beaman, everything is fine."

I knew this time something was wrong. Of course, when I got back to my room and looked into my sister's eyes that was my confirmation. At that point, having a mastectomy was a reality.

I guess my two fears were the same ones that most women face. I was concerned about my life. I wondered, "did they get it all, had it spread to some other place?" Secondly, and my least concern, was my femininity and my sexual attractiveness. I have been married forever and a day. I figured if my husband could grow that patch of hair back on top of his head, then I would work on perfecting myself. But I knew I had nothing to worry about because my husband was very supportive. We had learned to accept each other for what we knew we were — at the best of our appearances, and as time changed us. I was happy to be able to witness the changes.

I come from a family of eight girls, no boys. All of us are very close. I was very concerned because I felt at this point

I had increased their risk factor for breast cancer. But so far, I have been the only one to get it. I was also very concerned about my daughter. I wanted to know as much as possible about my cancer, so I could know if it was the type that would be easily passed on through a genetic link.

I was fortunate that I did not have to have any type of after treatment — chemotherapy or radiation. I credit this to my taking charge of my own health care. If I had waited three months, I could have had more of a development. Also this could have caused more complications and weakened my chances of survival.

Last year I found another lump in my other breast. Once again I flew to Los Angeles for a biopsy. I was concerned that my cancer had metastasised and it was in the other breast. Because I had already had four biopsies on that breast, I was a good candidate for a mastectomy by choice, even if the lump was benign.

I told my doctor no matter what they found, I wanted them to take my breast. I did not want to continue to go through this biopsy after biopsy. Each one was just as emotional, each one was just as draining.

After the surgery was over, I found out that I had made the right decision. Although the tumor was benign, the cells in my breast had shown pre-cancerous signs. It was almost as if there was a guardian angel watching over me. I don't give myself credit for anything. I thank God for steering me in the right direction. I just did my breast self-exam, had mammograms and bone scans.

I had decided to do everything in my power to get cancer before it got me. Whatever it takes, I try to stay on top of it.

We have to realize that early detection is our best weapon. I am a Reach to Recovery Volunteer. Whether a woman has a lumpectomy or a mastectomy I always encourage them to keep in touch with their bodies.

It is important that women not be overly concerned about their femininity or sexuality. If you are alive, coping and adjusting will come. But if you aren't alive, neither one will come.

Many times I wonder why I dealt with breast cancer so easily. It never really bothered me. I know that it wasn't because I was so brave. But now I realize I had already faced a major illness a few months before ... so breast cancer was just another phase for me to go through.

I had been having a secretion from my breast. I was aware of mammograms, so I decided to go in and have one. To my surprise instead of being concerned about my breast, the doctors were more worried about my left lung. There appeared to be a cyst on it.

I ended up having surgery on my lung right away. It was totally unexpected. Even though it was benign, they had to remove a piece of my lung. I was in intensive care for 10 days. I remember being very sick at the time. Once I got over that, I knew I had really been through something. But the doctors never said anything about my breast.

Ernestine Montgomery

Age:	76
Stage:	Unknown
Occupation:	Retired
Residence:	Los Angeles, California
Procedure:	Mastectomy
Treatment:	None
Survivorship:	22 years
Lymph Node Involvement:	None

A month before he was going to do my mastectomy, my doctor told me to go home and talk to my husband to find out what we should do about my breast. I thought to myself, "If there is something there I don't need to talk to him, I will *tell* him what we are going to do."

The first thing I did was let my husband know that I was going to have a mastectomy. He really didn't have a problem with it. Only four months before he had seen me at my lowest after my lung surgery. All he wanted was for me to be healthy. He did everything possible to make sure that he made things as easy as possible for me during both operations.

My husband did a lot of traveling, so even though he tried to be helpful, I was home many times alone. So, instead of being worried or concerned, I became very independent and I learned how to do things differently.

I quickly decided I wasn't going to let having one breast keep me down. Since I was poor and I could sew, I went out and bought some bras and cut the cup out and made a cover for them. Then I tacked those into my old bras. I used rubber form to fill them in ... no one knew the difference. The main thing was that I didn't feel any different.

Twenty-two years ago things were very different. A lot of women were ashamed to admit they had breast cancer. It was something no one wanted to talk about. I remember my neighbor's daughter came over to see me after I can home from the hospital, so I showed her my scar. She was totally shocked. I couldn't figure it out. We were both women, and I didn't have anything to be ashamed of. That is the way I felt then, and it is still the way I feel today.

When I look back at where I came from I have to thank God that I made it. But I think whenever you go through something like that it makes you stronger. You have to just double up your fist and go straight into it.

"I think whenever you go through something like that it makes you stronger. You have to just double up your fist and go straight into it."

$\mathcal{M}$yra Hayes Shelton

When the doctor says you have cancer, it shatters your whole world. All you can think about is that they haven't found a cure for cancer. It is not like someone is telling you that you have bronchitis, where you get some antibiotics and go home. All they can say is that they have proven treatments which have been successfully done on some patients. But you still wonder, is this going to work for me?

Then when you put into perspective that it is breast cancer, the questions began to flow. How am I going to look now? Am I going to be able to finish raising my children? Will I see them finish college? Am I going to be around when they get married?

Myra Hayes Shelton

Age:	47
Stage:	1
Occupation:	Executive Assistant DR&L
Residence;	Madison, Wisconsin
Procedure:	Partial Mastectomy
Treatment:	Radiation
Survivorship:	3 years
Lymph Node Involvement:	None

Since I had my first experience with a benign lump in my left breast, I became accustomed to doing routine breast self-exams. I was very conscious of anything that felt awkward. I developed a history of having cysts and having to have them aspirated. After they were aspirated several times, the doctor then would perform a biopsy. This made me very conscientious when it came to my breasts. I was always very attentive when it came time to have my mammogram.

One day a growth appeared. I watched it for a few months. It didn't hurt, so I didn't pay much attention to it. It seems that you usually don't have a sense of urgency about things that don't hurt you. Because it was an abnormal looking lump, I did bring it to my doctor's attention when I had my mammogram. The mammogram came out OK.

In the back of my mind I still felt that something was wrong. I was still concerned. My doctor was concerned also. He is very sensitive and a fantastic surgeon. He ordered an ultrasound. From the results of the ultrasound, it seemed to be a judgment call as to whether something was wrong or not.

My doctor finally decided that I needed to have a biopsy.

I was in recovery when my doctor told me, "It looks like it's OK, Myra." I sighed with relief. Since it was an out-patient service, I went home to rest up.

The next day I got a call from my doctor. They had finished examining all of the tissue and they had found one section to contain cancerous cells. He wanted me to come in and talk about my options.

"I think the hardest part after I found out I had cancer was actually telling my parents. I knew they would hurt. I think they hurt more than I did."

At that point, reality hit me. Whenever you have a biopsy you know that it could go either way, but you never think it is going to be anything wrong. I knew that there was something different about this lump from the very beginning. It seemed to protrude more than the cysts I had before. My breast took on a different shape. I knew that something had changed.

When I discussed my options with my doctor, he told me, based on the type of cancer I had, it wasn't contained so a lumpectomy wouldn't be an option. Yet he really wouldn't know if a complete mastectomy was necessary until he actually did the surgery. Therefore, I was prepared to have a complete mastectomy, if I needed to. I just wanted them to go in and do what they had to do.

I felt very fortunate that my children weren't babies but I still didn't want to have to leave them. I felt like I still had a lot to do here. All these things were going through my mind. I just told my doctor to do what he had to do. I wanted to live and I had a lot to live for.

I think the hardest part after I found out I had cancer was actually telling my parents. I knew they would hurt. I think they hurt more than I did. It is such a trauma to your family — each one displays it and deals with it in a different way.

I felt responsible. I had to be the strong one. I knew what my family was going through. It was like they were helpless. We all prayed a lot. We came together as a family and prayed and that helped us to get through it. Many people don't realize that cancer hits more than just the person that is diagnosed.

Some people think that by not being open about cancer, it will go away. I never denied it. I think it helps to tell friends and family that, "Yes, I have cancer. I am going through surgery and will do whatever it takes to live."

Some people feel as though they have been struck with cancer and there is some kind of stigma attached to it. They don't want anyone to know because it is something terrible that you don't talk about. I think it is healthy to keep yourself open and get your feelings out; it helps your body in the healing process.

I didn't attend a support group because I had a lot of support from my family and friends. If I didn't have that, I would definitely go to a support group. I also had a coworker who had dealt with breast cancer. Talking with her and seeing her doing so well was encouraging to me.

In working for Tommy Thompson, the Governor of the State of Wisconsin I also found it reassuring when I received support from him and his wife. Ironically, his wife Suezanne, was recently diagnosed with breast cancer. This time I felt that I could be a role model to her so that she could make it through this as well.

I feel that I value my time, what I give and how I give, a little bit more now. I have always been a giving and sharing person. I think now I have developed a little keener perspective on a lot of things. We take life for granted. We automatically think we are going to live to a ripe old age.

Now, I realize that you may not have time to say, "I didn't mean it" or "I wish I could have." You don't have that luxury. The main thing is that you realize that cancer can happen to anyone. It is not always something that happens to your neighbor. It can happen to you too.

When the doctor first told me that he was going to have to remove my breast, I went crazy. I was totally hysterical. My niece was pregnant at the time, and she was waiting for me in the hallway at the doctor's office. I was her favorite aunt. She overheard the conversation and fainted. They had to take her to the hospital. Fortunately, she didn't have the baby early.

I had surgery on July 17, 1950. Back then, the idea of having your breast removed was like someone telling you that you had another head ... it was totally unheard of. It wasn't like it is now, where everybody talks about breast self-exams and mammograms. Back then nobody said anything.

I don't know how I felt ... this was all of a sudden. It's hard to say how you feel when the doctor tells you [something like that].

I first knew something was wrong when I noticed blood on my gown. I realized I was bleeding from my nipple. When I went to the doctor, he told me that he was going to have to remove my breast and scrape the bone next to my chest wall.

Adell Puckett

Age:	89
Stage:	Unknown
Occupation:	Retired lunch counter worker
Residence:	Dallas, Texas
Procedure:	Prophylactic Mastectomy
Treatment:	None
Survivorship:	45 years
Lymph Node Involvement:	None

He said he could take the cyst off. But if he was me, he would have it removed because he would probably have to come back and remove the breast later anyway. If he removed it now and scraped the bone, he would be through with it.

I was so scared at first. I told him to go ahead and take both of them off. It wouldn't hurt me a bit. I knew I wasn't going to be having any children. So, rather than die, I would rather have them take 'em both.

My doctor, who was white, said, "No, Mrs. Puckett, we don't have to take both breasts. We just need to take the one."

I thought my husband, Elbert, was going to lose his mind when he found out. But once he realized I was going to be OK, he was fine with it.

I stayed in the hospital for three days. At the time I had good insurance through my husband's job at the Post Office.

I talked with a neighbor before I had surgery. She told me, "Baby don't worry about that, you're not going to die from any breast operation. I had mine 23 years ago." It made me feel good to realize someone else had been through this.

After my surgery I bought a bra with a pocket in it, then I got a prosthesis. When you looked at me, you couldn't tell a thing. At that time, prostheses were plastic with fluid in them. Whichever way you leaned, that was the way your prosthesis would go.

Now, when I think about it, even if reconstruction had been an option, I wouldn't have wanted it. I know too many people who ended up having it, and the implant started leaking. My prosthesis is just fine for me. I wear one all the time. I never go without it. I even sleep in it because my doctor said if I slept in it, it would keep my shoulder from drooping. So far, it's worked or it seems like it has.

I just stayed off work about a week or two because I didn't feel sick or anything.

I had not been on my job long, so I was eager to get back. They had just begun to hire blacks to work in white cafeterias. I had gotten a job downtown serving over the rail [counter]. Although we couldn't waitress on the main floor, we could still serve food over the rail. I worked at that cafeteria for 13 years and two months.

Even though I caught mine before it turned into cancer, my mother died of lung cancer, and my husband died in 1977 of prostate cancer.

If I live to see the 13th day of this coming August, I will be 90 years old. All I can tell other women to do is to trust in the Lord because He never fails. That's how I made it through. I have always put my trust in God and tried to live right. I know if you believe and trust in God, everything is going to be all right.

> **"I** *talked with a neighbor before I had surgery. She told me, 'Baby don't worry about that, you're not going to die from any breast operation. I had mine 23 years ago.'"*

Theresa A. Patrick

I had prayed so hard. I asked the Lord to let me get to know Him on a more intimate level. I needed to know that He was working in my life. I wanted to know that all the

things that I had done in the church would mean more than following a life-time habit simply because I was raised in the church. That was my prayer from the depth of my heart. Two weeks later, I was diagnosed with breast cancer.

I always had a history of health problems. At 3, I was diagnosed with VonWillebrands, a rare blood clotting deficiency. I learned I needed to take care of myself and be in tune with my body at a very early age. I could not ride a bicycle because a simple cut or scrape might cause me to bleed for three or four days, and I might have to have a blood transfusion.

As I grew older, I developed fibroid cysts in my breasts. At 35, I had my first mammogram. Even though I could not feel any lumps in my breasts, the mammogram revealed they were definitely there. At that point my doctor said, "Theresa, you need to have a mammogram done at least every year."

I knew that the norm was every two years, but at his recommendation I started having mammograms every year for six years. The mammograms were always negative.

At 42, I went in to have my first complete physical by a female doctor, and this included a mammogram as well. The cysts were still there, but they had not changed. I felt confident that I had nothing to worry about.

A year later, I began to experience pain in my right breast. For the next eight months I paid close attention to my

Theresa A. Patrick

Age:	44
Stage:	2
Occupation:	Administrative Director Richardson Independent School District
Residence:	
Procedure:	Mastectomy
Treatment:	Chemotherapy
Survivorship:	6 months
Lymph Node Involvement:	3 / 12

breast as I did my breast self-examinations. Something had changed. I felt a lump for the very first time.

I acted immediately.

The next day I made an appointment to have another mammogram. I also scheduled an appointment with my breast surgeon. The surgeon also felt the lump. She said, "It looks like something has happened because we have never been able to feel them before. It looks like we have gone from a pea size to a maraschino cherry. It is time to do something."

I said, "Fine."

Two weeks later we scheduled a biopsy. Before having the biopsy, my radiology report went to the wrong doctor. Instead of sending the report to my doctor, it was sent directly to me.

I had to hold back the tears as I read the report. It said, "Three masses, high in density, 2 centimeters each, possibly malignant. Recommendation: see a breast surgeon."

I was devastated. I kept remembering it said, "Possibly malignant!"

I remembered my prayer to the Lord to get to know him on a more intimate level. I never thought it would come to this, but if this is how He had chosen for me to get to know Him better ... I accepted it. I just asked Him to keep my mind clear because it appeared that I was going to have to make some decisions, and I was going to have to make them rather quickly. I knew I definitely needed a clear mind.

As I prepared for the surgery, the surgery itself was not my main concern. Due to my clotting condition, I was extremely concerned about bleeding to death. In fact, that was my primary preoccupation.

I took one look at my doctor's face after I had awakened from the biopsy and I was pretty sure that the news she was about to give me wasn't good. I also reflected back to the radiology report I had received in error.

My doctor said, "I have good news and bad news for you."

"I had to hold back the tears as I read the report. It said, 'Three masses, high in density, 2 centimeters each, possibly malignant. Recommendation: see a breast surgeon.'"

With all of the anxiety I was experiencing, all I could say was, "OK, let's get the bad news first."

She then said there were malignant cells in my right breast, and her recommendation was a unilateral mastectomy.

Being totally uneducated about breast cancer at the time, I asked, "What is that?"

She said, "I need to remove your right breast."

She let me know that she was going to give me 30 days to think about it because she was going on vacation.

I quickly informed her that I didn't need 30 days. With all the calmness and assertiveness I could muster up, I said, "I guess we need to do this before you leave." She didn't realize I would have done it right then if I could have.

I let her know that this was a big deal for me, and I did need to rush. I had just gotten a big promotion on my job. I was only in the position two weeks. On the very day I was sitting in the hospital my colleagues were at an important administrative meeting.

When I found out I had cancer, that word still sounded foreign to me. I called the American Cancer Society and asked for everything that they had on breast cancer — like, yesterday.

The night before my surgery I wrote a letter to my surgical team. I told them that I appreciated the planning and their abilities and everything they had put into the surgical process: finding a virus free blood clotting agent for me, transfusing me before the surgery, transfusing me after the surgery and making sure the drugs they used for doing this were synthetic and were all virus free for AIDS or anything like that. I let them know that I really appreciated everything they had done.

"But you just need to know this one thing, that I have asked people across the country not only to pray for me, but to pray for you. I have called you all by name. I know everybody has something going on in their lives. I don't care how professional you are, everybody is dealing with something ... and I understand that. It is important for you to know that I have taken care of that for you. I have asked the Lord to be with you and your families so you don't have to worry about them. Everything is taken care of.

"Janet, you are the head of this team and I expect you to do everything that you think you need to do. I give you my permission to do that.

"So in the words of Arsenio Hall, let's get busy and get this thing over with. And know that everything that you are worried about or that is going on in your life, I have already asked the Lord to take care of it for you. I have asked Him to make your life a little easier, and your burdens a little lighter."

I handed one of the members of my surgical team this letter before they wheeled me into surgery. I just wanted to make sure they were all on a spiritual level before they began. Even though I knew I had the best surgical team around, I needed them to know that I had already petitioned the Lord and it was no longer in their hands.

After my surgery, I asked my doctor was I going to be able to see my 4-year-old niece Whitney graduate. She said, "I don't know."

All I could think was, "Oh, my God!"

She then responded, "If you are asking me what your prognosis is, your prognosis is good. But I don't know, you could go out there and get in a car wreck."

I thought to myself this was not the time to be funny.

I ended up having three lymph nodes involved, which put me in Stage 2. I realized I was blessed, but again being human all I knew was that my breast was gone.

The Lord made the most devastating, traumatizing experience of my life a good one, if you can understand what I am saying.

I didn't think that anything could be more devastating than losing a parent. When I lost my father, I was daddy's girl and that was devastating to me.

I now realize that all those things were preparing me for something else. I think you have to prepare yourself for the crisis because as sure as you live, there is going to be another one.

> *"I now realize that all those things were preparing me for something else. I think you have to prepare yourself for the crisis because as sure as you live, there is going to be another one."*

A Spiritual Awakening
Becoming closer to Christ after cancer.

ohnnye Ridley

I never will forget. I was lying in the hospital bed and I had so much on my mind. My doctor had told me that he wanted me to have chemotherapy. Just the thought of it scared me to death. I was so afraid, and I did not know what to do.

I started to pray. I was staying in a Catholic hospital and there was a huge cross hanging on the wall in my room. As I prayed, I noticed that the cross began to illuminate. Then, for the first time, I felt everything was going to be OK. I knew that God had heard my prayers.

The next day I told my doctor I was ready to take the chemotherapy treatments.

I found my lump while doing a breast self-examination. Ironically, I had just had a mammogram three months before. I immediately called my primary care physician so that she could check it out. She confirmed that there was definitely something there. She then referred me to a surgeon for a biopsy.

Johnnye Ridley

Age:	54
Stage:	1
Occupation:	Teacher
Residence:	Houston, Texas
Procedure:	Lumpectomy
Treatment:	Chemotherapy & Radiation
Survivorship:	1 year
Lymph Node Involvement:	0/13

The surgeon was very familiar with my family and wasn't concerned about the lump. He knew that I did not have any family history of cancer; therefore, he wasn't in a big hurry to do a biopsy. But I was. I wasn't sure what this lump in my breast was, but I knew that it didn't belong there and I wanted it out.

Right after the biopsy I waited in the recovery room for my

doctor to give me the results. I waited and waited and waited, but he never returned. Finaly a nurse came in. She was surprised that we were still there. She informed me he had already left and gone back to his office.

A few minutes later he called me and told me that the lump was malignant, so he was going to have to do a mastectomy. He was leaving town, and he would be gone for a week. He assured me he would do the surgery when he returned. I went into a hissy. I screamed into the receiver, "Just stop!" then I hung up the phone. I had had enough. I kept thinking to myself, "My doctor is leaving town and I have to have a mastectomy."

I don't think some doctors realize that it is important how you give people information. Sometimes the information given to someone may have such an impact on them that it could make them do something irrational. Based on the matter-of-fact way he chose to tell me that I had cancer ... I thank God that I did not completely freak out.

"Finally I asked him, 'What's an R.D.?' He quickly responded, 'A real doctor.'"

I am one of those people who when something happens, I like to take care of it immediately. So, the next day I kind of went crazy calling pathologists because I wanted another opinion. My brother-in-law is a doctor and he was very helpful. He kind of walked me through everything.

I remember telling him how my doctor had given me the results of my biopsy over the phone. He asked me if my doctor was an M.D. I said, "Yes, of course."

Then he said, "That's the problem. You have an M.D. and what you really need is an R.D." I was so puzzled. What in the world was an R.D.? Was that some type of cancer specialist? Why hadn't I heard of an R.D. before? Finally I asked him, "What's an R.D.?"

He quickly responded, "A real doctor."

Well, I set out to find a "real doctor," and finally did. I was very fortunate — instead of having a mastectomy, the doctor I selected informed me that I could have a lumpectomy. He also suggested I follow my surgery with chemotherapy and radiation which would be just as effective as having a mastectomy.

I got through the chemotherapy and 21 days of radiation,

and I was never sick. However, because of poor circulation in my arm I began to develop swelling, which is called lymphedema. My doctor hadn't told me anything about it, so it was completely unexpected. Afterward, I found out that quite a few women who have breast cancer end up with lymphedema as a result of the lymph nodes being removed from under their arms. Unfortunately, it seems the doctors don't know a lot about it so many women are in limbo when it comes to how to reduce the swelling in their hand or arm.

My doctor recommended a pump, which I use on a regular basis, and that works OK for me. But now I have to be very careful not to lift anything too heavy with the arm I had surgery on because that could cause the swelling to increase.

Cancer really changed my life in more than physical ways. After 13 years, I got back involved with my church. I started visiting my priest on a regular basis. We all talk about having faith. We know that it is something you cannot see. But when something like cancer creeps into your life, all you have to hold on to is your trust in God and your faith.

I also stopped procrastinating. I was always putting things off until tomorrow. I always wanted to publish children's books; I got a partner and we started our own publishing company. I also wanted to sing in the church choir. So I joined the choir. Cancer put a new thrust in my life and made me go out and do all the things I used to just think about.

Many of us don't fear death, but we know it's possible. When you have cancer you know it is at hand. You start living life to the fullest because you know that tomorrow is not promised to anyone.

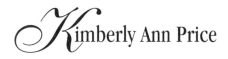

Kimberly Ann Price

A co-worker was diagnosed with breast cancer six months after I was. We became very close. We shared our experiences as she went through chemotherapy and radiation. The doctors told her they thought they had gotten it all. Then she had a recurrence. Because it was so close to her heart, they couldn't operate. Soon the cancer spread to her brain.

The most touching encounter in my life came eight hours before she died. I sat there at her bedside in the quietness of her room as she passed into a semi-conscious state. All I could think of was that she was so young, she had a family and she had put up such a hard fight to live. As I took one last look at her, I couldn't help but think only by the grace of God ... It could have been me.

Kimberly Ann Price

Age:	39
Stage:	1
Occupation:	Human Resource Management
Residence:	Bridgeport, Ohio
Procedure:	Bi-lateral Mastectomy
Treatment:	Radiation
Survivorship:	9 years
Lymph Node Involvement:	None

I had always had fibroid cystic disease, so I was used to examining my breasts. I had my first benign lump in my left breast when I was 21. Five years later I found a lump in my right breast, but my doctor assured me that it was nothing to worry about. According to everything that I read it should have been benign. We watched it for four years. Finally, I decided I didn't want it to be there any more. It shouldn't be there anyway. I wanted to have it removed.

I went in for what was supposed to be a routine operation. They removed the lump and found out it was malignant. My doctor explained that I had two options because I had caught it so early. I could either have a modified radical mastectomy or a lumpectomy with radiation. I opted for the later.

My doctor also let me know there was some calcification in my left breast, but it wasn't necessary to do anything.

He wanted to keep a close eye on it and see if anything developed.

We watched it for five years.

Every time I would have a mammogram done it would come back slightly suspicious. They would try to do a biopsy but they never seemed to get the right spot. The fifth year when I went in the radiologist was determined to get a clear picture. He had me do a Cleopatra stand. They did a biopsy. This time they finally got the spot. It was malignant.

Since I had already had cancer in my right breast my doctor figured if the cancer returned, it would come back in my right breast. Therefore he recommended I have a bi-lateral mastectomy. Because having both breasts removed was such a severe measure, I had five or six other opinions before making up my mind. They all confirmed his recommendation.

It was a very difficult decision to make. I also opted for immediate reconstructive surgery with silicone implants. I knew about the big scare with silicone implants but my doctor let me know that only 2 percent of the cases had any problem. I read all of the literature and I felt I definitely knew what I was getting into. I realize any time you put anything foreign into your body there is always a possibility for it to mess up. Because I had already had radiation, and the skin on my right breast was hard, he wanted to use the most conservative means for reconstruction possible. I didn't have enough skin and he thought a tummy tuck would be too severe.

Knowing what I was up against, I just prayed about it. I told God that if anything went wrong I wouldn't sue because I was leaving that 2 percent up to Him.

The one thing I know cancer did for me is, it totally cemented my relationship with Jesus Christ.

I recently had a birthday. One friend jokingly said, "Kim, I have never known anyone who broadcasts their birthdays like you do."

I said, "You know what, nine years ago I could have lost my life and I am still here. I have a friend who was diagnosed after I was and she is not here. Therefore, I look at every day as my opportunity to celebrate life."

"I said, 'You know what, nine years ago I could have lost my life and I am still here. I have a friend who was diagnosed after I was and she is not here. Therefore, I look at every day as my opportunity to celebrate life.'"

My outlook on life has changed drastically since I have dealt with breast cancer. I have five older brothers and I was the eldest of two girls. I always got a lot of attention, and I was very spoiled. I grew up thinking that everything revolved around me.

Breast cancer made me realize that I am not an island unto myself. I have learned to extend myself. Now my life is all about giving. I try to look at it as "what can I do to help make this a better place to live in? How can I help to make somebody's burdens lighter?"

I became a Reach to Recovery Volunteer for the American Cancer Society. I also joined Can Care and the Sisters Network. These organizations have given me an opportunity to help people who are going through the same thing I have experienced.

When it comes to breast cancer, I think a disproportionate number of African American women still believe if you don't think about it and don't talk about it, it will go away.

Yes, I am single. One day I would like to get married, but right now I have a life to live. Now I am committed to living that life more abundantly. I am learning how to live that life to glorify God.

I used to be very materialistic. I still like nice things but they are not as important to me. I have come to realize that the things that are really important don't have a dollar value on them. What's important to me now is preserving relationships and making the world a better place to live in.

As a breast cancer survivor, I have learned not to become preoccupied with having a recurrence. I don't think there is any such thing as a premature death to a child of God. We are here for a purpose and God knows from the beginning how many days we are going to have. As long as I am focused on Him and live my life accordingly, I am going to live out those days. When he decides to call me home, it is going to be OK because I have done what I was supposed to do. I know that you can hold on to something and become poor, and give everything and become richer. I am learning to give and become richer.

Dawn Elliott

In August 1993, I was on my way to work and the Spirit of the Lord came to me and told me to be prepared. I kept thinking to myself, "Be prepared for what?" There was nothing wrong. Everything in my life seemed to be going OK at that time. I never would have dreamed that six months later I would be diagnosed with breast cancer.

Dawn Elliott

Age:	36
Stage:	i
Occupation:	Sales Representative
Residence:	Missouri City, Texas
Procedure:	Mastectomy & Reconstruction
Treatment:	None
Survivorship:	1 year
Lymph Node Involvement:	0 / 10

My doctor discovered my lump when I went in for a routine examination. I asked him to check out a bump that I had been feeling under my arm. He felt under my arm and told me the bump was nothing more that an infection from shaving, but he did notice a lump in my breast that he felt needed to be checked out.

I was shocked. "What do you mean?" I shrieked.

He let me feel it, and it was definitely a lump. Although I periodically checked my breasts, I never really knew what a lump felt like.

When I went in to have a mammogram, they discovered there were two lumps instead of one. But that wasn't the problem. The problem was micro calcifications in the other breast that were picked up by the mammogram.

They did a frozen section from the tissue and found out the micro calcifications were cancerous.

After I found out, I didn't do a whole lot of crying. I really didn't do a lot of praying either. I just asked God to take care of me. I really didn't know what was going on. I just asked Him to fix it.

My doctor gave me my options of a partial mastectomy with radiation or a mastectomy. I gave him permission to do whatever was necessary.

Once they actually did the surgery, the surgeon realized the micro calcifications were not in one central location. They were all over my breast. At that point, he felt my best option was a mastectomy. He didn't want to take a chance and leave some cancerous tissue there.

In December 1994, I gave myself reconstructive surgery as a Christmas present. My husband had insisted that it didn't matter to him. He assured me that it didn't affect the way he felt about me in the least, but I knew this was something I wanted to do for myself.

At first I felt a little guilty because I had my surgery the week before Christmas and I hated to put my family through that during the holidays. Nevertheless, it didn't seem to matter to my family because everyone was very supportive, especially my father.

When I was young, my father and I were always very close. Through the years we seemed to grow apart for various reasons. I never would have thought that breast cancer would restore our relationship.

From the moment I told him about my diagnosis, he was right there at my side. Many times I would stop by to visit with him before I would head off for my doctor appointments. Ironically enough, he was the one who helped me make up my mind to have reconstructive surgery. He told me to "go for it." He knew that it wasn't something I needed to do for anyone else. It was something I needed to do for myself.

Compared to the pain of reconstruction, the mastectomy was a piece of cake. I have to admit I didn't have the surgery because I felt less than a woman. It wasn't about that. I really wanted a better shape. After having three children and three C-sections, I had a little flab in my tummy area. This way I got to kill two birds with one stone. I got rid of the flab and I got a new breast at the same time. Now, I am able to wear my own bras and swimsuits with no problem or extra hassles.

It's funny now when I run into people I haven't seen in a long time. They just look at me and say I look great. I just laugh to myself because I know that they don't realize all that I have been through.

I went in for one of my follow-up check ups and the MRI had picked up a spot on my left kidney. I said, "God, you brought me through this big hurdle. I am not going to believe this and I am not going to accept this."

When I went in for further tests, they did an ultrasound. They could no longer find anything. At that point I began to claim my healing.

I know when I was diagnosed many of my friends could not believe it. They kept telling me that I was too young to have breast cancer; breast cancer was something that was supposed to happen to older women. But I know now that the Lord was preparing me for something even greater.

Although it had nothing to do with my having breast cancer, my husband and I recently separated. That has been very difficult for me to deal with. With the cancer, I would say "God, here it is take it." With this I feel I can't do anything. The separation after seven years of marriage is much harder for me to deal with.

With the cancer, God taught me how to cast my cares on Him. I feel like now I am in His waiting room, just waiting for Him to manifest His blessings. I think sometimes the hardest thing for us to do is to wait on God to manifest what He has for us. I have already received the Prophecy that God has some great things in store for me. Now, I am just waiting for them to manifest.

The cancer was a great trial for me to deal with. God brought me through that. I know that God will bring me through this as well.

"With the cancer, God taught me how to cast my cares on Him. I feel like now I am in His waiting room, just waiting for Him to manifest His blessings."

Margaret Sanders

I remember waiting to go into the operating room when this white cloud appeared above my head. As they wheeled me into surgery the white cloud seemed to hover over me the entire time. The last thing I saw before I went to sleep was the white cloud. When I woke up the white cloud was gone, but I still felt the presence of the Holy Spirit with me and I knew everything was going to be OK.

My first signs of breast cancer started when my arm began hurting. Shortly afterward, my breast and my arm began to swell. I went to the doctor and he gave me some pills, and said that if the swelling didn't go down in 10 days to come back.

I took the pills, and the swelling went down some ... but it didn't go away. So I went back to the doctor. He then sent me to have a mammogram. Although I didn't have a lump, the mammogram revealed a mass in my chest. He then referred me to a surgeon for a biopsy, and they discovered it was cancer.

Margaret Sanders

Age:	58
Stage:	2/3
Occupation:	Assembly Worker
Residence:	Markham, Illinois
Procedure:	Modified Radical Mastectomy
Treatment:	Chemotherapy & Radiation
Survivorship:	7 years
Lymph Node Involvement:	Unknown

My doctor told me that if I didn't want him to he wouldn't remove my entire breast. But at the time I was very skeptical. I was afraid they might not get it all. I told him I didn't want to take any chances, so I opted for a complete mastectomy.

At the time I didn't realize how important things were, so I didn't ask a lot of questions. I just went with whatever my doctor had to say. After the surgery it was indicated that I had some lymph node involvement, therefore my doctor suggested that I take both chemotherapy and radiation.

After my first couple of chemo treatments I lost my hair, but I wore my wig gratefully. I didn't mind it at all because I was happy to be alive!

I responded very well to my treatments, and I was able to work the entire time. I felt fortunate that I had a good doctor. He told me things like: not to lift anything heavy, and get plenty of rest, which made my recovery go smoothly.

I still have to admit, I was a little bit afraid. But having the Lord with me, I knew that everything was going to be all right. Through it all, I always prayed and I had the Lord on my side.

I kept asking God to help me endure the things I could not change. When I did this I wasn't afraid any more.

"In my life now, the most important thing is my walk with the Lord, and I know that He already knows what I have, so having one breast doesn't matter."

I thought about reconstruction, but at my age, I didn't think I really wanted to do that. I looked at it this way — if I didn't tell anybody, nobody would ever know. I just fit my prosthesis in my bra and keep on stepping. In my life now, the most important thing is my walk with the Lord, and I know that He already knows what I have, so having one breast doesn't matter.

I felt fortunate that I was able to find my cancer because I never got sick and I never hurt.

My doctor told me that my life expectancy might be two to five years. He didn't say it in a scary way, but it was more matter-of-fact, based on my condition. But, I didn't dwell on it. He also told me that the cancer could recur. I didn't let that bother me either.

I thought to myself, "We all have to die from something anyway." I knew that I could not become obsessed with cancer.

I have seven children and they were all very supportive. They were right there when I needed them. Because of my support from my family I never focused on the fact I had cancer, I just knew I had something that I had to deal with.

I think one of the worst things about breast cancer is that women look at it as something very bad. But life is a gamble, anyway. Just the word "cancer" scares the average Black person. Therefore, when someone says you have cancer, people get upset and depressed. But you have to look at cancer just as you would any other sickness.

The Bible tells us that we are healed by His stripes. If we are already healed we don't have to be afraid. After all we know we are going to suffer because Jesus Christ suffered.

I know one lady who thought she would rather die than lose her breast. She decided not to have the surgery. She didn't last any time. I think her mental state helped to speed up the effects of the disease.

There is no doubt that it takes a toll on you seeing yourself with one breast. Then you have to face your husband with this. But if he doesn't understand, then that is just too bad. My husband always said it didn't matter, but it might have ... I don't know. But I would rather be alive than anything. I am just so thankful to be alive with one breast.

After dealing with cancer, life takes on new meaning. You don't have time to worry about little things like breasts or hair. I was just thanking God for sparing my life.

I don't feel no ways sad about it. No one wants to have cancer, but when it happens you have to have the strength to deal with it and keep on going.

Turning Negatives Into Positives
Becoming a breast cancer advocate.

everly Rhine

I would lie in my bed when I didn't think I would live another day. All I could hear echoing in my head were the words of Les Brown, saying, "Don't take your greatness to your grave." I knew then that I had not experienced the greatness God had invested in me. I just prayed for Him to allow me to live long enough to experience and develop some of that greatness. I just wanted to be a tool and an instrument to do something good in this world, and to be heard.

I now sit on the advisory council of the Breast Cancer Early Detection Program for the State of California. It was formed after legislation was passed a couple of years ago that add a 2 percent tax to tobacco. It is estimated that it will generate millions of dollars per year for cancer research, treatment and screening. I bring the voice of African American women to that board.

Beverly Rhine

Age:	50
Stage:	3
Occupation:	Criminal Justice Officer
Residence:	Compton, California
Procedure:	Modified Radical Mastectomy
Treatment:	Chemotherapy & Radiation
Survivorship:	5 years
Lymph Node Involvement:	Unknown

My lump was discovered by my husband one Sunday night while we were lying in bed. When he first mentioned it I thought he had lost his ever-loving mind. Then I thought, "How could he be so cruel as to play a joke like that on me?" I touched my breast and, sure enough, there was a lump there. Then he said, "Baby, it wasn't there three days ago."

The next day I was sitting in the doctor's office. He sent me for a mammogram. It took two weeks to get the results, which stated that it was "inconclusive."

Meanwhile, the lump had doubled in size.

My doctor suggested that I watch it for six months. He became angry when I had the audacity to demand to see a surgeon. On my referral papers he did not state that my situation was immediate, so I had to wait a couple of weeks for a referral to see a surgeon. I finally got tired of waiting, and I went to the surgeon's office to explain my situation. I had an appointment the next day.

The surgeon attempted to do a needle aspiration but he could not get any fluid out of the lump. At that point, having read enough material I felt that it was cancer. One of the signs of a cancerous tumor is not being able to aspirate fluid.

Two weeks later, I had a biopsy. By that time my lump had grown from 1 centimeter to 3.5 centimeters. That growth had all taken place in about a month.

After it was confirmed to be cancerous, I opted to have a modified radical mastectomy. I also had reconstructive surgery with silicone implants.

The next year, I went back and demanded they take the silicone out because of all the information that came out about it. I knew that God had not allowed me to beat cancer just to die from silicone poisoning.

During my experience with cancer I discovered a new purpose in life — painting. I had never painted anything in my life. I learned how to paint figurines when I was sick and I was determined not to die without having a hobby. For so long I had been a single, female head of household raising two children. If someone asked me what my hobby was all I could do was laugh. My hobby had been trying to survive and make it from day to day.

Many days between chemo treatments all I had time to do was paint. Every time I painted another figurine it was like I was connecting more to life. It became a symbol that I was either going to live, or leave a bunch of great figurines behind for people to remember me by.

I remember sitting up one night looking at television, while I was taking down my braids. I was just getting ready to wash my hair, and an entire braid fell off into my hands.

> *"Many days between chemo treatments all I had time to do was paint. Every time I painted another figurine it was like I was connecting more to life. It became a symbol that I was either going to live, or leave a bunch of great figurines behind for people to remember me by."*

For two seconds I thought this was the perfect time to nut up. No one would blame me for going absolutely insane.

By the third second, I had asked my husband to bring the clippers so I could shape my hair in a natural form. Then I started looking for big Afro-Centric jewelry. I thought if I had this wonderful jewelry it would take away from my head and the fact you could see my scalp.

A few months later, my husband was fired from his job for spending so much time with me. It was like the promise that God made Job in the Bible, "if you just hold on and don't deny me I will reward you ten fold." We have been rewarded. We started designing and manufacturing Afro-Centric jewelry, which had started out as just a hobby after I lost my hair. Now it is comforting to know that if something happened to my day job I would survive.

It seems that as cancer threw me into the bottomless pit of life, I found myself. I know now that there is something positive that can come from cancer — to bring out the power that is within you. From this disease I have developed into a marvelous human being ... but I was a pretty good sister before the disease.

I have decided that rather than spending my time thinking about a recurrence, I will convert that energy into activism that might translate into my granddaughter not being at risk for this devastating disease.

When I first found out I had breast cancer, I tried to be strong. I knew I was going to have to go through it alone. So, I really didn't take out time to deal with my emotions. Then I joined the Women of Color Breast Cancer Support Project in Los Angeles. The president of the organization stood up and began sharing her story with everyone. I never will forget the moment she broke down and started to cry ... I started to cry too. I realized through this whole ordeal I was trying to be a "Big Girl." She taught me that part of being strong was knowing when to be weak. I now know it is OK to cry.

I discovered my lump when I was getting ready to move into another apartment. In the process of packing boxes, my hand rubbed against my chest and I noticed a lump. The first thing I did after I moved was go to the doctor to check it out. My doctor thought I had bruised myself. She suggested that I watch it for a couple of weeks.

Roxie White

Age	67
Stage:	1
Occupation:	Retired Secretary
Residence:	Inglewood, California
Procedure:	Mastectomy
Treatment:	None
Survivorship:	2 years
Lymph Node Involvement:	0 / 9

The lump made me more conscious of my breast. I kept checking it to see if it had grown or changed in any way. As I was pressing against my breast, blood came out of my nipple. That frightened me enough to make me go back to my doctor. This time she referred me to an oncologist. The oncologist did not do a biopsy, he just did a needle aspiration. He let me know that he was going to be leaving town and I should come back in another month.

By this time I was so frightened I didn't want to wait a month to find out what was going on. I thought it was time to find another doctor, which is what I did. My new doctor immediately did a biopsy. That is when I found out it was malignant.

I had not really been doing breast self-exams. I had read pamphlets and articles about breast cancer. I guess I never thought it would happen to me. No one in my family on either side had it, so I never really thought about it. I just took my mammogram every year and kept on going.

Because I am a diabetic, my doctor suggested that I have a mastectomy because chemotherapy and radiation could cause some problems. She also suggested that I not wait too long in making my decision.

I think I went into a state of shock when I first found out it was cancer, because I took it so well. But I didn't have much choice. I had to deal with it. All I could think of was that I was going to have to deal with this by myself. All of my family was in Washington, D.C.

"I got to my room and there was no one there. That had to be the saddest moment of my life. All I wanted to do was to let them know I made it."

I had two friends go with me to the hospital the day of my surgery. They stayed there until the nurse told them I was going to recovery. I was so excited when I woke up. I wanted to let them know that I was OK. I got to my room and there was no one there. That had to be the saddest moment of my life. All I wanted to do was to let them know I made it. I had no one to share my excitement. There was no one to be happy that I was still around.

That was a painful experience, but it let me know that since I didn't have any family here, I needed somebody. That led me to join a breast cancer support group. It has been really helpful talking with other women who are going through the same thing.

Where I come from, everything was always hush, hush. But now I feel like it is time to talk about it. People need to know you can get breast cancer and it doesn't have to be hereditary.

I am so proud of my daughter and my granddaughter. When I went to visit them, I saw that they had their shower card hanging up in the bathroom to remind them to do their breast self-exam.

I had a little scare a few months ago. I was experiencing pain in my back and I thought maybe the cancer had spread. I had a bone scan and everything was OK. The test revealed that I have arthritis and I already knew that.

I think breast cancer changed my life for the better. It made me more aware of life. I try to live each day better, instead of not doing anything at all.

Carolyn Tapp

Now, when I go to the doctor I want to know everything: what type of cancer did I have, what stage was my cancer in, how many lymph nodes were removed. Before I was so passive I just listened to what the doctors had to say and I took that as gospel. For me that no longer works, I must know "why?"

Carolyn Tapp

Age:	54
Stage:	2
Occupation:	Retired Loan Officer
Residence:	Los Angeles, California
Procedure:	Lumpectomy
Treatment:	Radiation
Survivorship:	2 years
Lymph Node Involvement:	3 / 13

The last time I was in to see my doctor he told me that he was only supposed to give me three minutes of his time, maximum. I told him I needed more than three minutes because today I wanted to talk.

My bout with breast cancer began with an infection in my left breast. When I went in to have it checked out, my doctor ordered a mammogram. It revealed a mass in my right breast. The surgeon told me that it did not look cancerous; therefore, he suggested I wait six months before having a biopsy.

So I waited.

I began to feel a itching under my arm, and it bothered me. But I thought, "I only have a few more months to go." I noticed the lump seemed to be growing, but I thought, "I only have another month to go." After six months I went back for the biopsy. Not only did I find out I had cancer, but by this time it had spread into my lymph nodes.

I was kind of angry at first with the doctor and the hospital because I thought I should have had the biopsy right away. Then I got angry at myself. I thought maybe I should have taken charge and insisted on having the biopsy. I didn't push for what should have been done. Of course, I didn't know then what I know now about breast cancer.

I know now that any time a lump is found you don't sit on

it. I know now that breast cancer moves very fast in Black women, therefore many times you don't have time to wait.

For a year after my surgery I didn't want to know anything. Now I want to know everything. As a result of my experience, I want to help other young ladies get through this thing. Everything can become overwhelming to deal with if you don't know where to get information from or who to talk to.

As a result of poor circulation, I developed lymphedema in my arm. My doctor wanted me to get information for him about lymphedema. I didn't have time for that. I needed someone who knew how to treat it. I finally went to another doctor. She set me up with a specialist from Australia who was able to get my arm where I could move it again.

I have three daughters and I am very concerned about them because I know that there is a heredity factor with breast cancer. One of my daughters was thirteen when she had to have a benign tumor removed.

At first it was hard for my husband to deal with me having breast cancer. When I first told him he sat on the bed and cried. He wondered if they would have to remove my breast or not. No one in either of our families had ever had to deal with breast cancer, so we were both rather naive about it.

Since my lump was so small my doctor told me that I could have a lumpectomy, and I would have the same rate of survivorship as if I had a mastectomy. My husband wanted me to have the whole breast removed so that it wouldn't come back. But I opted to have the lumpectomy.

My doctor recommended I have 25 radiation treatments. Since my breasts are very heavy and I am overweight I got burned really badly.

Breast cancer definitely wasn't the easiest thing I have had to deal with, but I am just glad to be around. I only hope I never have to go through it again. But if I do, I know that God is going to go through it with me again.

There is a point when you are growing up that you don't think about death. But now I know that I am going to die; it could be sooner or it could be later. But I have made my peace with God and I have made my peace with myself.

"There is a point when you are growing up that you don't think about death. But now I know that I am going to die; it could be sooner or it could be later. But I have made my peace with God and I have made my peace with myself."

Wilhelmina Grant

I've been training in the martial arts for over four years. I had been kicked and punched so many times it would be hard to keep track. But I was sparring for this one match, and my partner accidently punched me in my left breast. At the time I tried to play it off, but it really did hurt. In fact I was about to double over from the pain. It bothered me for about two or three days then I forgot about it.

A month later, I started having a shooting pain through my breast. At the time I thought it was the pens I was carrying in my uniform pocket that were sticking me, so I just took them out and put them on the other side and kept on going. I kept getting the pains in my breast for two or three weeks. All this time, the thought of breast cancer never crossed my mind.

After the continuing pain, I went in to a breast clinic to have a mammogram. Since I was under 50, they let me know they could not do a mammogram. But I informed them of the pain I was experiencing in my breast, so they decided to do a ultrasound. The ultrasound revealed a complex cyst.

I was told I needed to have it aspirated. The technician who did the ultrasound was very paternalistic. He kept patting me on the hand and saying, "You don't have cancer, my dear. You are much too young. Just go home and forget about it." He assured me that once I got the cyst aspirated it would collapse and that would be the end of it.

Of course I was inclined to take his advice and forget about it. I kept hearing his voice say, "It is not cancer, my dear."

Wilhelmina Grant

Age:	38
Stage:	2
Occupation:	Flight Attendant
Residence:	Brooklyn, New York
Procedure:	Partial Mastectomy
Treatment:	Chemotherapy & Radiation
Survivorship:	1 year
Lymph Node Involvement:	5/21

My schedule was really hectic — I was flying full time, doing an internship at a museum, and attending school. But I decided I needed a second opinion because I was still having pain. I wasn't convinced that it was cancer, but I knew it wasn't just nothing, because nothing doesn't hurt.

I went to a radiologist to have the lump aspirated, but she again recommended a mammogram and an ultrasound. She was very thorough. She took about 15 views on the mammogram. Every time I thought she was finished, she asked me to turn in a different direction. Then she informed me that she would not be doing an aspiration, because it was not a cyst. It was a growth and they were going to need to do a biopsy.

The next week I got the results, ductal carcinoma.

At that point I went shopping for a surgeon. I interviewed three different doctors before making my final selection. To this day I feel I made the right choice. My surgeon and her staff were excellent. I haven't had any problems or experienced any difficulties as a result of my surgery.

Now in reflecting on everything, I feel grateful I got punched in the karate match. Of course, I know you can't get breast cancer from a blow to the breast. But what that did was bring my attention to what was going on. It was evident that the tumor had already been growing. If I had never been punched, the cancer might have still been growing today. In that case, I guess it was a lucky punch.

I went through radiation and four months of very aggressive chemotherapy. Because of my age, my doctor recommended a higher dosage of chemo and more aggressive treatment. I didn't mind because I did not want to have to go through it again.

It was kind of rough. I had to give myself an injection of Nupigon every morning in the leg in order to stimulate my bone marrow. (The chemo kept knocking my blood count down.) I don't know anybody who enjoys giving themselves an injection every day.

The alterative was getting a bone marrow transplant, and I definitely did not want to do that.

"If I had never been punched, the cancer might have still been growing today. In that case, I guess it was a lucky punch."

My fingernails turned black; the inside of my mouth, my tongue, and my cervix all turned blue or black. For the first few days I also got sores in my mouth.

I didn't have a problem with nausea, but the palms of my hands and the soles of my feet would tingle, and I would also suffer from short term memory loss.

I would get on the bus and forget where I was going. Sometimes it was so bad I couldn't find my way home. I would be talking to someone, then I would blank out in the middle of a sentence. At first I didn't know what was going on. I didn't know it was the medication until I began to talk to other people who had taken the same medication and they all experienced short term memory loss.

You want to hear something ironic? While I was going through all of this, my cat was diagnosed with breast cancer. She had to have a mastectomy. After her first surgery, she continued to have problems, so they had to go back in and remove more breast tissue.

I had never heard of a cat getting breast cancer.

After my surgery things didn't change much in my life. I am still going crazy with all the things I have to do. I now have added to that list several volunteer obligations connected with breast cancer.

I never thought about breast cancer before. Now that I have been through it, I am embracing the cause in so many different ways. I have always been busy working on different things. But now this is something that I feel I have to do, especially for women of color who think like I thought — that they would never get breast cancer.

I was extremely depressed and despondent. I went to the doctor and all he acknowledged were my external symptoms. Based on my severe depression he suggested that I see a psychiatrist. He never knew my depression was caused by my big secret ... I had a lump in my breast.

It was through a routine self-examination that I discovered my lump. I found a small one in my right breast. However, due to fear, I did not deal with it for at least six months.

Fortunately, I did not keep my condition a total secret. I did tell a very good friend. It was only through his support and encouragement that I sought medical attention.

I now know that cancer waits for no one. Based on the time I took, my condition could have been fatal. I have realized that cancer does not always allow one time to procrastinate.

Karen Williams

Age:	43
Stage:	2
Occupation:	Technical Assistant
Residence:	Fort Worth, Texas
Procedure:	Modified Radical Mastectomy
Treatment:	Chemotherapy & Reconstruction
Survivorship:	5 years
Lymph Node Involvement:	2 / 26

I was extremely fortunate — the type of cancer I had was very slow growing.

When I finally went to the doctor, he immediately recommended I have a comprehensive mammogram. He also did an ultrasound. Based on the results of both tests, he felt there was a problem and referred me to a surgeon for a biopsy.

The results of the biopsy, infiltrating ductal carcinoma ... in other words, breast cancer.

My doctor recommended a modified radical mastectomy with reconstructive surgery. Although I only had two lymph nodes involved he suggested chemotherapy as an extra measure.

I have to admit, the chemotherapy was the toughest part of my treatment.

Some people don't have a problem with chemotherapy; in my case it made me very sick. I was very depressed, I had very dry skin ... although I did not lose my hair.

Although the chemo was the toughest and most difficult for me to deal with, the surgery itself was not necessarily easy either. I lost something I have had all of my life. But when I consider I could have lost my life, losing my breast was nothing.

"I lost something I have had all of my life. But when I consider I could have lost my life, losing my breast was nothing."

Once I had finished chemo I wanted to celebrate so I decided to give myself a gift by having reconstructive surgery. I know reconstruction is not for everybody, but it was definitely for me. I was very happy with the results. If I had it to do all over again I would make the same choice.

I was in the hospital for five days after my surgery, and it gave me plenty of time to think. The first thing that went across my mind was, how was I going to get on with my life?

One of the major steps in helping me switch gears and get back in tune with reality was a visit from a Reach to Recovery volunteer from the American Cancer Society. For me, this provided me with a real-to-life model that indicated there was life after breast cancer.

The only thing I regret is, as a single parent, I wish that I was more conscious of my sons while I was going through this entire ordeal.

When I was diagnosed, both my children were in high school — one a sophomore, the other a senior. I was so busy trying to cope I did not deal with what they were going through at the time. I did not try to find a support group for them; it was hard enough for me to cope myself.

Later on my sons revealed that they felt my eating meat contributed to my cancer. As a result they both became vegetarians. It has not stopped me from eating meat, but they both have adopted a totally meatless diet.

Now that I am on the other side of my diagnosis the fear is gone. I am a five year survivor, and I am cancer free. But, one of the things I am really concerned with is reaching out to other women and helping them deal with their diagnoses.

In the African American community we tend to look at cancer as a death sentence. We need to see more women that are out there beating the odds so that we can realize we can make it too.

We definitely need to negate the myths and become a more informed people. There is no reason why breast cancer mortality is on the increase for African American women while it is decreasing for the rest of the population.

The reality is: If we don't deal with it, we can expect our children and grandchildren to be without mothers and grandmothers.

We have got to become proactive rather than reactive. We can no longer continue to fall back on the socio-economic excuse, because now more than at any other time in history, there are resources being made available. The Bible says we have not because we ask not.

I know that, in my case, fear and denial played a major role in my not getting help as soon as possible. I was always considered a strong and logical person, but people don't realize that cancer goes beyond logic.

We must remember that God has not given us a spirit of fear, therefore, we need to walk the faith that we talk. We must truly believe that God can do anything! I had a great team of doctors, but I also believe that God uses doctors, too.

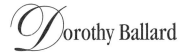

Dorothy Ballard

I taught Sunday School for over 30 years, I was president of my church choir, but there was still an emptiness in my life. I was routinely teaching Sunday School and I was half singing in the choir. One Sunday, when I got home from church, I got down on my knees and prayed. I told the Lord I wanted to apply for a job. I wanted to do something He wanted me to do, not just something I wanted to do.

I didn't want anything that was going to build myself up. I said, "Lord, you made me. You know my strengths and my limitations. You know I am not an academic person but I can read and write. I know how to count two bits, four bits, and six bits. Lord, I want you to put me to work. I want you to give me a sign so I will know that it is what you want me to do, not what I want to do."

After that prayer, I went on about my business and I didn't hear a thing.

Dorothy Ballard

Age:	70
Stage:	1
Occupation:	Retired Assembly Worker
Residence:	Little Rock, Arkansas
Procedure:	Lumpectomy
Treatment:	Radiation
Survivorship:	11 years
Lymph Node Involvement:	0 / 9

Two years later, a doctor and her colleague came knocking on my door. They asked me how to get the word out to the African American community about breast cancer. I sat and looked at them and said, "Witness to them."

They didn't understand what I meant. Coming from a basic religious background, I knew the African American community would understand the concept of witnessing. Because of my experience, I was willing to witness to the world that cancer does not have to be an automatic death sentence. I knew that God can heal the entire person mentally, physically and spiritually. I let them know this concept would be best started in the church.

When they left, I went in my bedroom and got down on my knees and thanked God. When I prayed to God to be of better service to Him, I didn't have breast cancer. I knew he had healed me and was allowing me to be of better service to others.

I had gone in to have a pap smear. My gynecologist found out it was abnormal and he suggested I come back every six months instead of once a year. The next time I went back he found a lump. He then suggested I see a surgeon.

I told him I would get back with him after the holidays were over. He looked at me kind of funny and said, "No, Mrs. Ballard, you are going to do this now."

At that point I knew it was serious. My daughter is a nurse in Little Rock. I called her to let her know that the surgeon had detected a mass in my breast and wanted to do a biopsy. She went ahead and selected a team of doctors for me.

When I went in for the biopsy, they asked me, if it was malignant, did I want to be awakened and given the results, or did I want them to continue with the surgery? I told them, "I am scared. I am 60 years old, and I have never been in the hospital other than childbirth. If you find anything you need to take care of it. If you don't, I won't be back." I was just that frightened.

> "*I told them, 'I am scared. I am 60 years old, and I have never been in the hospital other than childbirth. If you find anything you need to take care of it. If you don't, I won't be back.' I was just that frightened.*"

The surgeon told me I had the option of a complete lumpectomy or a mastectomy. My cancer was contained, so I selected to have the lumpectomy followed by 28 treatments of radiation.

There is one thing that left a bitter taste in my mouth. I was working in a factory at the time I was diagnosed. I had ample insurance. Every year I got my annual check up. My doctor never did suggest I have a mammogram or examine my breasts or teach me to examine my breasts.

Three years after I was diagnosed with breast cancer, I got a notice from my physician telling me it was time to have a mammogram. I never knew anything about mammograms, or breast self-exams. I was looking to him for guidance about my health care.

Each year when I would go to him he would pat me on the back and say, "Mrs. Ballard, you are just fine." He gave me a false sense of security. If I had had any knowledge about breast cancer, I would have been on the lookout for it.

I know of two 15-year-old girls who had babies and developed breast cancer. I think when girls start their period they should learn how to do breast self-exams. It should become as routine as brushing their teeth and putting on deodorant.

Now, I am just happy to be alive. I never would have known that anything was wrong with me. I was feeling good. I didn't have any pain. In fact, I went through half of my treatments in complete denial. My doctor suggested I would be off from work for 12 weeks, I went back to work in eight weeks.

I don't want you to think I am crazy; nobody wants to get cancer. But there is no doubt that spiritually, cancer is the best thing that happened to me. It made me take an inventory of my life and my values. Before cancer it was always "I, me, and my" ... it's not that way now. It also gave me the initiative to be a part of the Delta Witness Project.

I felt that God gave me another chance at life. I had been a member of my church for 56 years, but I was just going through the motions. Now, I can say I am truly born again. I know that if the Lord comes and gets me the next minute, my soul is all right. I don't have to guess about it, I know that God is love. Sometimes the thing that we fear the most is the best thing for our soul.

Even if I stayed here another 150 years, this is going to be a short time to be with Him forever. I know I am going to die that first death, that is given to mankind. But sweetheart, when He comes back to claim His own, I hope He will carry me back with Him. He said, "I am going to prepare a place for you and where I am you can be there also." There will be no more crying, no more worrying ... everything will be all right. I don't worry about the golden slippers and the streets paved with gold. If I am with Him, I am going to be all right. I know Jesus is alive because He lives in my soul!

Alice White

When I stood up in church and told everyone that I was going to have a biopsy, everyone looked at me strangely. They all acted like I had done something drastically wrong. I know people thought I was deathly ill and that I was going to die soon. They didn't realize that breast cancer isn't an automatic death sentence.

I had been bothered with a real bad sinus infection for quite a while. After I finally realized that it wasn't getting any better, I went to the doctor for a complete physical. My doctor ran all kinds of tests on me. Then he told me that I had a bad case of bronchitis, and he was going to write me out a prescription for it. I asked him, "Are you finished, doctor?"

He responded, "Oh, yes."

Then I let him know that he had not given me a mammogram. He said he didn't know that I wanted to have one. But I reminded him that I had asked for a "complete" physical.

Alice White

Age:	62
Stage:	2
Occupation:	Retired Teacher
Residence:	Helena, Arkansas
Procedure:	Mastectomy
Treatment:	Radiation & Chemotherapy
Survivorship:	7 years
Lymph Node Involvement:	5 / 17

We, as women, must take charge of our own lives. We must tell doctors everything that we want. If we don't, sometimes they might miss the boat, and that might actually be our fault.

The mammogram revealed I had a mass in my right breast. It didn't blow my mind when my doctor gave me the news. I had already had two cysts removed in the 1960s. Now *that* blew my mind. This time I was conscious of it, and it didn't really bother me.

I proceeded to tell him that I couldn't have a biopsy right

away because I was a teacher and I had a very important workshop that I needed to attend. At that point, I didn't look at this as being life threatening in any way.

Before the biopsy, I went to church and asked my church family to pray for me. Then I let the doctors know they could do whatever they had to do.

My doctor was concerned. He wanted to know if he should wake me up after the biopsy to give me the results or not. I told him to give the results to my family. I just wanted him to do what he needed to do so I could do what I had to do, which was to recover and get on with my life.

After the surgery, they recommended I take chemotherapy and radiation. I didn't have a problem with the chemo, but it was hard for me to make arrangements to have the radiation done because I needed to have it every day.

My doctor is in Little Rock and that was 120 miles from my house. I wanted to see if I could have it done closer to home so that I could mingle with my family and friends. I knew that if I had to have treatments in Little Rock I would have to stay there the entire time. I didn't know anybody there, and I knew that would be hard for me to deal with.

At first my doctor tried to jive me. He told me he didn't know any doctors who could administer the radiation in Memphis, which was only 60 miles from my house.

I called one of the major cancer facilities. They gave me the names of three doctors. I just picked a name out of the three. I wasn't sure if this was the person I should use or not. I called a doctor I knew and I asked him "If you were going to send a patient to have radiation, which doctor would you recommend?"

He called the name of the doctor I had selected. I said, "Thank you Jesus!" I knew I had made the right choice.

While I was taking my radiation treatments, I would teach school half a day. Then I would drive 60 miles, have my treatment, then turn around and drive 60 miles back. I kept that routine up for six weeks.

I had seven other surgeries in my life span. I guess that is why breast cancer didn't completely blow my mind. You

"I had seven other surgeries in my life span. I guess that is why breast cancer didn't completely blow my mind."

know where you put your trust and your faith. From that point, all you can do is go on.

I think my sisters were more upset than I was. They all went and had mammograms and pap smears after I was diagnosed. I come from a family of four brothers and six girls, but I was the first person to get breast cancer. Ironically, I was the one who seemed to stay in the doctor's office all the time.

After 39 years of teaching, I finally retired. My husband had a massive heart attack and a stroke this year.

Sometimes I think my breast cancer may have contributed to his bad health. I know it made him depressed, and he picked up some other bad habits that he had never had before. It seems that he really had a hard time dealing with it.

We had planned to do so much together when we both retired. I am not going to let this stand in our way. I just figure we might be walking slow but we will still fulfill our plans.

In the seven years since my surgery, I haven't had any problems. I don't ever think about a recurrence. I know my surgeon felt very confident that he had gotten all the cancer. He told me, "Mrs. White, you might die, but you won't die of breast cancer."

I looked at him and said, "That's good, because I don't intend on dying any time soon."

Karen Eubanks Jackson

I attended several breast cancer support groups following my surgery. And the more I went, the more I noticed that not enough information was being disseminated to African American Women. These groups left a void in me. Plus, the more I learned about breast cancer the more I wanted to know. And there was no doubt that I wanted others to benefit from my accumulated knowledge.

I was in my mid-30s when I first had benign tumors removed from both breasts. At that time, the doctors recommended that I have a mammogram every other year. So I did.

All the time I was having mammograms no one ever told me that 10 percent of women who get cancer don't have it show up through mammograms. So, every year I would sigh with relief after I would have my mammogram. I felt I was taking care of myself. Every time my results were negative, I felt like I was passing the test.

I was wrong!

Lo and behold, my cancer had been there all along but it was never detected. I never considered myself a candidate for breast cancer even through there was evidence of a history in my family. I always thought, like many Black women, that it is a white woman's disease.

I eventually found my cancer because it hurt. It was like a nagging toothache. It never came at any particular time of the month. And it didn't appear to have anything to do with my menstrual cycle. I thought it was a cyst, but it still bothered me.

Karen Eubanks Jackson

Age:	52
Stage:	2
Occcupation:	National President of Sisters Network
Residence:	Houston, Texas
Procedure:	Lumpectomy
Treatment:	Chemotherapy & Radiation
Survivorship:	2 years
Lymph Node Involvement:	0 / 12

I took my concern one step further. I went to the book-store and read up about breast cancer. The first thing I read was that cancer does not hurt. Once again, I thought I had passed. This had to just be another cyst.

I really wanted to be sure my diagnosis was correct. I then made an appointment with a cancer specialist. He did a needle aspiration. The results showed cancer cells.

My particular lump was 3.5 centimeters, which is a considerably large tumor. Although I have met women who have had larger growths, this was too large for me. The thing that bothered me most is that I had been getting regular mammograms while it was growing and it still got to be 3.5 centimeters.

I blanked out for nearly a month when I found out it was cancer. I didn't get hysterical, I just went into a nothingness state. I didn't hear anything. I wasn't thinking about anything. I didn't know who to call. I didn't know who the best surgeon was, or where the best cancer center was. Thankfully, at that point, my daughter and husband stepped in.

I was living in Los Angeles and my daughter was working as a journalist in Houston. I remember she called me and said, "Mom, the best cancer facility is right there in Los Angeles." She arranged everything. Because of her diligence, I found out where I should go and what doctors I should use.

I never really knew how long I had gone "blank." I functioned in my every day life just as normal: I dealt with everything. I went to work, I was a mother and I was a wife. I did everything except make decisions about my cancer.

When they finally gave me the option of having a lumpectomy or a mastectomy, I didn't even know the difference. With the size of my tumor I could do either. I chose the lumpectomy. I also started chemotherapy and radiation at the same time.

Because I was in good health, my doctors felt I could deal with both at the same time. Of course, I was the only African American woman I knew who was getting both at the same time. I wondered, "Am I sicker than everyone else? However, the combination of both caused the same reaction in me as it does in nearly everyone else.

*"**I** went to work, I was a mother and I was a wife. I did everything except make decisions about my cancer."*

I was really sick. I just managed to bite the bullet and keep on going.

Also, after my surgery the doctors told me there was no lymph node involvement. They only took 12 lymph nodes. Maybe the cancer was in the 13th one, but I chose to say I had 12 negative lymph nodes and be done with it. Then I realized that I could torture myself if I wanted to by thinking about the "what ifs." But I didn't.

Because I had a very sensitive surgeon who walked me through everything, and a very supportive family, I think I fared better than most women.

I did form some scar tissue. I think scar tissue is something that many African American women deal with; however, it is still something we don't expect. When my hair began to thin from chemotherapy, I decided to take the American Cancer Society's "Look Good, Feel Better" program.

I was already a cosmetologist so I thought that I could help other women who were not doing so well and didn't know what to do with their loss of hair and eyebrows. I knew that when I looked better, I felt better and I wanted other women to feel better too.

The more I became involved with breast cancer survivors the more I found the disparities in how women in different facilities were being treated. The type and quality of care depended on the facility they went to. And, some women were told, "Don't worry, let's watch it," while their cancer was growing and spreading all the time.

It was these concerns that led me to become a founding member of the Sisters Network. I was committed to working with other survivors and helping other African American women take responsibility for their own health care.

I have come to realize that if we don't stand up for ourselves, then who else will?

Brandyn Barbara Artis

Two months after my surgery I was scheduled to do a television show, but I hadn't been fitted for my prosthesis. I didn't know what to do. So, I took a silk scarf and filled it with coins and stuffed it in my bra. When I walked on the set it was very early in the morning and everything seemed so quiet.

The sound man was there and I knew that he played one of the most important roles in any production. Plus, the equipment is very sensitive to any type of noise or strange sound. My biggest fear was that I would walk up to the set and the coins would start to jingle. The sound man would start going crazy trying to find out where the noise was coming from. Then in front of everyone he would turn and point at me and ask, "What is this?"

To my relief, nothing happened. The production went as planned.

I had always been aware of breast health care because my grandmother died of complications from breast cancer at the age of 35. I have always examined my breasts and gotten my routine mammograms.

Brandyn Barbara Artis

Age:	Not Disclosed
Stage:	1
Occupation:	Actress / Writer
Residence:	Los Angeles, California
Procedure:	Mastectomy
Treatment:	Chemotherapy
Survivorship:	7 years
Lymph Node Involvement:	None

One day I was in the shower and I discovered a lump. I immediately went to my gynecologist and had it X-rayed. Because the X-ray looked a little suspicious, he had me hand carry it over to a surgeon. The surgeon aspirated the lump and drew a little fluid from it. Since the fluid was clear, he assured me I didn't have anything to worry about. He just recommended we watch it for the next year.

I didn't feel comfortable with that conclusion. Therefore, I took the X-ray to another surgeon. He also agreed that I didn't have a problem and there was no need to worry.

With two people having told me that I didn't have anything to worry about, I decided I wanted to believe the "good stuff."

For the next year I just coasted along. Then I had my mammogram and the cancer showed up.

Once I was diagnosed, it was very difficult for me to deal with. In my mind I thought I had always done the right things. I ate the right things, I had a positive outlook on life and I constantly exercised. Of all the women I knew, I thought I would be the least likely to get breast cancer ... despite my family history.

There is no doubt that this totally devastated me, but I have a strong tendency to bounce back. That is exactly what I did.

The sad thing is that cancer does not just affect the person being diagnosed. It affects your entire support system, as well as your family. Anyone that really cares about you is affected by the disease. My husband collapsed when the surgeon told us it was cancer. I had been with him for over 20 years, and I had never seen that side of him. That hurt. Now we can find some humor in that, but we have come to believe that cancer is our common enemy. Together we look at this as something we have just got to beat.

Ultimately, I think as a result of dealing with breast cancer our relationship has become stronger. We have learned to cherish each other and each moment.

I don't know that having cancer has changed my outlook so much. But I do know that it has made me more appreciative of little things. Little mundane things don't bother me anymore. I know I can't be Little Mary Sunshine every day. There have to be some valleys to appreciate the peaks. Yet, every day I wake up I know that I am extremely blessed. I can't spend a lot of time being negative. No one really knows how long we have to linger here ... least of all myself. In some way I try to make sure that I am giving back.

People usually laugh when I tell them that I am a very private person because I developed a play called *Sister Girl* around my personal experiences with breast cancer. In the

*"**M**y husband collapsed when the surgeon told us it was cancer. I had been with him for over 20 years, and I had never seen that side of him. That hurt."*

play I share some very intimate things, all of which are absolutely true. I realized a long time ago that if you hold onto something, something negative can destroy it.

I have met women all over the world who suffered from breast cancer, and we have shared intimate pieces of our lives. It is a give and take situation. The audience experiences the play together and we have a common bond.

We have got to move beyond the fear of breast cancer. As a Reach to Recovery volunteer, I come in contact with a lot of women. I would never give medical advice to anyone, but it is difficult when I see a sister with a growth the size of a grapefruit but she is afraid to do anything about it. Franklin D. Roosevelt once said, "There is nothing to fear but fear itself." Fear can prevent you from doing a whole slew of stuff.

In actuality, when it comes to dealing with cancer, the thing that is going to kill you is non-action.

In our culture the word "cancer" in itself has become a very mighty word. Just the word has the power to truly devastate people. I met a lady who told me that after her mastectomy some relatives came to her house, but they didn't want her to play with their baby. They were afraid that the baby would get cancer from her.

It is not hard to realize why so many women have a hard time dealing with losing a breast because society has put such an important value on them. We use breasts to sell everything from car wax to potato chips.

Unfortunately, some women buy into the concept that if something happens to your breast you are useless ... rather than worry about their health. They think that if they do a breast self-exam they may feel something. Therefore, they feel it is better to ignore it — then maybe it will go away, and that is the worst thing to do.

The earlier cancer is detected the better chance you have for survival.

I had a hard time accepting the fact I had to have my breast removed. After seeing four different doctors, and having four mammograms, I finally realized the diagnosis was correct. It still didn't make it any easier to accept.

Even after I finally did accept it, I still thought that silence was golden. I wasn't going to tell anybody about my surgery. After all, I had never known anyone who had her breast removed. Of course, I had heard of Happy Rockefeller, Nancy Reagan and Betty Ford, but I didn't know them. They were people that you read about in the newspapers and you see on television. Besides, they weren't African American women.

I found the lump on a Sunday afternoon. I had brushed my hand across my chest, when I felt something odd. I touched it again, and I thought to myself, "Gosh, it feels like a lump." I immediately called my doctor. He assured me that it was nothing to worry about, but I could come in the next day to have it checked out.

I decided that I was not going to let it rest. The next morning, I went to see a different doctor whom I had heard was very good. Although I had been told that he would not see me without an appointment, I went anyway.

When I walked in to his office several women were waiting in the reception area. Because I was a teacher I was used to taking charge, so I just proceeded to the receptionist's desk. The receptionist stopped me in my tracks, assuring me that the doctor did not see anyone without an appointment. However, I informed her that the doctor would see me, because I had a lump in my breast!

Lois Smith-Williams

Age:	56
Stage:	1
Occupation:	Professional Prosthesis Fitter
Residence:	Allen, Texas
Procedure:	Modified Radical
Treatment:	None
Survivorship:	20 years
Lymph Node Involvement:	None

I know now that this was silly and I should not have responded in that way, but I was desperate. I was scared out of my mind.

Finally, and after much persistence, the doctor agreed to see me. I quickly told him that I had discovered this lump and I knew that something needed to be done. Without any delay, he ordered a mammogram.

I was still in a daze at the time. I didn't know anything about a mammogram, so I just followed the nurse as she escorted me to the X-ray room. When the doctor received the results of the mammogram, he told me the area was very red and inflamed ... and he was going to have to remove my breast.

I was totally hysterical by this time. I told him there was no way he was going to remove my breast. He just looked at me like I was crazy.

To make things worse, not only did I insist he was not going to take my breast, but with a stern voice I told him, "Not only do you not know what you are talking about, but you are ugly ... and I am not going to pay you." Then I fainted.

When I came to my senses everything was in a blur. Needless to say, I was very embarrassed. I realized I had made a fool of myself. I apologized to the doctor and his staff, and I assured him that I was going to pay him. But, I let him know that he still was not going to take my breast.

I spent the next two days going to see different doctors. Each doctor gave me a mammogram, and then told me the same thing. I was going to have to have my breast removed.

Finally I went back to my original doctor, who had on the phone assured me everything would be all right. I never told him I had already had three mammograms. So, of course, the first thing he suggested was to have a mammogram. After he received the results for the mammogram he diagnosed me. He said he was going to need to hospitalize me, because he needed to remove my breast.

I had not been in the hospital since the birth of my children. Without a doubt, I was probably one of the worst

"...with a stern voice I told him, 'Not only do you not know what you are talking about, but you are ugly ... and I am not going to pay you.' Then I fainted."

patients they had ever seen. The night before my surgery I tried to jump out of the window, and the next day I thought I was in a funeral parlor because of all the flowers ... the nurses were trying to console me. Despite the fact that I had a hard time dealing with my original diagnosis, I never missed a beat after my surgery. After I was released I decided to become a volunteer for the hospital to repay the staff for putting up with me and all of my crazy antics during my stay. At that time I also decided to become a Reach to Recovery volunteer for the American Cancer Society. I picked up and I kept on going, and I have been going ever since. I eventually became a breast cancer advocate.

After several years, I left my teaching career to become a professional fitter of prostheses. I even turned my barn into a boutique so that I could fit women in the community.

Two years ago my husband died. Soon after that I opened a shop in the city. That gave me the opportunity to cater to more women. I thought it was so important to make women feel good about themselves after their surgeries.

Now, it seems hard for me to realize that 20 years ago I didn't even know how to pronounce the word mammogram. Breast cancer at that time was something that you whispered about. If you had it you definitely did not want anyone to know. It seemed that cancer was an automatic death sentence. If you had cancer people always assumed you were going to die.

Well, anyone who knows me knows I am very much alive!

Ruth Morrison

I found an article in the newspaper about a breast cancer support group in my area. Even though I had not had my surgery, I decided I was going to attend their meeting. When I called the number listed in the paper, I got a answering machine. So I just left my name and number hoping someone would call me back right away. I never received a call. The next day, I was just sitting in my room thinking about all the things I was going to have to deal with. Then my step-daughter walked in. She asked if there was anything wrong? Before I could answer, she told me she had taken a call from someone with a breast cancer support group. At first I was a little surprised, then I broke down and told her about the tumor the doctor had found during my physical.

Then she shocked me. She told me that she had a mastectomy.

For eight years I thought she only had a lump removed. I was quickly finding out that it seemed like breast cancer was one of those things people didn't like to talk about, not even to their family.

Ruth Morrison

Age:	65
Stage:	1
Occupation:	Customer Service Rep.
Residence:	Rockland, Massachusetts
Procedure:	Lumpectomy
Treatment:	Chemotherapy & Radiation
Survivorship:	1 year
Lymph Node Involvement:	0/15

I was in for my annual physical when my doctor discovered a tiny lump. I was already scheduled to have a mammogram the next day, so it didn't seem to be any big deal when she recommended one. Everything at that point seemed rather routine.

After the mammogram, I had my confirmation that there was a small lump in my breast. My doctor said it was small, especially in comparison to some of the lumps she had seen. Many times I think women are so embarrassed when they find a lump that they don't go in to have it checked out. They wait until they can't stand the pain any more or they have fluid leaking from their breast. I guess by that time, the only thing the doctors can do is keep them comfortable. I felt very fortunate to be catching mine so soon.

At first my surgeon tried to do a needle aspiration but they could not get any fluid. Then, they did a biopsy. I was told I would get the result in about a week.

The next day I was at work, and I got the call informing me that my tumor was malignant. I thought that as long as I live I would never let anyone give me that kind of news at work again. I was just sitting there in my cubicle in my own little world. I kept thinking to myself, "Oh, my God, I can't believe it."

For a week I didn't tell anyone, not even my husband. I just went along with my everyday tasks just like everything was normal although in reality, I knew that it wasn't.

It seemed like once I was diagnosed it was like stepping into a totally different world. I just wanted to find out everything that I could about this disease. I had not been aware that as you get older the incidence of breast cancer is more likely. There had never been any breast cancer in my biological family. There had been lung cancer and prostate cancer, but no one had breast cancer. It seems this had caught me totally off guard.

I have two daughters and I had heard about the heredity factor with breast cancer, so that made me want to know even more. As I got the information, I passed it on to them so they could be aware too.

After keeping everything to myself for a while, I finally came to the conclusion that I couldn't worry about it any more. I was surrounded by doctors and medical personnel using medical terms I had never heard, like "dirty margins, needle aspirations, lymph node involvement." But I was determined to find out what everything meant.

After my biopsy, I was sitting on the table and the surgeon ran off all these options to me. She said, "You can have a full mastectomy, a partial mastectomy, or a lumpectomy with lymph nodes removed." She rattled them off so fast it was hard to think about it. So finally I asked her, "What would you do?"

She coldly responded, "I can't make a decision for you. It's not my body."

I asked her what would be the preferable option to take. She

> "*I was surrounded by doctors and medical personnel using medical terms I had never heard, like 'dirty margins, needle aspirations, lymph node involvement.' But I was determined to find out what everything meant.*"

stated, "It depends on how you feel. You have to make the decision. When you do, call my secretary and we will perform the operation."

I thought to myself, "Lady, you have had your one shot at putting your knife on me. That's your last shot."

I immediately started looking for a second opinion. Then I found another surgeon.

When I met with my new surgeon, she discussed the size of my lump with me and she charted my mammogram for the last four years. She assured me that there was nothing there prior to the lump being found. She also did a liver scan and bone scan to verify the cancer had not metastasized. She let me know that the liver and the bone were the two areas where breast cancer would gravitate to after leaving the breasts.

They removed 15 lymph nodes, but none were positive. From that point on, my prognosis was very good. I had six weeks of radiation and six months of chemotherapy.

I thank God that the company I work for was very understanding. My manager is a young man, and he is just as understanding and concerned as he can be. When I first found out I had cancer, I spoke with my supervisor and laid all my cards on the table. From that point on we never had any problems.

I didn't have to ask for time off. I just gave him a list of my treatments. I tried to make my treatment schedule accommodate my work schedule as much as possible. But with chemo, I didn't have a choice. It had to coincide with my doctor's schedule. But I still let my manager know ahead of time what my schedule was and he was always understanding.

I have had a tremendous amount of support from my family and friends. My husband was also extremely supportive.

When I was first diagnosed, I would lie awake at night and think, "I won't be here next year. I won't know what it is like in 1997 because I won't be around." But I don't have that feeling now. I realized that before, I was just existing instead of living my life. Now, I try and get as much out of life as I can. I dropped out of an organization that I really didn't want to be a part of anyway, I was just paying the dues for the sake of it.

Now, I do what I want to, when I want to.

Men Get It Too

A male breast cancer survivor speaks out.

Michael Price

It was Breast Cancer Awareness Month and there were a group of women marching in front of the race track where I worked. They were walking and waving their signs. Well, in the meantime we guys were just kicking back looking at them on the monitor from the jockey's lounge. Then one co-worker yelled out, "I bet there isn't a tit in the crowd!" Everyone started laughing. Everyone except for me. I just glared at the guy.

"I guess you think it's funny, huh?" I raised up my shirt to reveal the incision that I had been keeping a secret for two months.

I said, "I've got the same thing they got ... and you think that's funny?" All their faces dropped to the floor, they didn't know what to say. At last my secret was out. I, a man with a big chest, firm biceps, and a hearty grip ... had breast cancer.

Michael Price

Age:	49
Stage:	2
Occupation:	Self Employed
Residence:	Edmond, Oklahoma
Procedure:	Radical Mastectomy
Treatment:	Chemotherapy
Survivorship:	4 years
Lymph Node Involvement:	4/33

For two years I ignored a knot that rested right underneath my nipple. I watched it grow from the size of a small BB to that of a pencil eraser. Being the most physically fit person that you could ever meet, I never even dreamed I could get cancer. I jogged, I swam, I biked and I hunted. I did everything you could think of when it came to sportsmanship and physical activity. But my favorite job and pastime was working with horses. In fact, I figured the knot in my chest was really the result of a kick from a horse, or blow to the chest during a karate class.

During a routine physical my doctor suggested that I get it checked out because men get breast cancer, I just blew it off. No way ... not me. I couldn't get cancer.

I don't know why I didn't see the writing on the wall. Breast cancer wasn't a stranger to my family. My sister had been diagnosed a few years before I acknowledged my lump. It was during her second bout with breast cancer that I found myself by her bedside in Houston.

I remember being at the hospital with the family gathered around. I jokingly patted myself on the chest and said, "I guess I'll be next." But nobody thought it was funny.

They told me to get it checked out. Yet, I still didn't take them seriously.

When I returned home my brother phoned me. It was my wake up call. He said, "Man, as health conscious as you are I can't believe that you are walking around with something in your chest and you won't get it checked out."

"He said, 'Man, as health conscious as you are I can't believe that you are walking around with something in your chest and you won't get it checked out.'"

I guess he was the one who pushed the magic button. I finally agreed to go to the doctor. The shocker was my doctor didn't know what it was either. He referred me to a surgeon. Fortunately it was a surgeon who was very familiar with breast cancer. She suggested I have a biopsy.

At first it seemed simple enough. It was only going to be day surgery. She explained they were just going to lift up the nipple and remove the lump. Then I would go home.

I went in on Thursday, and I was told they would give me a call on Monday. But the telephone rang on Friday morning. My doctor said, "I am sorry I have some bad news for you. The nodule we removed was cancerous and it is all the way to the perimeter; so therefore, it had to have spread in your chest. And we don't know if it has gone to your other organs yet."

I was in total shock.

She wanted me to have the surgery right away. Four days later I was in the hospital preparing to have a radical mastectomy. To be honest I wasn't really afraid. I had already come to grips with the fact I had breast cancer. I had the Lord on my side, so I figured the doctors just had to do what they had to do.

Then all of sudden it hit me: I was preparing for a "cancer" operation. Even though I knew I had breast cancer, it was the "cancer" part that got me. I must have asked the doctor four different times, "You really are saying I have cancer."

They assured me there was no doubt that "Yes" indeed I did have cancer. I said "OK, let's get it on!" as they wheeled me into the operation room.

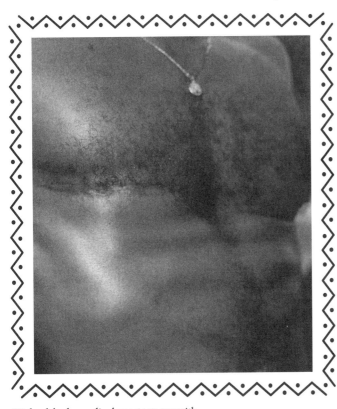

Michael had a radical mastectomy with 33 lymph nodes removed from under his arm.

The next morning I was starving to death. I hadn't eaten anything in two days. At first they brought me this little breakfast of sausage, eggs and toast. I quickly slammed it down and was looking for some more. I winked at one of the nurses and asked her to see if she could find me something else to eat. Sure enough, she brought another one. Then I attacked my second breakfast for the day.

I was totally surprised when about an hour later this guy shows up with a bottle of milky, chalky white stuff and he asked me to drink it. They were going to take me down to have a CAT scan. After I drank it they took me down for tests.

A little while later another guy came back to the room and said, "Mr. Price, we are going to have to take you down again and run some more tests."

By this time I was wondering what the heck was going on. I said, "For what?"

He said, "Well, the test you took earlier revealed there was something in your stomach, and we are not sure what it is. It could be from your disease."

I completely lost it. All I could think of was, "They found something in my stomach." I was prepared for breast cancer, but I wasn't prepared for this. It scared me so much that I just laid there for a moment. All the time he was patiently standing by this wheelchair waiting to carry me back down for more tests.

Finally, I said, "Man, could you just hold on for a minute?"

I threw my head back down on the pillow, and I tried to pull myself together. This had caught me completely off guard. I know it had to be something else ... not cancer again.

Shortly after the tests were finished, my doctor walked in the room with this big smile on her face. I just said, "What's up now?"

She said, "The X-rays showed that all you had in your stomach was that big breakfast you ate this morning."

When she walked out of the room, I jumped up and did a dance. I was happier than a runaway slave. I told my sister who was sitting by my bedside, "I feel pretty good now." I stood up and bent down doing a stretch to touch my head to my knees. Then I bounced back into bed. The first thing I saw was — blood. I said, "Oh, I guess I shouldn't have done that."

My sister was so upset. In her maternal voice she scolded me, "Mike, that didn't make any sense." Before I knew it she had the nurse in my room and on my case. For the rest of my stay I was determined to be a good guy. After all, I knew nothing else like that was going to happen.

They originally wanted me to stay in the hospital for 10 days, but I figured that just wasn't happening. I only ended up staying for four to five days. My sister was with me for a while so she helped change my bandage. I was glad to have her with me. I couldn't stand to look at my scar let alone change it every day. It looked like some kind of giant navel or something. I avoided looking while she was changing it, but she let me know I was going to have to see it. She was going back home.

When my sister left, I had my introduction to chemo. I think Superman would rather have a double dose of Kryptonite than to have to go through chemo. I had my treatments on back to back Mondays, then I would have two Mondays off. I recalled how people would say it wears you out. But I thought, "Not me. Those people aren't like I am. They aren't in great shape. They don't work out a couple of times a day."

"I think Superman would rather have a double dose of Kryptonite than to have to go through chemo."

After I had my first treatment, I couldn't understand what everybody was talking about. I thought, "There is nothing to this." I didn't even think I was going to need the anti-nausea medicine. I felt so good I came home and ran four miles.

That evening it hit me. I laid on the couch and I said to myself, "In a little while I am going to get up and get a drink of water." Two hours passed before I was able to pull myself together enough to actually get up and get something to drink.

After plastic surgery to stitch up a hole where his nipple was, Michael now feels comfortable not wearing a shirt.

Each week it seemed it got worse. On Monday when I had my treatment I was fine. Tuesday through Friday it was all down hill. I was used to working out really hard five days a week. While I was taking my treatments it took everything in me just to walk.

They gave me a book with helpful hints on how to eat while you are going through chemo. I threw it away because that was how I ate anyway.

There is no doubt that going through chemo was Hell, but I knew I couldn't give up.

One thing that kept me going was one of the nurses told me to imagine that when they put the IV in my arm there were a lot of little Pac Men being let loose and they were going to eat up all the poison in my body. She said, "They may eat some of the good stuff too, but you can always build that back."

Psychologically that imagery helped me out. When things got bad, I just thought, "It's just those Pac Men at work."

My doctors were determined that I was going to have a long recovery period. But I knew that wasn't happening. I had arranged my surgery during a month-and-a-half seasonal break on my job. When that was over, I let them know I had to get back to work.

When it was time for me to go back to work, they still thought I needed three more weeks to recover. But I did everything in my power to persuade them otherwise. I finally won.

Once I got back to work I was determined that no one would ever know that I had breast cancer. That was something I was going to keep to myself.

The first day back I had to saddle up a horse. When I raised my arm and extended it, I felt like I had ripped my chest apart. I just grinned at the gentleman that was standing by, then I walked away. When I got to an area where I knew that nobody could see me, I doubled over with pain. As soon as I heard a noise, I quickly pulled myself together and acted like nothing was wrong.

Once some of my co-workers actually found out I had cancer, they were ruthless. One guy said, "I used to think about killing you while you were out jogging, but now I don't have to worry about it, that cancer is going to kill you."

Ironically, last year after he had been complaining of back pains he went to the doctor. They found a huge, malignant tumor in his back. The next week he was dead.

When I used to work out I just thought I was doing it for myself. I wanted to have this great body. But now when I do anything I have to thank God. When I go biking or swimming, I say, "Lord I am trying to take care of your temple so I can give you better service." Because I know it was God that pulled me through all of this. I have always liked to live a peaceful life style, but now I know I am at total peace because I am at peace with God.

"The first day back I had to saddle up a horse. When I raised my arm and extended it, I felt like I had ripped my chest apart."

When The Doctors Say It's Too Late

Dealing with a terminal prognosis

I still remember my doctor telling me I only had six months to live. I couldn't believe it. At first he had assured me that the symptoms I was having weren't anything to worry about. Now, he was telling me that I was going to die.

"You can't tell me that I am going to die. I haven't spoken with the Lord about it yet," I told him, angrily.

He just looked at me like I was crazy and said, "That's all I can say."

I discovered my lump while doing a breast self-exam. But due to fear, I waited a year before I said anything about it to my doctor. My breast had started leaking by that time. It was not really white, but it was a liquid substance. I kept putting off going to the doctor, but when I finally told my doctor about it he said it was nothing to worry about ... ladies do that all the time.

Nine months later, I called him and told him there was something

Annie Pearl Foster

Age:	65
Stage:	3/4
Occupation:	semi-retired care giver
Residence:	Dallas, Texas
Procedure:	Radical Mastectomy
Treatment:	Chemotherapy
Survivorship:	21 years
Lymph Node Involvement:	Unknown

wrong with my breast because it was getting sore. By this time there was a definite lump in my breast. When I lifted my arm I could feel a knot the size of a kernel of corn, and I had never felt anything like that before in my breast.

After my insistence, my doctor told me to come to the hospital the next day, and he would do an X-ray, but he was sure there was nothing wrong.

I said, "What if it is cancer?"

He just insisted, "The ladies all say that."

But he kept assuring me that I had nothing to worry about. He ran several tests. Then he gave me the news ... it was cancer. Inoperable cancer. In fact, he said if they operated, I would die shortly afterward because the cancer was at such an advanced stage.

I am sure he was used to people not wanting to accept bad news, but he didn't know that I really meant what I said. There was no way I was going to let him dictate to me what my life expectancy was going to be. Nobody knows that, but God.

My doctor sent me home and told me there was nothing else that he could do.

> *"The one thing I do know is that God is a healer. Once my doctors gave up on me, I turned to the Lord and asked for his divine healing power."*

It was at that moment I decided I was going to ask God to spare my life. I had already asked him for two sons, and he had blessed me with two fine boys. I knew that he didn't bless me with them to leave them here for someone else to take care of.

That night I prayed from the depths of my soul. I asked the Lord to spare my life and to allow me to live and fulfill my purpose.

Three days later, one of the doctors from my team called me and asked me to come back in. They wanted to run some more tests to see if there was anything they could do.

I let him know that I was not in a rush to get back because they had already let me know that I was going to die. I ended up waiting a week before I went in.

They ran all sorts of tests on me. They did X-rays and scans, and anything they could think of.

Then something happened.

My doctors told me they thought they could help me now. It appeared my X-rays had changed. It seemed my prognosis was no longer as grim as it was a week before.

The one thing I do know is that God is a healer. Once my doctors gave up on me, I turned to the Lord and asked for his divine healing power.

After the doctors ran additional tests and no longer felt my case was terminal, I knew the Lord had answered my prayers and had begun to heal my body.

Before my surgery, I remember telling my team of doctors I didn't want any one fooling with me that didn't believe in the Lord. I knew that God had healed my body. They told me that they knew the Lord could help me, but he wasn't there to do the operating.

I let them know the only way they could come near me with a knife was if they had faith for my healing. I already knew what the Lord had done. But I didn't want anyone touching me that didn't believe it, too.

After the surgery, I recovered very fast. The hardest part for me was learning to use my arm all over again. They had taken all the lymph nodes from under my arm, so it was very difficult and painful to even raise it. Like most people, chemo made me sick. I lost my hair ... but I got over it.

I have to admit losing a breast was the worst. It is heart-breaking when you wake up and have no breast. It was also hard for me to get used to wearing a pad for a breast. For a while I even had a hard time getting my clothes to fit right.

Back then, it was hard to find someone to fit you properly. I had a very large chest, so I always felt one-sided. Then I would get frustrated and start crying. I guess I was self-conscious because I thought everybody could see how I looked.

The one thing that helped me make it, in spite of what the doctors said, was that I had faith in God for healing me. I didn't become afraid. I think when most people find out they have cancer, they give up and accept the fact that they are going to die. But you can't give up, you always have to be willing to fight for your life.

When I first heard my cancer had returned I was shocked. I was so overwhelmed with emotions, I decided to throw myself a pity party. It seemed I had been through so much in my life: I had to deal with a drug addicted husband, raising a son alone ... all the while trying to keep him off the street. There were so many times when all I could do was turn things over to God. Yet, I felt I was always trying to do the right thing.

This time I felt I really needed to feel sorry for myself. I decided I wasn't going to try and be strong any more, I was going to break down and cry. I was already taking a lot of medication, so I decided to mix that with some wine coolers. Despite my depression my main objective was not to kill myself ... I just wanted to get some much needed rest.

The most ironic part of this entire situation was, I couldn't go to sleep. I ended up staying up all night watching television. Then, it seems my punishment was a massive headache. All of a sudden it hit me: this wasn't me. Why was I sitting here ready to kick the bucket? I am not the one!

My maiden name was Frazier, and I decided to call myself "Smokin' Joe" Frazier. So, I decided this time I wasn't going down for the count. I was ready to kick butt and take names. If cancer was ready for me, then I was ready for it.

My original bout with breast cancer started three years ago, when I began to feel pains under my arm. I didn't think much about it because I had been working out. By the next month I developed a sharp pain under my arm and through my breast area. I touched the area that was hurting and,

Yvette Frazier Eason

Age:	41
Stage:	3/4
Occupation:	Cost Control Manager/Construction
Residence:	Houston, Texas
Procedure:	Modified Radical Mastectomy
Treatment:	Chemotherapy & Radiation
Survivorship:	3 years
Lymph Node Involvement:	1 / 17

sure enough, there was a lump. The next day I went to the doctor and had a mammogram. The doctor said it looked like a cyst. I had never heard of a fibroid cyst. My breast was very red and irritated. My primary care physician put me on antibiotics with hot and cold packs for five days and he told me to come back if there wasn't a change.

There was no change.

My doctor then referred me to a surgeon. Unfortunately he didn't think I met the criteria for having cancer, so he ordered an ultrasound. The person who read the ultrasound also thought it was a fibroid cyst; he recommended hot and cold packs. If that did not work, he concluded, the lump was malignant. My doctor knew we had already done that, so he ordered a biopsy.

After the biopsy, the surgeon apologized because it was not what he had anticipated. Not only was it cancer, but the tumor was so large that I had to have four chemotherapy treatments before surgery could even be done. I also had two additional chemo treatments after the tumor was removed, as well as five weeks of radiation twice a day.

After all of this, I was cancer free for two years.

In August of 1994 I went in for my regular blood work, and my tumor markers had increased. The doctor ran several tests but found nothing.

Three months later I nicked my finger while cooking, this aggravated my lymphedema. It later turned into cellulitis. Within a few days it switched to streptococcus, a flesh-eating form of bacteria. This was undoubtedly the most severe pain I had ever experienced in my life.

I remember my arm got as big as my thigh, and my temperature rose to 104.7 degrees. When I was admitted to the hospital they called in an infectious disease specialist.

Two days before I left the hospital I started complaining about my back and the back of my neck. When I returned to work my back was still hurting, so they changed my chair to make me more comfortable. After the back pain continued, I got a massage, but the pain was still very persistent.

Finally, I decided to go back to the doctor. He ran some more tests, and once again my tumor markers were up. They found out the cancer had returned. The cancer had traveled from the auxiliary nodes under my arm to the back of my neck.

This time they started me off with five treatments of radiation because the cancer was in the bone — but it was not in the marrow 100 percent. I still felt fortunate, because there had not been any nerve damage.

I realize now that the cellulitis might just have saved my life. If I had never gotten sick, they might not have found the cancer.

When I first found out the cancer had returned I couldn't believe it. My first treatments had been so aggressive. But I remembered my form of cancer was diagnosed as inflammatory cancer. This was considered one of the more aggressive cancers, and it did not respond to chemotherapy very well. There was a 60 percent chance of it returning within three years. The prognosis from that point on was extremely grim.

The first time I dealt with cancer, I was prepared for it. This time to be honest, I am scared, because it is in my system. I feel sick when I didn't feel sick before. I also know I have to fight it, I can't just give up.

I have enough faith to know that God can cure anything. But I have also faced the fact that this may not be something he chooses to cure for me. I realize I may die. He has given me the art of being able to celebrate life, so I can't worry about death. When I get up in the morning my prayer is to thank God for this day and to give me the strength and courage to endure whatever I need to ... that's all I ask for.

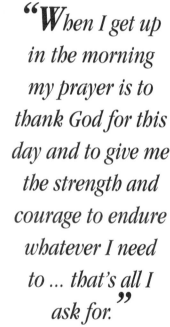

"When I get up in the morning my prayer is to thank God for this day and to give me the strength and courage to endure whatever I need to ... that's all I ask for."

Deborah Green Woulard

I knew that I had to go see my doctor for some test results. But, it was December 21, and I was getting ready for the holidays. In order to keep my spirits up, I planned a fun activity after my visit. I decided I was going to decorate my tree. I got all of my things ready for decorating, then I headed to the doctor's office.

Deborah Green Woulard

Age:	39
Stage:	3
Occupation:	Service Sales Representative
Residence:	Houston, Texas
Procedure:	Lumpectomy
Treatment:	Chemotherapy & Radiation
Survivorship:	6 years
Lymph Node Involvement:	16 / 19

The nurse escorted me to the examining room, but I thought it was strange that she didn't give me a gown to put on. She just told me that the doctor would be in to see me shortly.

When the doctor came in, she asked me to follow her to the conference room. I turned around and looked at her and I noticed there was a tear in her eye. She said, "I don't have good news for you. The cancer has returned."

She then took a stick and pointed to a slide which showed where the tumors were located. There were tumors in both of my lungs. I asked her what the possibility was of having surgery. She informed me that unfortunately surgery was not an option. By now the cancer was throughout my blood stream.

I started to cry. Then I gathered up some strength to ask her what my life expectancy was. She told me I had possibly 8 to 10 months; if I had chemotherapy, maybe a year.

This was a heck of a way to start out the holiday. But it was evident I needed my family now, more than I had at any other time in my life. So, I headed home for the holidays where I was given encouragement and a lot of prayers.

My aunt and I set aside a certain time every day to pray, and we began to thank God for the healing that had already taken place.

Right after New Year's Day, I returned to my doctor. I let her know that I was going to start the chemotherapy treatments. Then I looked her straight in the face and told her, "I'm going to be your miracle patient."

Thinking back to when I was first diagnosed, it really caught me off guard. Although I had a family history of cancer, I never really thought about getting it. I was having my annual physical and my gynecologist found a lump in my breast. He then scheduled me for a mammogram. The mammogram results were confirmed by a surgeon.

The surgeon performed several tests. He then informed me there was a 50/50 chance that I may have cancer but he couldn't be certain until he did a biopsy. However, if it was cancer he told me that he would have to remove my left breast.

At that point I started reading all kinds of material from the American Cancer Society. I then learned about lumpectomies. I thought this was great. I wouldn't have to lose my breast.

I told my doctor that I wanted a lumpectomy. If that would not be possible, I wanted to be awakened after the biopsy and told that my breast would have to be removed ... but my first option was a lumpectomy.

I was thankful when I awoke; my doctor told me that a lumpectomy was performed. There were 19 lymph nodes removed, 16 of them positive. This meant I was going to have to have radiation and chemotherapy as after treatments.

When I finally reached the five year mark I was bombarded with tests. I had a liver scan, bone scan, chest X-ray, ultrasound and all kinds of blood work. But the consensus of all the tests was that everything was fine. I was now considered cancer free!

The next month I developed a hacking cough. I had been really bothered with sinus drainage, so my doctor just recommended I double my dosage of cough syrup.

"Then I looked her straight in the face and told her, 'I'm going to be your miracle patient.'"

But the cough was persistent. It finally got so bad that I went to the emergency room. They performed a chest X-ray to rule out pneumonia.

I filled my prescription for antibiotics and went home to be with my family for Thanksgiving. My cough, in the meantime, did not go away.

I called to check my messages and found out my doctor was trying to reach me to schedule an appointment to review some tests.

Once I returned to Houston, I called my doctor's office to find out what tests she was referring to. That is when I found out that it was about my recent chest X-ray.

After I found out that my cancer had returned, I knew that I could not just take it lying down. A friend took me to a health food store. The manager of the store performed a test on me to tell me what type of vitamins and minerals my body needed.

I took everything she suggested, including shark cartilage. Shark cartilage smells like the bottom of the ocean, so it was not the most pleasant thing to deal with ... but I took it anyway.

I was scheduled to take six doses of chemotherapy. After my third treatment another CAT scan was done. My doctor informed me that most of the tumor was gone. I still continued to take the shark cartilage as much as possible, but because of the nasty taste and odor I had a hard time trying to do it on a daily basis.

After my last treatment, another CAT scan was performed. This time nothing showed up in my lungs. My doctor told me I was in remission. I could tell she was shocked. She had never been one for words, but it was all over her face that she was totally elated.

I think my case really hit home for her, because last Christmas she sent me a personalized greeting card. I guess she could think back to a year before when Christmas wasn't so happy for me.

Nancy Garner

In June of 1993, the doctors had only given me six months to live, so I knew that it was out of their hands now. I had to seek a higher healing power. I had heard of this young minister that was running a month-long revival at his church. I wanted to go. I knew that I had already received man's prognosis. At this point, the only other thing I knew was to turn it over to God.

Before I left for the revival, my husband warned me not to let anybody lay hands on me. But I knew that I had to do this for myself. My sister decided to go and lend moral support.

As long as I live I will never forget that night.

Everybody seemed to be overflowing with the Holy Spirit. I was just sitting on the pew keeping to myself. Then all of a sudden, I felt this force going through my body. I felt like someone was pressing me tight between two slabs of metal. My body got so hot I thought I was going to explode.

Nancy Garner

Age:	56
Stage:	3/4
Occupation:	Homemaker
Residence:	Chicago, Illinois
Procedure:	Mastectomy
Treatment:	Chemotherapy
Survivorship:	1 year
Lymph Node Involvement:	None

I sat there perspiring like crazy in the midst of the congregation, but no one was paying attention to me. Everyone was really getting into the service. For a while I thought I was having a heart attack. I was in so much pain I thought I was going to die. It seems I was completely out of control. I did not know what in the world was going on. Then this powerful surge shot through my body. It was so strong it knocked my shoes off my feet.

All at once I began to feel revived. It was like giving birth to a baby. I felt totally new. When I left the church I didn't say anything to anybody. Little did I know I had been healed. I would no longer show any signs of breast cancer.

I first noticed something was wrong with my breast after I had an accident. While I was washing my car I fell and injured my breast. I had opened the car door and stepped up to clean the top of my moon roof. I guess I lost my footing because I fell backward. As I fell my breast caught the edge of the opened car door. At the time the pain was so severe it felt like I had ripped my breast off.

Although there was no broken skin, there seemed to be some internal bleeding. I noticed a nice size bruise in the area of the injury. There was also a knot in that area of my breast. I watched it for five weeks, but it seemed like the healing process was going very slowly. I kept feeling this pain. It wasn't in my breast, but it was in the back of my neck.

Finally, I decided to go to the doctor to find out why it was taking so long to heal. I ended up seeing three specialists. They all felt I needed to have a biopsy before they could really tell the extent of the damage to my breast. They all believed my symptoms were a result of the injury, but they still recommended a biopsy.

At first I opted for a needle biopsy, but they couldn't aspirate any fluid. So, I ended up having to have a surgical biopsy. Afterward, they told me I had cancer. That was the shock of my life.

It seems the cancer had been embedded in my rib cage, but when I injured my breast that caused it to come to the surface. Even though I had had a mammogram three months before, it still was not picked up, because the tumor was too far back to be detected.

The doctors told me it was in stage 3 to 4; they also said I actually had *two* types of cancer. Based on these factors they felt I only had six months to live.

When I was diagnosed it was so strange. I kept saying, why me? I have gone through my life trying to do the right things. I eat the right food. I never smoked. I only take an occasional drink of wine at dinner. I have never lived around a chemical plant. Why would I have to get the type of cancer that could kill you so fast? Some people get cancer and live for years.

Nevertheless, I was determined that I was not going to let this get the best of me. I set out to find the best team of doctors to handle my case. But as I was searching for excellent

> *"As I fell my breast caught the edge of the opened car door. At the time the pain was so severe it felt like I had ripped my breast off."*

medical attention, my health was constantly declining. The pain kept getting more persistent in the back of my neck. Finally it got so bad I could hardly turn my head. After a while I could no longer drive my car. My nights became sleepless because I was in so much discomfort.

After I had selected a team of doctors they suggested I have a series of chemotherapy even before they attempted the surgery. That was hard for me to deal with. They didn't believe I was going to live, but they wanted me to have chemo anyway. I couldn't quite understand the reasoning behind that, but I went ahead with the treatments.

The confirmation of my healing had come three months after my diagnosis, when I got home from the revival. I was laying in bed and I heard a voice call my name three times. At first I thought it was my husband, but when I looked at him, he was snoring.

I heard the voice again. This time it was saying, "You are healed." I got up and I washed my face. I thought this was weird. I am hearing voices. People will think I am cracking up or something. I lay back down, then the voice got louder. This time it was saying, "Nancy, you are healed, go in peace." At that point I realized that is what happened to me at the church. I fell out of the bed and began praising God. There was such a commotion my husband woke up. At first he thought I had passed out. But I let him know what had happened, and he started praising God with me.

From that point on I could lift my arms. I could do everything I did before I had been diagnosed with breast cancer.

At first I didn't know if I should have the surgery any more or not. But my husband and I agreed it wouldn't hurt to have the operation. I knew it wouldn't bother me to lose a breast anyway. I was through having my children. I looked at it as being nothing more than an abstraction of a tooth. Some people live with one eye, or one leg. I was definitely prepared to live with one breast.

I did ask them to test me before the operation to make sure that it was necessary. They refused. My diagnosis had already been confirmed by three specialists; therefore, they felt there was no need for any additional testing.

After the operation they informed me that my breast was no longer cancerous. It had not been necessary for my breast to be removed. I reminded them that I had advised them that I had been healed and I had asked to be tested again. Then I said, "In other words I could sue you, right?" One person said, "Yes."

But I let them know that was the last thing on my mind. For I counted everything as a blessing from the Lord. I had not experienced a pain in my breast, my back or my neck since I had left the revival. So all of this was like a process I was going through. I guess it was my way of verifying what I already knew ... that I was truly healed.

Even though my doctor had recommended I stay in the hospital for two weeks, I was home in less than three days. They sent a visiting nurse to my house. I let her know that she didn't need to come back because I didn't need her. I was going around doing everything that I had always done.

My doctors still have a problem understanding what happened to me. At the time I was diagnosed with cancer, my close friend, my sister-in-law and some members of my church were also diagnosed with cancer. We were all fighting for our lives at the same time. My sister-in-law didn't make it, my friend didn't make it, the members of my church didn't make it. But I am still here!

I went to all of their funerals except for one. Each time I would say to myself, "Oh my God" because I knew what the doctors said my prognosis was and I felt I would be next. But I never let fear take over me.

I know that I am supposed to have five years of follow up treatments, but that doesn't bother me either. Because I realize the doctors only thought I had six months to live anyway. But one thing I know for sure, when God does something He doesn't undo it. I don't fear death, and I definitely don't intend to let cancer take my life.

"We were all fighting for our lives at the same time. My sister-in-law didn't make it, my friend didn't make it, the members of my church didn't make it. But I am still here!"

Oleary Hasson Osibin

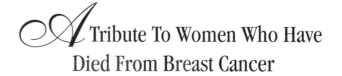Tribute To Women Who Have Died From Breast Cancer

My sisters of the sun, indeed every member of the sisterhood, and especially those who have gone on. You were always greater that the universe. Shining so brightly that the moon and the stars must whisper your names. We hear with our hearts as they tell us to be strong ... and so on and so on and so on ... what do you say to someone? I have learned to say if you need me I will be there I love you.

A quote from the play *Sister Girl*, written by Brandyn Barbara Artis

Louise Baker	*Brenda Ward-Jackson*
Zorata Talbert Basey	*Ida Kelly*
Jessie Broussard	*Annie Lou Lewis*
Donnie Brown	*Audre Lorde*
Leona Brown	*Jo Lozella Mars*
Bettye Capers	*Millie Martin*
Lauretta Clarke Davis	*Janice Mickey*
Robbie Davis	*Cora Curry Moore*
Sharon E. DeGourville	*Betty L Newell*
Barbara Doss	*Annie Reid*
Helen Eaton	*Minnie Riperton*
Jackie Franklin	*Albertina Robinson*
Debbie Ann Brown-Gaster	*Maisy Dawkins Strawn*
Bettye Jean Gaston	*Danitra Vance*
Lila Mae Gee	*LouDella Williams*
Annie Holmes	
Cleo Hosick	

Bettye Capers

Mildred Blackmon

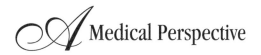

A Medical Perspective

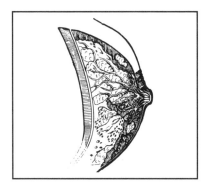

A cross-section of the breast

After the diagnosis

Changes In the Breast

Fibrocystic Condition, also referred to as Fibrocystic Disease, can cause changes in the breast. These are benign cysts that are not cancerous. This may also cause discomfort during or around the menstrual cycle. Reducing caffeine intake my help in making this condition more bearable. To date, there has been no direct link between this condition and breast cancer. There are other conditions such as menstruation and pregnancy that may cause changes in your breasts. It is important to know your breasts and know what is normal for you.

Once you're diagnosed

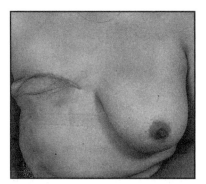

Lumpectomy

Lumpectomy

If the cancer is localized and the lump is small enough, a lumpectomy may be a valid option. If the cancer is multifocal this may not be the best option because of the possibility of leaving other affected tissue in the breast.

Mastectomy

If the cancer is not contained, a mastectomy may be a more viable option. This is the complete removal of the breast. For a woman with very small breasts, a lumpectomy may not give the desired cosmetic result. Therefore, a mastectomy may be necessary. In both a lumpectomy and a mastectomy the lymph nodes are sampled for metastasis.

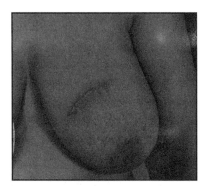

Mastectomy

Recurrence or Chest Wall Involvement

For someone who has had a mastectomy or there is chest wall involvement, there are other things that may need to be considered. Sometimes additional therapy is needed. It is also important to know if there is any lymph node involvement. Factors to be considered are: how long the tumor had been there, whether there are estrogen or progestogen receptors on the cells, the DNA analysis, family history and the aggressiveness of the tumor.

Chemotherapy

Depending of the staging of the cancer, chemotherapy may be a precautionary option or a life-prolonging necessity. This is something that should be discussed with your doctor. Your previous health and family history may play a major role in what after treatment you receive. The possible side effects should also be talked over with your physician.

Radiation

Radiation may be used by itself or in conjunction with chemotherapy as an after treatment for breast cancer. There may be side effects to this treatment.

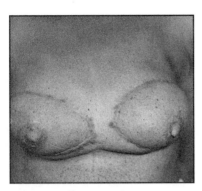

Reconstruction

Reconstruction

This procedure to rebuild the breast is done by a plastic surgeon. Although this gives an impression of a breast, it is still not a real breast. However, it may look natural and give a woman more flexibility in clothing. Because some African American women have a problem with keloid skin, it is also important to realize it might not look like some of the pictures or film that you have seen of women of other races.

Reconstruction can be done with either an artificial substance or with your own body fat. Sometimes a tummy tuck is done when body fat is used.

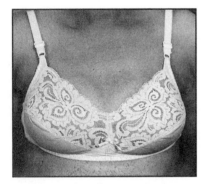

Wearing a bra after reconstruction.

Support

Breast cancer is not just something that affects the patient's body, it also impacts the emotions. It is essential to have a good support network.

Follow Up Treatments

The follow up treatment may vary depending on your procedure and your doctor. Many cancer patients have three-month check-ups with their oncologist or surgeon for the first few years after the procedure. The visits are then reduced to every six months up until the fifth year. When a patient reaches the five-year mark, often considered the point of remission, visits are only once a year.

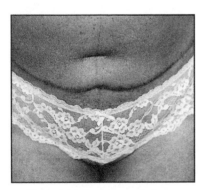

The incision for a tummy tuck may extend from side to side.

A Special Thanks To

Dr. Cheryl Harth
Clinical Hematologist Oncologist
Methodist Medical Center

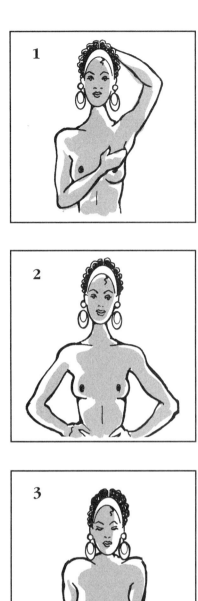

A Personal Touch
A guide for doing breast self-exams.

1. *Standing*

   With your right hand behind your head use your middle three fingers to examine your breast. In a circular motion press firmly against the breast (in toward the chest wall) to check for knots, lumps, or swelling. Repeat this with the opposite side. Pretend your breast is the face of a clock and go around the entire breast in a clock wise fashion, making sure to cover the entire breast area including under the arm.

2. *In Front of A Mirror*

   Visually inspect your breasts. Look for any noticeable changes, dimpling or size differences.

3. Tense your chest muscles to make any changes in your breasts more prominent.

4. *Lying Down*

   While lying down on your back place a pillow under your right shoulder. Again use your three middle fingers to examine your breast by pressing firmly against your breast in a circular motion.

   Make sure that you examine the entire breast area, including the area under your arm. Also, gently squeeze each nipple to check for any discharge.

   It is very important that you get to know your breasts, by repeating this procedure on a monthly basis. Therefore, you can be the best judge of noticing a change.

   The American Cancer Society also recommends that you have your breasts examined annually by a physician, and after the age of 40 you start having mammograms.

   In having mammograms it is also important to consult with your personal physician. If there is a history of breast cancer in your family, a base line may need to be done before the age of 40.

uestions To Ask Your Doctor

1. What, specifically, did my biopsy show?

2. What are my treatment options?

3. What are the potential risks and benefits of these procedures?

4. Which procedure are you recommending for me, and why ?

5. Where will the surgical scar or scars be located?

6. Will the lymph nodes under my arm be checked for cancer? If so, how will this affect my treatment options?

7. What tests were done on the tumor and what were the results (estrogen and progesterone receptor assays, DNA analysis, S-phase fraction)? What effect will the results of these tests have on my treatment options?

8. Will I need additional (adjuvant) treatment with radiation therapy, chemotherapy, and/or hormonal therapy following surgery? If so, can you refer me to a radiation oncologist and/or medical oncologist?

Courtesy of The Susan G. Komen Breast Cancer Foundation.

It's A Family Affair

Genetics role in breast cancer.

Dr. Funmi Olopade, an assistant professor and director of the Cancer Risk Clinic at the University of Chicago, has studied women who have a family history of breast cancer, and has researched the genetic link that is responsible for this family connection.

Robyn Paige and Kimberly Price share the common bond of being the only girls in a family of seven. They also have another bond – they both have had breast cancer. Their brother Michael is also a breast cancer survivor.

The medical community has known for a long time that breast cancer can run in families. About 5 to 10 percent of all breast cancer diagnosed has a genetic link. If your mother, your grandmother and aunts had breast cancer, there is a strong possibility that you have inherited the same mutated or defective gene.

Not all breast cancer is inherited. Some cancer, what we call sporadic breast cancer, develops without a family history. We are hoping to get more understanding of the inherited genes to get a better handle on sporadic breast cancer as well.

These breast cancer genetic studies have become very important in our search for a cure for the disease. Researchers hope to determine how these genes become abnormal, what makes them cause breast cancer and if they can be used to prevent the disease.

So far scientists have identified four genes that pre-dispose a person to develop breast cancer.

BRCA1: This gene, discovered in September 1994, causes both ovarian cancer and breast cancer in families. It doesn't depend on your race because anyone can inherit a defective form of these genes. It is believed that having a defect in this gene is equivalent to having broken cell brakes. The cells undergo uncontrolled growth. Defective BRCA1 genes are responsible for 5 percent of all inherited breast cancer.

Several scientists estimate that 600,000 American women are at risk from the inherited form of the disease. At least 85 percent of the women who have this mutated gene have a chance of developing the disease. The risk factor for the general population is 12 percent. Male carriers of the gene have an increased risk of prostate cancer, but not breast cancer.

BRCA2: This gene pre-disposes a family to breast cancer, but not ovarian cancer. BRCA1 has been cloned so its effects can be further studied, but BRCA2 has not been cloned at this time. Female carriers of this gene also have an 85 percent risk of developing breast cancer.

p53: This is a protein molecule that holds cancer in check when it is working. It is defective in cancer cells of more than 50 percent of women who develop the disease. Some people inherit the mutated gene, in others it is damaged by radiation or chemicals.

The interesting thing about this gene is that it does not just cause breast cancer. This gene is associated with about half of all human cancers. It can be found defective when people have brain cancer, leukemia, bone cancer or cancer of the adrenal gland. Scientist say it is probably only one of a series of genetic changes necessary to transform a normal cell into a tumor cell.

AT or Ataxia Telangiectasia: An international team of researchers reported on the finding of this rare gene in June 1995. An estimated 2 million or more Americans are thought to be carriers of this defective gene. Their risk of developing some form of cancer is three to four times higher than the general population. The risk of breast cancer for female carriers has been estimated to be five times that of the general population.

These women are also sensitive to excessive radiation. Unfortunately, at this time, we don't quite know how much radiation would be considered excessive. It is important to identify these women ahead of time. Medical procedures such as CAT scans and mammograms could increase their risk of breast cancer. They are definitely not the ones you would want to order mammograms for every year.

Women need to begin to have their risk assessed. This can be done at clinics, like the one at the University of Chicago.

The first step is finding out which diseases family members have suffered from. You should look at breast cancer, ovarian cancer and colon cancer in your family history.

Also, it is important to look on both sides of the family. People sometimes make the mistake of thinking because their mother hasn't had breast cancer they are not at risk. You get your genes from both parents. Your paternal aunts may all have developed breast cancer but your dad didn't. Your dad could still be a carrier for the same defective gene and could have passed it on to you.

If your cancer is hereditary, you will find that it will be diagnosed at an early age, usually under 45.

We can tell you if having a genetic test will help define your risk more precisely or if you will benefit from that type of test. Having one relative with breast cancer does not mean that it is an inherited condition. You have to see that the cancer has gone from one generation to the other.

You shouldn't get too excited if you discover your family carries one of these defective genes.

If you are a carrier you should know and do something about it. Having this information can help you plan a course of action much more precisely.

As much as I emphasize genetics — because I believe that genetics are going to help us — I also like to say that every woman is at risk. Some may have a much higher risk than others. Most of the breast cancer that is diagnosed will be in women who are older than 65 and who may not have a genetic risk factor. However, because they are older, age is the most important risk factor for them. They need to get their mammogram every year.

Everyone needs to practice the three things that the American Cancer Society recommends: doing breast self-exams, having a doctor examine your breasts once a year, and getting a mammogram. It's recommended that women between 40 and 50 get a mammogram every other year. Women over 50 are urged to get one annually.

For The Health Of It

Diet plays a role in breast cancer.

Maxine Willie
Registered Dietician
Martin Luther King Family Center
Dallas, Texas

Food habits are very personal. Once we establish our eating patterns, it is very hard to change. A doctor will send a patient to me, but they will pass by my office several times before they come in. Finally, when they do come in their diets are so out of control they have limited choices.

Most of us don't even realize how much fat we take in on a daily basis. The average person is unfamiliar with a low-fat diet. Most of them are eating one to two pounds of butter per day. And without sitting down with a nutritionist, they will not make any attempt to reduce the fat. They think they are only eating about a tablespoon or two.

It is extremely difficult for someone who has spent a lifetime of frying their food to stop and begin baking it instead. It is like you have just told them to die and go to Hell or something.

I have some suggestions and guidelines that will help proactively reduce the risk for cancer. They are in line with the American Cancer Society guidelines.

1. Avoid Obesity: African Americans tend to be 40 to 60 percent heavier than other ethnic groups. We really need to work with our children. Often times, we are chubby as kids, weight-conscious in our 20s and heavy again in our 30s. At the downhill of 30, we become more susceptible to lifestyle and diet related disease. If we want to effectively change our diets and eating habits, we have to change our lifestyle at a early age.

2. Reduce Total Fat Intake: Sit down and plan a menu. If you are going to have a chitterlings dinner, make that a special occasion, not something you do every week. For most people, the total fat intake needs to be reduced to between 20 to 30 percent of the total caloric intake. Most people don't know what their total caloric intake is.

3. Eat a Variety of Foods: Eating only meat and bread or meat and potatoes will kill you for sure. If not, it will cause you a lot of pain because you are setting yourself up for disease such as gout, cancer and diabetes. A balanced diet includes vegetables and fruits.

4. Eat More High Fiber Food: High fiber diet includes soluble and insoluble fibers. Fibers help to rid the body of fat and toxins. It's a great way to clean the colon. Most fat that is not removed from the intestine will be reabsorbed and returned to the blood stream.

Remember to drink plenty of water too, that helps move the fiber through your system.

5. Limit Alcohol and Tobacco Use: I truly believe these should be eliminated from your diet. If it is a must, definitely use in moderation. Excess in this area tends to weaken the body, providing a way for cancer to get in.

6. Use Salt Sparingly: Use more herbs and spices to season food and cut out the salt, often listed as sodium on packaged foods. Also watch out for nitrate cured foods, which are artificially smoked foods. We think we can use smoked turkey legs instead of fat back to season our greens, but we don't realize that we are using an artificial chemical. Our diet would be much better if we used Liquid Smoke or boullion cubes in our greens. We can also use broths, onions, garlic, thyme, rosemary, oregano and other spices to add zest to our food without adding salt.

7. Supplements: Your basic vitamins should come from the food that you eat. If this is impossible or not practical, supplement your diet with vitamins. It is very important that these are vitamins that are missing because you can overdo your vitamin needs. If you are reducing your caloric intake, then you can supplement your diet with a good multi-vitamin. But you must do this on a regular basis for it to be effective.

Eartha Kitt
(Photo courtesy of the JBAAL archives)

Even in her 60s, actress Eartha Kitt maintains her diet and exercise regime. She has her own garden that provides many of the fruits and vegetables she eats. Her secret for her great looks and beautiful skin: "It is not what you put on your face that counts, it is what you put in your face.

"Sometimes we spend a lot of money on facial products; there is nothing wrong with that. However, the main thing we must remember is that if we take care of our bodies, our bodies will take care of us. We need to let our bodies talk to us. If we eat something and it makes us feel lethargic or it makes us hyper, then we are eating the wrong thing.

"We must pay attention to the messages our bodies are sending us, because it will truly tell us what we need."

A Perfect Fit

Prostheses and other attire.

The first thing that I try to do when a woman comes into my boutique, is make her very comfortable. If this is her first visit, she may not quite know what to expect. There is no telling what she may have heard from other people. I try right away to ease her fears.

I start out in a very conversational manner by asking who her doctor is, and how long it has been since her surgery.

Then I take her into the fitting room. At this point I want to make sure she is relaxed. I begin asking her more questions, so that I can become familiar with her. Has she been seen by a Reach to Recovery Volunteer? Has she been doing her exercises? How far can she raise her arm? Does she have a prescription for her prosthesis? It is very important that she have a prescription for her prosthesis. This lets me know that the doctor feels she has healed enough to wear one.

I always let the physician know that I have seen their patients, and how they were doing. Therefore, if there are any problems they can follow up with them.

Lois Smith-Williams
Director & Professional Prosthesis Fitter
Creations - Ladies Health Boutique
St. Paul Medical Center,
Home Health Care
1-800-856-7841

Getting fitted for a prosthesis can be a very sensitive issue emotionally, so I really want the woman to be totally at ease before we get started. Then I finally get around to asking her to pull off her top. If there is any uncomfortableness, there is a cover top I put over her. If she does not want to strip down the gown can be left over her, and I can work under the gown. I realize some women don't feel they want to look in the mirror quite yet.

A woman always needs a fitting in order to be able to feel and look like she did before her surgery. There is no reason a woman should be lopsided, have an uncomfortable bra, or a bra that is not doing her prosthesis justice. Once she has been properly fitted, she starts looking really good and she starts feeling good as well. At that time, at least 99 percent of my clients will completely take the top off and look at themselves in the mirror. Their confidence level is usually restored at this point.

I can't stress enough to women how important posture is. After their surgery a lot of ladies get relaxed and start to slump. This problem gets considerably worse if they don't feel good about themselves or they get a little depressed.

I usually have the women come back in two weeks after their initial visit so that I can find out how their bra is working and how their prosthesis is looking. Then I have them return in another month just to be sure everything is OK. At that point, they don't come back for six months, and then it is time to get some new bras.

Brandyn Barbara Artis is wearing a swim suit designed for a woman who wears a prosthesis.

It is very important that the prosthesis be the same size as the remaining breast. The prosthesis can come in sizes 32, 34, 36 ...., or it can come in number 1, 2, 3, 4,... it depends on the manufacturer.

I would never ask a woman what size bra she wears. To me that is insulting. First of all only one out of every seven women knows what size bra they wear. Almost every woman I run into is in the wrong size bra. I prefer doing the fitting myself, so that I can find their correct size.

An inappropriate bra size can cause circulation problems, dropping in shoulder, neck pains, bulging of the breasts out of the cup and back problems. A bra is like a harness on a horse. It really supports the top part. Whatever happens, whether it is right or wrong, it affects the upper part of the body. It might not feel like it makes a difference, but take it from me, it does.

If a lady goes too long with one breast, and the other cup is being stuffed with tissue, socks and other stuff, where the weight is, it pulls the body. This has a tendency to make the shoulders droop.

For today's woman on the go, there is also a prosthesis that you can attach to the skin. It attaches directly to the chest wall.

Now, prostheses also come in a variety of colors. Because we as Black women are so many colors, the prosthesis may not match your skin tone. However, that does not matter, because the cover can be dipped in tea to tint it to a shade of brown. You can play with the cover and tone it down by dying it.

Prostheses are varied in price and can run anywhere from $80 to $400. I look at it as being good, better, best and ultimate best.

The average life span of a prosthesis is usually from two to three years. I would hate to see a woman wear a prosthesis five or six years and brag about it. With normal wear, I think it should be replaced every three years. At that point, it still remains firm and it moves with you.

Very few women stay the same size for six or seven years; with weight changes you also need to consider changing your prosthesis. Also, you should be fitted every six months to a year with new bras. Surgical bras usually run between $36 and $42.

I recommend that the bras be washed by hand and drip dried to protect their longevity. Also I believe women should keep at least three bras on hand: one to wash, one to wear, and a spare.

Some women are concerned that they may not be able to wear lingere. But this is not a problem. There are gowns made with pockets so that you can slip the prosthesis in. For the lady that wants that sexy look there is always the option of the prosthesis with a velcro adhesive patch that sticks directly to your skin.

For the active woman, there is nothing that can't be done once you have a good prosthesis. Even swimming is not a problem. There are swimming suits made with cups that can easily hold your prosthesis.

I don't recommend hot tubs. It is very important to know about the manufacturer's warranty of the prosthesis before getting into a hot tub because the heat could damage it.

If a woman has reconstruction or a partial mastectomy she can also wear a prosthesis for an extra lift. There are special bras and prostheses designed to accommodate just that. They are designed to fill in whatever part of the breast the woman needs the extra fullness in.

I also recommend a scar cream, which is high in aloe vera and vitamin A & E. I encourage the women to massage the area with the cream. I also encourage them to have their husband massage the cream in, so that he can become as familiar with the breast being gone as he was with the breast being there.

There is no doubt that if a woman is properly fitted she will enjoy wearing a prosthesis, and look like she did before she had her surgery.

A wist of the Cloth

Scarves, wigs and other alternatives after hair loss.

Many people don't realize the most traumatic component of cancer for many women is hair loss. A good prosthesis or reconstructive surgery can help keep the loss of a breast from being noticed. But oh, Sister, when the dark and lovely locks begin to fall, it creates an entirely new dilemma. It's especially hard for women who have spent hours perming, curling, braiding or just plain brushing their mane. Many of them have never considered wearing a wig. For them, losing their hair becomes a frightening thought.

Chemotherapy patients may lose all or some of their hair on their heads, including the scalp, beard, mustache, eyebrows and eyelashes. Body hair may eventually thin out or disappear completely from the arms, armpits, legs and groin. Though far from being medically dangerous, this hair loss (alopecia) often has a devastating psychological impact.

Breast cancer survivor Minnie Pryor refers to her hair as Africa. Despite what the doctors said, she was convinced that she was not going to lose her hair. "I just knew that Africa wasn't going anywhere," she said. "Then one day I was combing my hair and pulled out a whole handful of hair. Then I realized that Africa too was going to desert me."

Beverly Rhine, another survivor, says she was sitting down unbraiding her hair when: "As I reached up to unbraid my hair, an entire braid came off in my hand. I realized at that moment if I decided to lose my ever loving mind, no one in the world would blame me. If I went stark, raving mad, I would have just cause."

As with other side effects from dealing with breast cancer, survivors say hair loss can provide an opportunity to bond with family members.

It's painfully embarrassing, but hair loss doesn't have to be the end of the world. Many women quickly adjusted by shaving and trimming what remained to highlight their natural hair line.

Others have found alternatives. It is almost like the song, "I'm Every Woman." The possibilities are endless. You can go from casual to chic with the simple twist of a scarf or change of a hat. Breast cancer survivor Charlotte Brewster has lost her hair twice from chemotherapy. She has become a pro at using all the options available to her. Look at some of the

intriguing things Charlotte does to make herself look glamorous, despite the hair loss.

"One day after my hair had started doing what it was going to do, I looked at my head and it was like looking at something in a movie. I only had three long strands of hair on my head," said survivor Audrey Montgomery. "I was devastated. I went into the bathroom. I was feeling down at the time. I took a mirror and turned around to look at the back of my head. At that point, it really hit me. I could always see the front and the side, but I had never looked at it in the back. I was just about to fall apart. My husband peeked in to check on me. He walked over to me. 'Baby, my hair ... it's just — gone.'

"He bent my head down and kissed the top of my head and said, 'It does not matter. I love you anyway.' We have been together for nine years and I will probably remember that more than anything he has ever done."

VonDonna Bircher says she used to have a lot of pride in her hair. "I went to the beauty shop every week. I had called my beautician the day before I was scheduled to go in to let her know that I was probably going to be losing my hair. It was thinning a great deal. The next day when I went to the beauty shop, my beautician thought everything was going to be OK. She washed and conditioned my hair as normal. I had a conditioning treatment under a heat cap. When I had finished, my beautician rinsed my hair. I raised up and I had no hair — it had all come out. Everybody started looking at me. My sister was with me at the time ... I started crying, my sister started crying, my beautician started crying and the customers started crying. The entire beauty shop ended up in an uproar because of me losing my hair."

Shirley Levingston had never worn a wig. Just the process of getting one became a major ordeal because spiritually she was not claiming the potential hair loss. Yet when it actually happened, she was already prepared with two wigs on hand. She says she was able to take it all in stride. "The Bible tells me that what we say with our mouth shall come to pass. Therefore, I didn't want to say I would lose my hair, even though I realized it was one of the side effects of chemotherapy. I came home one day and I was getting ready to wash my hair. I was wearing my hair pulled back with a barrette in the back. As I pulled my barrette off, along with it came an entire batch of hair."

Behind Closed Doors

Intimacy after breast cancer.

This book wouldn't be complete if we didn't talk about preconceived notions of femininity and sexuality. Many women who are facing breast cancer often wonder whether sex will ever be the same or not.

I've found it depends on who you ask. Many survivors profiled for this book say sex gets better! For a mature woman who understands where the sexual feelings come from, losing a breast doesn't mean you're no longer sexy or your mate won't find you desirable.

Casting for actress Brandyn Barbara Artis hasn't changed. She travels the world performing her one woman play, "Sister Girl". After viewing her photo on page 32 you can see she is just as alluring with one breast as many women are with two.

Chemotherapy, as we already discussed, causes hair loss even in the pubic area. What most people don't realize is that it can also cause hormonal imbalances which may lessen the sex drive. As we tackled this challenging topic of intimacy after breast cancer, we sought advice from a sexual relations expert as well as some very candid comments from several breast cancer survivors about the intimate details of their lives.

Dr. Gwendolyn Goldsby Grant

Essence magazine advice columnist

Author: The Best Kind Of Loving:
A Black Woman's Guide to
Finding Intimacy

Photo Credit: Dwight Carter

Dr. Gwendolyn Goldsby Grant is the *Essence* magazine advice columnist, author of the best-seller "The Best Kind Of Loving: A Black Woman's Guide to Finding Intimacy," a certified sex educator, mental health educator and psychologist. She frequently lectures to women's organizations, church groups and corporations across the country. Here's what she has to say:

"I just really believe that women in this country have been sexually objectified. They advertise our legs, our breasts, our hips and our feet. In other words women have become compartmentalized instead of being taken as a whole person. I think that is due to the fact each part becomes marketable for sexual reasons. That is why I call it Kentucky Fried Chicken sex. Guys even speak of it as "I am a leg man, I'm an ass man, I'm a thigh man, or I'm a breast man."

"So, when a woman loses something like a breast, she then feels she is no longer able to attract a man. She becomes victimized by this Kentucky Fried Chicken sex mentality that we have. It is from that concept that I developed the idea of 'Whole Person sexuality.' Sex is not about pieces and parts. Sex is a whole concept, of a whole person. It is not just one little place or two little places, one place between your legs and another place between your arms. Sex is about a whole person.

"If you fall victim to the concept of being a pieces and parts person, you never really get to the whole person. When there is a piece or part missing, the whole thing falls apart. People who spend their life looking for pieces and parts have a endless lifestyle because they never find the whole person.

"If there is a Whole Person concept, when the part goes, like a breast, you realize the person is still there. It is like building a statue. As long as you have the base, it can still stand, no matter if one piece falls off or not. Relationships have to have a strong base, a foundation, because no matter what piece is missing the Whole Person concept comes from within.

"Often in my workshop I hold up a blank piece of paper with a big black dot on it and ask people what they see. They all say they see the dot. Then I ask them why they see the dot. They may say the dot stands out or the dot is more prominent. Then I let them know that is how they are programmed about sexuality. You are focused only on your dot. I call it dot sex. You have allowed yourself to be programmed on one spot. Therefore, one to two spots define your sexuality. That is so unfair to the rest of you.

"We need to get rid of the dot syndrome mentality. When we buy into the dot syndrome, then we become 'poked a dots'. It means someone is poking you in your dot, and they are not thinking about the rest of you.

"I believe that is how breasts fit into this picture. Because usually someone is poking you in your dot and nibbling on your breast, all of that from the dot to the breast becomes sex to him. All of the rest of you is not regarded.

"As a result of this type of sexual concept, some women may develop a 'missing part' mentality after a mastectomy. If the main part goes, you feel are not really a whole because you are defining yourself through your parts.

"Missing parts don't mean a missing person. If we internalize this type of socialization where we are pieces and parts, then we buy into that concept as well. That allows the missing part to become more important than the total person. That is not fair to the whole person that you are, and that has to do with self-esteem. You are giving your whole self a very bad break, because you are letting your parts define you.

"If there is a whole person concept, when the part goes, like a breast, you realize the person is still there."

"On the other hand some people are very spiritual in their relationships, as are many of the women in this book. When you are spiritual, you don't internalize this mess. You see relationships as being something more than physical. You realize that relationships are psychological, emotional and spiritual. Therefore, when someone loses a part they are still a whole person. That is what spirituality teaches us."

Here's what the survivors said:

Augusta Gale says she had a 3-dimensional chest before she had both breasts removed. She went from a Double F, to a 0, then to a C after reconstruction. Despite all this she jokingly says, "The men say more than a mouth full is excess anyway!"

VonDonna Bircher:

I would never let my husband see my bald head. Whenever I took off my wig, I would go into the bathroom and put on a turban. I went months without him seeing my head. One particular night we were in bed, making love and the turban came off. I went crazy struggling trying to grab the turban. He grabbed my hand and said leave it alone, do not put it back on. He turned the light on and said, "I want to see your head." He looked at my head, and he said, "From now on when you are in this house, I do not want you to put that on your head. There is nothing wrong with your bald head."

I don't know, but I really felt a genuine sense of closeness to him that night. I realized this man was willing to accept me in any form or fashion. No breast and no hair — I guess if I had one leg or one arm it wouldn't have mattered to him either.

Charisse Cossey:

I try to get men into my spirit first. By the time they see the nudity, the spirit is so overwhelming and intoxicating that any disfigurement is so minute. I feel that this whole process starts from within myself. I can't tell women they need to take their blouse off first and their panties off second ... all of this is an internal process. I think it is about knowing sex past an orgasm. I truly believe that sharing is sharing whether it is a dollar bill or a million dollars.

Beverly Rhine:

I lost my sex drive. My body no longer produced estrogen or any other hormone. Hormones are in direct relation with a woman's sex life. When many women lose their hormones, it causes vaginal dryness which makes sex painful. So they take estrogen to rectify this problem, which then puts them at risk for a cancer recurrence from the estrogen. I continue to enjoy sex ... I just don't feel the sexual drive and motivation that I used to have. I used to have a very high sex drive.

~~~~~~~

Odell Lee:

I did have a lot of second thoughts about intimacy, and it was challenging when I did date. I was usually overly sensitive. I had learned to live with my body for 38 years and all of a sudden it had changed. I resolved within myself to say "this is me, take it or leave it."

~~~~~~~

Alpha Thomas:

My sexual partners are females. Usually, they are very curious about breast cancer and they ask me a lot of questions. I have had some partners who even stroke the area where my scar is.

~~~~~~~

Michael Price:

Chemo made me horny. When it came to my sex life, breast cancer didn't change anything for me. And I do mean, it didn't change anything.

~~~~~~~

Marian Mostiller:

Marian spent a lot of lot of time in denial before and after her surgery. Immediately after her surgery her mother helped bathe her and take care of her incision.

After my mother left, my husband came and said it was ridiculous that when I saw him I covered my breast. I told him I was so ashamed of the way I looked. He said, "I can take care of you." He removed my hand and started kissing my incision. I will always be grateful for that.

~~~~~~~

Stephanie McKissic:

Stephanie had a hard time having her first breast removed at 19, but it was even more difficult to have her remaining breast removed at 29. However, now she realizes her sexuality did not reside in her breast.

When I am intimate with someone, I still get pleasure from it. I have realized that if I am comfortable with the guy, he is usually comfortable with me. If I exude a certain amount of uncomfortableness, which I can do at times because I am very self-conscious, then my partner feels that nervousness and he becomes uncomfortable as well.

Sex is still good for me. I realized that I have to use my imagination. You have to use your imagination whether you have breasts or not. Because I don't have breasts, I realize I have to do different things and try different things to make it more exciting, so that it won't get boring. People with two breasts have that same problem. I think because I don't have breasts it has made me more sensitive in other areas. Probably the sensations I used to have in my breasts have gone to other areas of my body. It is up to me to tell my partner what works for me.

△▽△▽△▽△▽

Zora Kramer Brown:

Zora recalls one talk show when the commentator asked her to be candid about sex after breast cancer.

In the middle of the interview he asked me, "How must it feel to make love to a woman with one breast?" I caught my breath and said, "Probably like it feels for a woman to make love to a bald-headed man. My sexuality never started with my body and it was always in my head."

We have no problem about dating a bald-headed or overweight man. I think it is unfair we have to be relegated to our sexuality being defined by what part of our bodies are acceptable or not.

△▽△▽△▽△▽

Shirley Levingston:

Women need to truly wait for the Lord to send them a man. Because if He sends you a man, you can bet he will stick by your side even if you have all your toes cut off!

△▽△▽△▽△▽

Cynthia Vaughan:

At the time I had my first mastectomy I was 29, and single. I wanted to get married, and I worried about how I was going to be received. I worried about that for about a day. It then became clear to me if there were those that didn't want to be around because of the cancer, I didn't need them anyway. If someone would run from me because I had a mastectomy, then they were not with me for the right reasons. The essence of me was still there. I was still Cynthia.

△▽△▽△▽△▽

Brandyn Barbara Artis:

Upon seeing me for the first time after my mastectomy, my husband walked up to me and kissed me where my breast used to be and said, "Baby, you can only put one in your mouth at a time." Then he turned around and walked out the door. That was it. There was nothing else to say, and I knew everything was going to be OK.

> **"*I*n the middle of the interview he asked me, 'How must it feel to make love to a woman with one breast?' I caught my breath and said, 'Probably like it feels for a woman to make love to a bald headed man.'"**

Turning The Tables
A male point of view.

urtis King

Cancer is difficult to talk about. The difficulty lies in the fact that the word "cancer" unleashes an eerie, emotional fear. It triggers a strange reality inside that sort of forces one to come to grips with one's own mortality.

It is even more emotionally and mentally draining to watch family members, mostly women, literally deteriorate before your very eyes. It seems to only take a matter of seconds for this untamed species to feed itself on the flesh of others.

I find it truly remarkable that women who have lived through this eventually get to a stage where they can talk about it publicly. Discussing it freely is probably the greatest healing medicine.

Recently, I experienced an interesting observation in a Washington, D.C. park. On several occasions, I would take my daily walk to Loggin Park to read and meditate. Over the course of 10 to 12 months, I had noticed two middle-aged African American women sitting in the park chatting and breast-feeding their babies. I would speak and sometimes stop and talk to the women. From the surface, all seemed to be well ... the babies were smiling as they received nourishment from their mother. The mothers seemed happy and undisturbed as they breast-fed their babies.

Curtis King

Founder and Director of the Junior Black Academy of Arts and Letters, Dallas, Texas

My activities kept me away from the park for a few weeks. When I returned on a more consistent basis, I no longer saw the women. I wondered what had happened to them. Their park visits seemed to have been a part of their weekly routine. I concluded that they probably had moved out of the neighborhood. A couple of days later, one of the women re-appeared with her baby. I was sitting in their spot. She spoke and we had a brief conversation. I asked about her friend.

There was silence and then tears as she struggled to get the words out,

"She died a couple of weeks ago!"

"What happened?" I asked.

"She had breast cancer!" the woman replied.

I was stunned. "I'm sorry to hear that!"

"That's life," the woman responded.

We didn't say very much to each other after that because I could see that it was painfully difficult for her to talk. I closed my book, nodded good-bye, and started walking back to my temporary home. I thought to myself, how could this be ... the woman seemed to have been in perfect health. But something unusual kept nagging at me about this experience. I think it was the fact that here was a mother shamelessly breast-feeding her child ... exposing her breast in a public park and perhaps realizing that she was dying at the same time.

I have to confess that even though I was a breast-fed child, I too have gotten caught up in the aesthetic imagery of a woman's breast. But it was not until I had the park experience that I really came to grips with breasts as a profound function of life. I think that we, as African American men in this country, are gradually coming to understand that things which affect women also affect us. Certainly cancer is not just a woman's thing ... men too are victims.

Finally, I am glad that the women in this book represent strength and courage and that they are allowing themselves to again be personally exposed. These actions will benefit many others, even those who dare not to speak out. As African American men, I believe that we recognize the external image of a woman is beyond sexual gratification. We are learning to embrace the inside as well. Continue to speak truth ... it will heal and set us free.

Erven Davis

My wife Robbie died of breast cancer when my son Chris was seven months old and my son Erven was 5 years old. I became a mother and a father. My wife handled a lot of the household chores, but after six years of marriage I had to learn how to cook, pay bills, do laundry and go to PTA meetings. I had to do all the things I didn't do or didn't know how to do.

Initially, we had found her lump after we realized she was pregnant with Chris. It was really small, and she didn't pay much attention to it. But then it started to grow. I finally convinced her to go to the doctor after two months.

When they told us it was cancer, she was already six months pregnant.

Her doctor talked to us, and let us know that he felt he could remove her breast and everything would be OK. But Robbie refused to have anything done until after the baby was born. Her doctor wanted to, but she didn't want them to.

Two weeks after the baby was born she went in to have the mastectomy. But, now it was too late — the cancer had metastasized.

That was probably the roughest thing I have ever had to go through, watching her go down like that. She began to lose her energy. I had to bathe her, and I also had the baby to worry about.

I really tried hard to let her know that she was no less of a woman because she had lost a breast. I loved her so much that it didn't bother me. All I wanted was for her to be OK. I did everything I needed to do and had to do.

I think losing a breast really bothered her more than it bothered me. For a while she didn't even want me to see it.

It was hard to cope with her illness because she never did anything to cause it. She didn't smoke. She didn't drink. She was a church-going person. I couldn't understand it.

Seven months later, she died at the age of 31.

After her death, I think I got stronger than I had ever been. It was unreal, but I had a strong faith in God. Emotionally, if it hadn't been for Chris and Erven, I might have lost it

Erven Davis flanked by his two sons Chris 14 (left) and Erven Davis Jr. 19 (right). Because of the trauma they have been through, Erven says they are more like brothers than father and sons.

myself. Robbie's mother wanted them, my mother wanted to keep them, but I felt they were my responsibility.

Now Chris is a sophomore in high school and Erven is in college. I believe that we are much closer because of what we have been through. It is more like we are brothers than father and sons.

There is a lot we don't know about breast cancer. We never know when it is going to pop up. I think we, as Black men, need to be very supportive. We say our wedding vows "for better or worse." We don't need to just say that if we don't mean it.

We need to be more supportive of our wives, and have God in our lives. There is nothing to be ashamed of when a woman loses a breast. As long as you have your relationship in order, that is all that counts.

Turning Back The Hands Of Time

A historical look at how breasts have been valued in the African American community.

Sometimes, in order to look at where we are or where we are going, it is important to realize where we have been. In examining African American women's high mortality rate from breast cancer there seem to be some very distinctive historical and culturally-based issues that may have played a contributing role in this extremely distorted scenario.

First of all, we must examine self-disclosure in the African American community — the amount of information that we tend to share with each other. Dr. Bertha Roddey took a close look at her family and discovered that her paternal and maternal families handled things differently.

"My grandfather on my mother's side was the son of a slave. On my mother's side of the family everything was hush hush. On my father's side of the family there were more Native Americans and they tended to be more open. My grandfather on my father's side would tell us everything. But when I was on my mother's side of the family, there was almost no self-disclosure at all."

Dr. Roddey says the disclosure issue was instrumental in shaping her personality. She had to learn when and where she wanted to take the risk of sharing information.

Many people do not realize that our self-disclosure pattern can affect our medical history. It is important to know about your medical history so that you can adequately assess your risk factors. Some of the subjects in this book acknowledge that they did not know about intimate members of their families who had breast cancer. Disclosure was given when the subjects were diagnosed with the disease.

Some historians feel this lack of openness goes back to slavery times. Many slaves were reluctant to mention an illness for fear that they or their family members would be punished or traded. This concept is also brought out in movies and books on slavery.

In looking at slavery, it is important to realize the emphasis that was placed on slave women's breasts. Noted historian Dr. Marvin Dulaney mentioned slave woman's breasts were often inspected during the auction or trading process. The woman with the larger breasts was considered more valuable. Slave women not only fed their children, but they also breast-fed the children of the plantation owners. This may be why even now, as we near the 21st Century, large breasts are still considered to be better.

Breast cancer survivor Minnie Pryor recalls as a student nurse having a patient with large breasts come into the hospital. The woman was suffering from breast cancer. When she was told that her breast would have to be removed, the woman left and said she would just take her chances. She returned a few months later, but by then it was too late. Minnie said all they could do was make her comfortable.

Minnie decided then that as an African American woman her breasts would never mean more to her than her life.

— *Taylor Turley*

et's Talk About It

It's now time to move forward. We've given you personal accounts from breast cancer survivors, a get-acquainted session on medical terms and a quick lesson on genetics role in developing the disease.

Our next step is to take charge. Breast cancer knows no race, sex or socio-economic status. It crosses all boundaries. But it can be stopped. Listen to those who are on the front lines:

Survivor Augusta Gale, gives this anecdote on how we can form teams to combat this disease:

The day after my surgery, my hospital roommate had expressed a desire to wash her hair. To me, there didn't seem to be a problem. But she seemed very concerned that we both were recuperating from surgery. Finally, I told her, "Look, there is nothing wrong with your right side and there is nothing wrong with my left side. Let's go in that bathroom and I'll get my left hand up there and you'll get your right one up there, and we will get your hair shampooed." Before we knew it, there we were, this Black hand and this White hand over her head. Together, we got the job done.

Breast cancer survivors have to form a chain across nations, across cultures and language barriers to fight the environmental causes of breast cancer, to fight the big chemical polluters, the pesticides, the toxic and nuclear waste dumps because breasts are rapidly becoming an endangered species.

Pam Ferguson
President of the Breast Cancer Action Group

It's an epidemic, we are dying and I am sick of it!

P. J. Viviansayles
President of Women of Color Breast Cancer Survivor Project

To me breast cancer was a very positive force in my life. It made me stop and smell the roses. It gave me an opportunity to stop and tell every one how much I loved them. But mostly it has given me the opportunity to make a difference in the world.

Bobbi de Cordova
Breast Cancer Advocate

One of the most devastating things that has ever happened to me in my life was losing my sister to breast cancer. I can't stress enough that everyone needs to become more educated about breast cancer and should become more aware of preventive measures you can take to circumvent any type of cancer. It is imperative that all women do self breast exams on a monthly basis.

Dr. Marilyn Kern-Foxsworth
Author/Associate Professor

~~~~~~~~~

The chance to prevent breast cancer begins with every moment.

Beverly Bulliner
Breast Cancer Prevention Trial

~~~~~~~~~

If we are to continue to be the primary caretakers to the world, we first have to become the primary caretaker to ourselves, because no one else will.

Dr. Cheryl Ewing
Surgical/Oncologist, University of Chicago

~~~~~~~~~

The women in this book prove that a woman can be a diva whether she has a lump removed, a breast removed, or both breasts removed ... for true sexuality begins in the mind, not in the body.

Darien Goode
Marketing Rep./Sony Music

~~~~~~~~~

My main concern is that people seem to be ignoring some of the statistics that relate to Black women and breast cancer. We have a higher number of Black women dying under the age of 45 to breast cancer, but nobody seems to be paying any attention to that fact.

Linda Finney
President of African American Breast Cancer Alliance

~~~~~~~~~

lossary

Along with the diagnosis of breast cancer comes a whole slew of medical terms, procedures and phrases that could totally baffle the average person. Below is a list of some of the most common breast cancer terms and their definitions.

Alopecia: Hair loss. It usually happens during or after chemotherapy. Some forms of chemotherapy are not as strong and may only cause the hair to thin.

Anesthesia: Drugs or gases that cause you to lose feeling. Sometimes it is administered to a specific area of the body. Other times, it puts the person to sleep.

Antiemetic: A medication that relieves vomiting and nausea that may occur from chemotherapy.

Areola: The dark colored area surrounding the nipple.

Axilla: The armpit, sometimes used to describe portions of the under arm.

Benign: This means noncancerous, not malignant. A benign tumor is not life threatening.

Big "C": Slang for cancer. (also see cancer)

Big Red: Slang for Adriamycin. A form of chemotherapy which is red in color.

Biopsy: A surgical procedure to remove tissue for further examination. This is done to give a more accurate diagnosis. Although mammograms, ultrasounds, and needle aspirations may give an indication of cancer, a biopsy is essential in making a final diagnosis.

Bone Scan: A special camera is used to take pictures of the bones after a radioactive material is injected in the bloodstream.

Bone Survey: This is an X-ray of the entire skeletal system.

Breast Cancer: A tumor or group of cells that have abnormal growth patterns in the breast area. They may have the potential to travel to other parts of the body via the lymph node system.

Breast Implants: Substances used to restore the breast form. Silicone, saline and body fat are most commonly used.

Breast Self Exam: Most commonly referred to as simply BSE. This is a procedure that women follow by examining their own breasts on a monthly basis. If they are pre-menopausal, the exam is done seven days after their period. If they are post-menopausal, the same day of the month every month.

Breast Reconstruction: The rebuilding of the breast to recreate a natural form. This may be done with silicone implants, saline implants or body fat. Reconstruction may be done immediately following surgery or much later.

CAT Scan: An X-ray that gives a section view of the entire body.

Calcification: Calcium deposits that are found in the breast. These may easily be detected by mammograms.

Cancer: Any one of several diseases that can result from abnormal cell growth.

Carcinogen: A substance that may produce cancer.

Carcinoma: Any one of several types of cancer.

Cellulitis: Infection of the soft tissue.

Chemotherapy: This is a drug treatment that can be given through the veins with an IV or through a porta cafe to destroy cancerous cells. It can also come in pill form. Depending on the stage of cancer, doctors often prescribe it in conjunction with radiation.

Cyst: This is a fluid filled sac or lump, which usually collapses when aspirated. It is not considered life threatening.

Cytotoxic: Kills the cells.

Duct: A pathway in the breast through which milk passes from lobes to the nipple.

Estrogen: A female hormone that plays a major role in reproduction. It is also referred to as the female sex hormone. It is produced by the ovaries and the adrenal gland.

Estrogen Receptor Assay (ERA): This is a test to determine if the breast cancer is dependent on estrogen.

Fibrocystic Breast Condition: This is a benign condition, where lumps are present in one or both breasts. Many times this may cause discomfort during the menstrual cycle. This is not a life threatening condition. This is also referred to as "Fibrocystic Disease" or "Benign Beast Disease."

Fried: Slang for severe radiation burns.

Frozen Section: A sample of tissue is frozen and cut for immediate examination by a pathologist.

Halstedad (Radical) Mastectomy: The original form of mastectomy, which is rarely done today because it is so extreme. Many doctors opt to preserve the breast whenever it's feasible. This form of a mastectomy removes the entire breast area and the lymph nodes under the arm.

Hormones: Substances produced by the glands which enter the bloodstream.

Infiltrating Cancer: The cancer can grow into areas other that its original site. This does not mean it has spread.

In Situ: In reference to breast cancer, cancer that has not grown from its original area.

Invasive Cancers: Cancers that have the potential to spread to other areas.

Intravenous (IV): Fluid, medicine or food, that is given through the veins.

Liver Scan: A test to examine the liver to check for metathesis.

Lump: An abnormal mass that can either be benign or malignant.

Lumpectomy: This is a more common procedure today because many doctors opt to preserve the breast as often as possible. This surgical procedure only removes the actual lump and a small amount of surrounding tissue. Also, some lymph nodes are sampled from the underarm area.

Lymph Nodes: Glands found throughout the body to help defend against foreign invaders, such as bacteria. An area that is usually tested for cancer.

Lymph Edema: Swelling of the hand or arm after the loss of lymph nodes from under the arm. The lymph nodes help the body to fight off infection. A person who has lost lymph nodes and gets a small cut could get lymph edema.

Magnetic Resonance Imaging (MRI): Magnetic resonance imaging hasn't been proven successful with breast cancer diagnosis. This is a machine that takes a picture of the entire body.

Malignant: Cancerous, can be life threatening.

Mammography/Mammogram: X-ray taken of the breast.

Mastitis: Inflammation of the breast that causes pain and tenderness.

Mastectomy: Surgical removal of the breast.

Menopause: Usually referred to as the "change of life." This is the point when a woman no longer has a menstrual cycle. There are other hormonal changes that may take place at this time.

Metastasis: When the cancer spreads from the original site to another organ.

Microcalcification: Small deposits of calcium in the breast that can appear on a mammogram and may sometimes indicate breast cancer.

Oncologist: A doctor who specializes in the diagnosis and treatment of cancer.

Oncology: The study of cancer.

One-Step Procedure: When a malignant tumor is found after a biopsy, and it is immediately followed by a surgical removal, whether it is a lumpectomy or a mastectomy.

Palpation: Feeling the breast for any changes or abnormal growths.

Partial Mastectomy: Instead of the entire breast being removed, only a portion of the breast is removed. This includes the cancer and some surrounding tissue as well.

Pathologist: A doctor who specializes in making diagnoses from tissue samples.

Permanent Section: A thin slice of tissue is removed for a pathologist to examine in order to determine a diagnosis.

Prosthesis: Although this refers to any artificial limb or form, in terms of breast cancer it is a form that replaces the breast. It may fit into the bra or be attached directly to the skin.

Prophylactic Mastectomy: Surgical removal of the breast as a preventive measure to keep cancer from developing.

Rad (Radiation Absorbed Dose): Method of measuring the amount of radiation that is absorbed.

Radiation Therapy: X-ray used to destroy cancer cells.

Radiologist: A doctor who specializes in the diagnosis of disease by the use of X-rays.

Recurrence: The cancer returns to the same site or another part of the body.

Red Devil: Slang term for Adriamycin. A form of chemotherapy that is red in color.

Saline: A substance used for implants in reconstructive surgery.

Side Effect: Unwanted and undesirable results that occur while taking medication. For example: the loss of hair may be a side effect of chemotherapy.

Silicone Gel: Substance used for implants in reconstruction or breast enlargements.

Staging: Process to decide progress of cancer. This is usually determined by (T) Tumor Size (M) Metastasis and (N) Lymph Node Involvement.

Tamoxifen: Estrogen blocker used in treating breast cancer.

Thermogram: The process where heat from the breast is used to detect abnormality.

Tumor: An abnormal growth or mass. They may be benign or malignant.

Two-Step Procedure: The biopsy and breast surgery are performed as two separate surgical processes.

Ultrasound: A sound wave imagery process to examine parts of the body. Sometimes this is done after a mammogram to confirm or further explore questionable results.

Sources: The National Institutes of Health/National Cancer Institute, Susan G. Komen Breast Cancer Foundation and The American Cancer Society.

$\mathcal{I}$ndex

upport Groups

God Cares Support Group
Church of the Great Commission
10137 Prince Place, #402 • Largo, Maryland 20772
Contact: Carolyn P. Harvey
301-350-3113 • 301-735-7398

African American Breast Cancer Alliance
P.O. Box 8987 • Minneapolis, Minnesota 55408
Contact: Linda Finney
612-731-3792

Sisters Network
National Headquarters
8787 Woodway Drive, Suite 4297 • Houston, Texas 77063
713-781-0255
Contact: Karen E. Jackson
Other Locations:
Long Island, New York
Dallas, Texas
Los Angles, California
Lake Jackson, Texas

Women of Color Breast Cancer Survivors Support Project
8610 S. Sapulveda • Suite 200 • Los Angles, California 90045
Contact: P. J. Viviansayles, Beverly Rhine

Sisters Breast Cancer Survivors Network
YWCA Greater Los Angeles
2501 West Vernon Ave. • Los Angeles, CA 90008
Contact: Patsy Harris
213-293-9408

Rise Sister Rise
1765 N Street, N.W. • Washington, D.C. 20036
Contact: Zora Kramer Brown
202-463-8040

Embracing Life
Contact: National Black Leadership Initiative on Cancer
University of Illinois at Chicago
2121 West Taylor Street • Suite 512 • Chicago, ILL 60612
Aunita Hill
312-996-8046 • 800-799-2542

Other organizations for information and support.

The American Cancer Society (ACS)
National Office
Tower Place
3340 Peachtree Road, NE • Atlanta, GA 30026
(404) 320-3333 • (800) ACS-2345

Cancer Care, Inc., and the National Cancer Care Foundation
1180 Avenue of the Americas • New York, NY 10036
(212) 221-3300

The National Alliance of Breast Cancer Organizations (NABCO)
1180 Avenue of the Americas, Second Floor • New York, NY 10036
(212) 719-0154 (messages only)

The National Lymphedema Network
2215 Post Street, Suite 3
San Francisco, CA 94115
(800) 541-3259

The Susan G. Komen Foundation
6820 LBJ Freeway, Suite 130 • Dallas, TX 75240
(800) I'M AWARE

The Wellness Community
1235 Fifth Street • Santa Monica, CA 90401
(213) 393-1415 • (800) PRO-HOPE

The Y-ME National Organization
for Breast Cancer Information and Support
18220 Harwood Avenue • Homewood, IL 60430
(708) 799-8228 • (800) 221-2141

The YWCA Encore Program
National Headquarters
726 Broadway • New York, NY 10003
(212) 614-2827

Beauty and The Breast
American Cancer Society
241 Fourth Avenue • Pittsburgh, PA 15222
(412) 261-4352

Z Talbert Basye Foundation
(Rainbow Runners)
500 S. Ervay, Suite 428 • Dallas, TX 75201
National Black Leadership Initiative on Cancer Headquarters
(214) 761-8435

National Institutes of Health
NCI, SPSB, ESN-240
9000 Rockville Pike • Bethesda, MD 20892
Program Manager: Veronica Y. Brown

The Breast Cancer Prevention Trial (BCPT) is a national trial whose headquarters is in Pittsburgh, PA. The organization is called the National Adjuvant Breast and Bowel Project (NASBP) The University of Chicago was chosen to be one of the more than 100 centers in the United States and Canada to be involved in the Breast Cancer Prevention Trial. Currently there are 11,286 women on the trial. The goal is to recruit a total of 16,000 women by the end of 1995. This very important Trial will determine the worth of Tamoxifen in preventing breast cancer.

Program Coordinator: Beverly Bulliner
University of Chicago
5841 S. Maryland, MC5031 • Chicago, IL 60637
312-702-4949

The American Federation of Teachers
and Cervical Cancer Project
The AFT Women's Rights Committee
555 New Jersey Ave. N.W. • Washington, D.C. 20001-2079

Breast Cancer Resource Committe
1765 N. Street, N.W. • Washington, D.C. 20036
Contact: Zora Kramer Brown, Les Butler
202-463-8040

Additional information on cancer: 1-800-4-CANCER

Reading List:

The Race is Won One Step at a Time
by Nancy Brinker

The Breast Cancer Companion
by Kathy LaTour

The American Cancer Society Cancer Book
edited by Dr. Arthur I. Holleb Support Groups

Self-Shiatsu Handbook
(Post-Mastectomy Exercises) by Pam Ferguson

Sylvia Dunnavant is a writer, photographer and poet who lives in Dallas, Texas. She has a communications degree with an emphasis in journalism from the University of Wisconsin, and has been published in national and state magazines and newspapers, including *JET* Magazine. The former Miss Black America contestant is a recipient of the Kizzy Image and Achievement Award. The Kizzy Award is presented by the Black Women's Hall of Fame Foundation in recognition of young women who have achieved excellence in their academic and professional undertaking in spite of racial and sexual discrimination. She has received a citation from the State of Wisconsin for her journalistic accomplishments. She is also listed in the 1982 Outstanding Young Women of America reference book.

Her other works include *An Affair of the Heart*, and she was the editor for *The Pastor's Pen*, by the Reverend J. Lee Foster. She also coordinated the photography in the Emmitt Smith 1995 16-month calendar which included many of her personal shots. Her photographs also appear in *The Emmitt Zone*, the autobiography of Emmitt Smith.